Nancy
Ring

Walking On Walnuts

BANTAM BOOKS   NewYork Toronto London Sydney Auckland

WALKING ON WALNUTS

A Bantam Book / August 1996

Grateful acknowledgment is made for permission to reprint "Nancy—1992" and "Independence Day"
by Dorothy Ring. Copyright © by Dorothy Ring.

Book design by Donna Sinisgalli.

Library of Congress Cataloging-in-Publication Data
Ring, Nancy G.
Walking on walnuts / Nancy G. Ring.
p.   cm.
ISBN 0-553-09664-8
1. Ring, Nancy G.   2. Artists—New York (N.Y.)—Biography.
3. Cooks–New York (N.Y.)—Biography.   4. Jews—New York (N.Y.)—Biography.   5. New York
(N.Y.)—Biography.   I. Title.
CT275.R6065A3   1996
974.7′1043′092—dc20
[B]   96–4280
                                                                                                    CIP

Published simultaneously in the United States and Canada

Bantam Books are published by Bantam Books, a division of Bantam Doubleday Dell Publishing
Group, Inc. Its trademark, consisting of the words "Bantam Books" and the portrayal of a rooster, is
Registered in U.S. Patent and Trademark Office and in other countries. Marca Registrada. Bantam
Books, 1540 Broadway, New York, New York 10036.

PRINTED IN THE UNITED STATES OF AMERICA

FFG   10 9 8 7 6 5 4 3 2 1

or

Great-Grandma Esther Hanna

and

In loving memory of

Edward Ring

and

Max and Rachel Kasoff

Acknowledgments ———◦

A book is like a cake. One is always testing the recipe over and over, trying new methods, and adjusting the amounts of ingredients. The development of my recipe depended on the help of many people, and I owe them all a world of thanks.

To my editor, Linda Gross, for realizing that there was a book inside me even before I did, and for her priceless enthusiasm and friendship. To my agents Frances Goldin and Sydelle Kramer, for their belief in the project from the very start. Special thanks to Sydelle for her insightful editing, talent for diplomacy, and sense of humor. To the art department at Bantam, especially Jim Plumeri, Donna Sinisgalli, and Glen Edelstein.

To Selma Ring, my beloved grandmother, for her mandelbrot and memories. To my father and mother, Frank and Dorothy Ring, for their unwavering support of my life's dream to be an artist. Extra thanks to my mother for the stories and for being an outstanding research assistant, and to my father for the photographs. To my sister and brothers, Janet, Bruce, and Michael Ring, for caring about my book as much as I do. Janet, thank you for the daily e-mail, feedback, and moral support. Bruce, thank you for the computer and research help, and for rustling up recipe testers. To my niece,

Leilani Wuestefeld, for taking time during her vacation to read the manuscript.

To my aunt and uncle, Norma and Richard Daniels, for the stories, great wine and food, the snowy week in Vermont, and sunny weekends in New Jersey. To my cousins, Jeff and Anne Daniels and Barrie and David Markowitz, for the loan of a computer when I didn't have one of my own. Extra thanks to Jeff and Anne for the great dinners and for playing hooky with me when I needed a break. To cousins Cathy and Steve Zukerman and Dale and Steven Daniels for always being supportive. To cousins Connie deSwaan, fellow artist and cook, and Ellen Bogen, cook extraordinaire, for their delicious dinners, stories, and recipes. To my mother-in-law, Jackie Kaplan, for being a mom as well as a friend and fellow artist.

To Peritz Ravitz for your loving letters from Israel.

To Naomi Schechter for your help cracking open the black walnuts and for your wise guidance.

To the Women Artists' Group: Karen Martin, Carole Murray, Janet Villani, Anne Watkins, and our honorary member, Karen Page, for the camaraderie and strength to get me through it all. A special thanks to Carole Murray for her restaurant reviews, advice, and endless rereading of the manuscript.

To my recipe testers: Anne Hughes-Daniels, Karen Martin, Carole Murray, Ellie Dickson, Eric Kaplan, Dorothy Ring, Connie deSwaan, Evelyn Hollidge, Maggie Potter, Charlotte Ring, Judy O'Sullivan, Terri Krajcar, and fellow chef Mary Shoenlein.

To the following people I owe thanks for help with my research: Henry Kleinman; Rana Werbin; Elizabeth Aisles of the Walnut Creek Historical Society in California; Zvi Shevet, the director of the Slonim Jews' Association in Israel; the librarians of the YIVO Institute for Jewish Research; and the librarians of the New York Botanical Garden Library: Susan Fraser, Anne Rumsey, Melanie Singer, and Luis Serrano.

To Ani Buk for the brilliant suggestion for the drawings. To Ray Stone for the gift of his book. To fellow pâtissier Liesl McGinn for taking me under her wing. To Susan and Michelle Horowitz of the Quilted Corner for the great selection of vintage aprons. To Yvette L. Walton of the Crafts & Talk store for crocheting the lace that appears in the drawing for Chapter 9.

Special thanks to Jack Rudin, cousins Mimi and Sid Yeuson, Aunt Carol and Uncle Norman Ring, Dave Gelber, Sue and Steve Rothbart, Robin Frost, Deb Koltenuk and Chris Merrow, our beloved Sammy, and to all the friends and family who sustained me through this enormous project. I only wish I had space to name each one of you. Last but not least, thank you to my husband, Eric Kaplan—my fellow chef, artist, and soul mate—"At last."

Now, as Grandma Rae would say, *Ess, mein kinder, ess.*

Nancy Ring
October, 1995

Author's Note ⟶

I would like to point out to the reader that the characters in the restaurant stories, and the restaurants themselves, are based on real people and real restaurants. As I have no wish to invade anyone's privacy, however, I have changed the names and the descriptions of the people as well as the restaurants involved, both to help protect the privacy of their staff members, and because what is said about each one is true of many others as well. This book is not meant to be an exposé of the restaurant business.

Even though this is primarily a work of nonfiction, I have also slightly changed events or chronology in a couple of brief sections of my restaurant experiences in deference to the development of the story.

However, all the names and descriptions of my family members are real, and the events of their lives are true, based on my own extensive research and the colorful reporting of the wonderful—and sometimes conflicting—storytellers of my family. Regarding Zahava Ravitz, though she was a real person and a member of my family, her story as it appears here is a composite pieced together from her husband's letters to me from Israel, the memories of my family who met her, and my own research. I am indebted to *The Book of Jewish Partisans,* edited by M. Geffen and others, pages 329 to 333, in which Zahava herself is quoted at length about her time spent in the forest as a partisan.

Family Tree

(ABRIDGED)

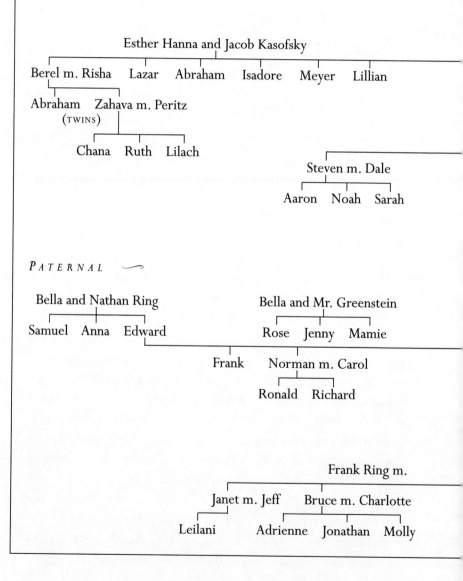

MATERNAL

Esther Hanna and Jacob Kasofsky

Berel m. Risha   Lazar   Abraham   Isadore   Meyer   Lillian

Abraham   Zahava m. Peritz
(TWINS)

Chana   Ruth   Lilach

Steven m. Dale

Aaron   Noah   Sarah

PATERNAL

Bella and Nathan Ring

Samuel   Anna   Edward

Bella and Mr. Greenstein

Rose   Jenny   Mamie

Frank   Norman m. Carol

Ronald   Richard

Frank Ring m.

Janet m. Jeff   Bruce m. Charlotte

Leilani   Adrienne   Jonathan   Molly

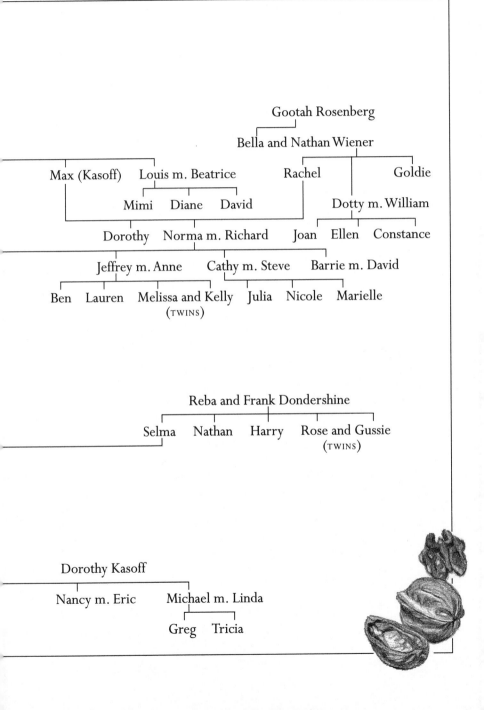

Gootah Rosenberg

Bella and Nathan Wiener

Max (Kasoff)   Louis m. Beatrice   Rachel   Goldie

Mimi   Diane   David   Dotty m. William

Dorothy   Norma m. Richard   Joan   Ellen   Constance

Jeffrey m. Anne   Cathy m. Steve   Barrie m. David

Ben   Lauren   Melissa and Kelly   Julia   Nicole   Marielle
(TWINS)

Reba and Frank Dondershine

Selma   Nathan   Harry   Rose and Gussie
(TWINS)

Dorothy Kasoff

Nancy m. Eric   Michael m. Linda

Greg   Tricia

Scullion

One

"*It was said that in the 'golden age,' when men
lived upon acorns the gods lived upon Walnuts.*"

A MODERN HERBAL,

VOLUME 2, GRIEVE & LEYEL,

1931

 can still hear them. It's as if I could just walk into the next room and see them again, that's how they live in my memory. Each one still impossibly here, stopped in time like a painting, like *The Last Supper*. Only it's not the same picture Da Vinci painted, it's Grandma Rae, the matriarch, at the head of the dinner table surrounded by her apostles— the agitated stew of her family.

Children as tiny and green as baby peas or as broad and thick as carrots, surfacing above the table for a moment to tear off a handful of yellow challah bread, or grab a square of schmaltz-laden potato kugel, then diving below the table to climb into laps, steal shoes, scrabble with each other, or feed the panting maw of the ever-grateful dog. Aunts like bubbles of foam skimming the edges of the table with a tureen of soup or stuffed cabbage. Plumped uncles, ready with a fork or ladle to nab the fattest dumplings or the juiciest bits of conversation. My mother and father, the bouquet garni, a bundle as spicy as hot peppercorns or as subtle as thyme, and never one without the other. And the grandparents, the little old men and women bobbing up and down like misshapen potatoes in a boiling broth of family, everyone gossiping, eating, arguing, stage-whispering into the closest ear what they never dared say to each other's faces, trading recipes, interrupting, gesturing and shouting and talking over each other.

You know, Selma, it's just as easy for Nancy to marry a rich boy as it is for her to marry a poor boy.

Ach, money doesn't mean anything to her, Rae. She wants love.

When the money goes, love flies out the window.

Grandma Rae and Grandma Selma and Papa Eddy and Papa Max. They don't make them like that now, like discontinued patterns of blue-veined china, faded and chipped, from long ago. They're lost or broken and you can't replace them anymore. All you're left with is rough fragments to try to glue together: odd-shaped glossy photographs from old cameras, yellowed handwritten letters with pages missing, a necklace or a watch you would never wear—it's not your style—but keep safe in a box, a check you never cashed in a card you thought you'd lost, a rolling pin, a linen tablecloth bunched up in the back of the closet. It has a stain.

And recipes.

Where did Nancy get a meshuga idea like that anyway, Rae, to be an artist? What kind of life is that?

God forbid she'll end up an old maid yet.

And I'll never see my great-grandchild.

You should live so long.

There were others too. Not just the ones who sat around the

table, but the ones who made their grand entrances later. Notorious great-grandmothers and great-aunts and cousins who had long ago had a handful of dirt thrown into their graves or else had traveled so far away that they couldn't make it back to our table. One by one they would return as Grandma Selma's mandelbrot cookies were dunked and the stories unfolded. These stories were like big weather, like events that could change your life forever in a few minutes, like earthquakes or hurricanes with names. Bella. Esther. Nathan. And at every holiday dinner they would tell those stories, sitting around my mother's big dining room table dunking mandelbrot in cups of tea, the table spread with the creamy linen cloth—a wedding present—that Grandma Rae had hand-embroidered with a thick yellow thread as rich as egg yolk.

When Nancy gets married, Rae, I have beautiful things for her. My silver, my lace.

I wouldn't hold your breath.

My mother kept her sterling silver in a velvet-lined box. She would take it out and tediously polish it just for holidays. My mother would polish slowly, thinking maybe this was the holiday that would work out all right—without "scenes," without tears. Working late into the night in her quiet kitchen, she would infuse her hope into the filigreed pattern of the silver with the soft, worn cloth, polishing the veins in the silver leaves, the hard edges of the silver petals on the spout of her teapot. She brought her flowered bone china out of the glass breakfront, where it usually sat like objets d'art in a museum. Grandma Rae would call.

What should I bring?

Bring yourself.

I'm bringing stuffed cabbage.

Then Grandma Selma would call.

What should I bring?

Bring yourself.

What's Rae bringing?

The next day Grandma Selma and Grandma Rae would put their stuffed cabbages into my mother's oven and hover over them, each making sure her dish was heated up just right. They would race each other to the table as we all sat to eat. The heavy silver clattered on the good china with a satisfying thunk.

Someone would say how good the stuffed cabbage was.

Which one are you eating? Hers or mine?

Back and forth to the kitchen we went for more brisket or tzimmes or the rest of the gravy. Sometimes we finished Grandma Selma's stuffed cabbage before Grandma Rae's.

I brought stuffed cabbage because Rae did.

If everybody jumped off a roof, would you go too?

Then we'd hear over all the noise the clink-clink-clinking of my father's spoon on his crystal glass, just long enough to stop the clamor. He and my grandfathers would make a toast. We'd all raise our glasses. *L'chaim.*

To life.

Just as fast as we cleared the savory dishes away, the table was groaning with the weight of homemade desserts. My mother poured from her ornate silver teapot, then reverently returned it to its silver tray in the middle of the table, where it sat surrounded by towering cakes. Aunt Norma's apple cake, Great-Aunt Dotty's chocolate cake, Great-Grandma Bella's honey cake, platters of candy and nuts and homemade cookies. And mandelbrot. Always mandelbrot.

Yesterday I made the mandelbrot standing in my kitchen with my walker. I was so tired, but if I just sit all day, I can't get up! How long can God help me go on?

Oy, vey is mir, Selma! Stop talking so much and eat!

Papa Eddy liked a thick, warm slice of golden-crusted apple pie, a scoop of vanilla ice cream snuggled up and melting against its glistening side. Papa Max liked stewed prunes, and walnuts. When Papa cracked the dark, sculpted walnut shells, I was reminded why the ancient Romans saw the nuts as tiny heads—the outer green husk, like the scalp; the paper inside, the membrane; and the nut itself, the brain. As Papa cracked the small skulls, he would begin to speak.

When I was a little boy in Argentina—

Then he would pause, and cough, as he often did, a bit of cookie stuck in his throat. Grandma Rae would interrupt, as she always did.

Stop choking, Max.

Papa would respond without looking at her with a dismissive wave of his arm in her general direction, and then continue.

We ran out of firewood for cooking and—

Shut up, Max, you're boring the children.

No, he wasn't. Not ever.

Take some more cake, Max. Nosh it up, Max.

Once, one of the children asked, "Papa, how long do you bake the mandelbrot?" Grandma Rae laughed.

That's a question? What kind of a question is that? Papa doesn't bake, he eats!

I listen to them laugh; it's like the gentle simmer of a soup. But the laughter fades suddenly, the voices drift away, out my open window like steam from a whistling kettle silenced in the thick blue paint of night. I'm alone. Alone in my kitchen.

I knew time would pass, but somehow I clung to the belief that we were special. Time would pass us by, leave us untouched. Now the old house has been sold, the good china and silver tea service are packed away in boxes in my aunt's basement, my name scrawled on the side. They're saving them for me. For what?

We'll all come for dinner. Someday you'll have a house big enough, you'll see.

But I still don't, and the dining room table isn't in the next room anymore. It's wedged in my body, in my hips, the ornate legs extending down my legs, and everybody's sitting around it, pressing against my stomach and my back like I'm nine months pregnant, like I'm bursting with the stories. I flip through my recipe book, and when I lift my hands, all their hands rise with mine. So many fingers—wrinkled, ringed fingers, old fingers like long, knobby roots—rustling the pages, so many that it makes me dizzy trying to see the recipes through all the hands that once patted my head, that once reached for mandelbrot at the holiday table, that once handed me these very recipes. Bakers' hands, mothers' and fathers' hands. Grandmothers' and grandfathers' hands. None of them like my hands, the hands of a childless artist. My hands, that haven't felt the worn satin ribbon marking the pages of a prayer book since I was a child.

Tsk. Sigh.

God must be tired of hearing me pray for my children and grandchildren.

Still, the old hands flutter around mine, echoing mine, refusing to leave me. This is family I'm talking about. Suddenly I find the recipe I'm looking for and their voices seem to chant together with mine.

Mandelbrot. Here it is.

For a moment I'm startled at how loudly they speak in my memory. Then I feel pleasure. And relief.

I can still hear them.

What? You expected maybe Golda Meir?

I smile to myself, then begin reading the recipe.

Grandma Selma can't remember where she got the mandelbrot recipe. Maybe it was from a neighbor. Maybe it was from Newark, New Jersey, or the Lower East Side of New York, or Romania, where her parents came from. I am the granddaughter of an immigrant family, a family that moved in order to survive. Who knew where the recipe was from? That was part of its mystique. It was an artifact, with edges worn from repeated use, with ink blurred by drips of oil or dimmed by the dust of flour. It was handed down, copied over and over in different hands in different kitchens, in different, overlapping, connected lives. Where was the recipe from? It was from the past. Our past. Mine. Though that past didn't always seem to have a whole lot in common with me.

I was taught that to tell a story well, you need a good strong cup of tea and a plate of freshly baked mandelbrot. The fragrant cookies sink into the steaming tea, the good china cups clink and scrape on their delicate saucers, the sugar lumps plunk, and the sweet alchemy begins. Long-ago events become stories, bigger than the lives once lived, from a time studded with tales as rich as chunks of chocolate in Grandma Selma's mandelbrot. That's why I have to bake mandelbrot now. Because I, too, have a story to tell.

Grandma Selma's Mandelbrot

2 cups flour
2 teaspoons baking powder
1 ½ sticks of unsalted butter (6 ounces), softened,
      not greasy

1 cup sugar
3 eggs
3 ounces sliced almonds
4 ounces semisweet chocolate chips

Prepare the dough: *Combine flour and baking powder and set aside. Cream butter and sugar until light. Beat in eggs, one at a time. Add flour and baking powder to egg mixture, mixing only until the flour is incorporated. Do not overwork the dough. Divide dough in half. Add almonds to one half and chocolate chips to the other. Refrigerate the dough for several hours or overnight.*

Bake the mandelbrot: *Preheat oven to 375 degrees. Remove dough from refrigerator and wet hands slightly. Roll each piece of dough into a two-inch-wide log. Place logs on a parchment-paper-covered, nonstick, or greased sheet pan. To prevent overbaking of the undersides of the logs, place another sheet pan upside down under the one the logs are on. Bake logs until medium golden and firm, 25 to 35 minutes, turning tray once during baking to ensure even color and temperature. Place the sheet pan on a rack and cool the logs for about 10 minutes.*

Rebake the mandelbrot: *When the logs are still very warm but not so hot that they crumble, carefully cut the logs into slices about 3/4 inch thick, using a very sharp serrated knife and a gentle sawing motion. Let these slices cool completely. Bake the sliced mandelbrot again, cut side down, at 375 degrees on doubled sheet pans. After 5 minutes of baking, turn the slices over and bake another 5 to 10 minutes, until the slices are light golden and feel slightly firm to the touch. Cool slices completely on a rack. Store in an airtight container for up to ten days. Yields approximately three dozen cookies.*

Two ⁓

"Why, 'tis cockle or a Walnut-shell,
a knack, a toy, a trick, a baby's cap."
THE TAMING OF THE SHREW,
WILLIAM SHAKESPEARE,
1594

he scene: Bistro Redux, a dimly lit, smoky New York City restaurant, circa 1989. The avant-garde beginnings of the colorful sixties revival, though black was still the color of choice. Dark red lips, white-powdered faces, and thick black eyeliner, on the top lid only, surrounded by birds' nests of hair. Clunky black leather shoes with huge silk organza bows for laces. T-shirts under suit jackets. Stubble beards. An ordinary Friday night—a perpetual flow of empty plates being lifted and full ones replacing them, cigarettes being lit and put out and then new ones lit again, chairs being filled and left and then refilled again. And the dance of the waiters and waitresses as we wound and twisted our way through the closely spaced tables.

It was not long after that night that I swore I would never waitress again. And I wasn't kidding. I think that if I had opened my kitchen cupboard and seen nothing in there but one bean in the bottom of a crumpled paper bag, and if I were cast from my home with nothing but this bean in my pocket while the Hudson overflowed and the trees snapped in gale force winds, I still would not have waited tables. And even if the mayor of New York City himself had come to me personally and said, "Ms. Ring, if you'll waitress, peace and prosperity will be restored," there would still have been no way I would tie an apron around my waist and sashay down a tiled floor to a cloth-covered, forked and knifed and salt-shakered table and say, "May I help you?"

What I do now, how I got there, and the saga of the once bare fourth finger of my left hand is a story that began at Bistro Redux, at the end of eight long years of waiting tables to support myself as an artist. Although sometimes when I think about it, it may have started long before that, before I even came into this world on Christmas Eve in 1956, when people I couldn't possibly have been aware of—my ancestors—were already helping to shape me into who I would be.

I hated my waitress uniform, but I loved telling the customers that although I was schooled as a painter, I really wanted to be a waitress and this was my big break. Getting a laugh was a lot easier than explaining the precarious position artists occupy in our society to a group of drunk executives, holding glasses of 1985 Burgundy aloft with manicured hands in an expensive bistro. Grandma Selma would say that's because I'm a lot like my Papa Eddy, who always greeted us grandchildren with jokes and a smile, passing out hard candy from his wide-legged-pants pockets.

The characters: He, a middle-aged businessman, charming smile, meticulously dressed. She, his wife, stylish and modern. And me, their waitress.

"Hello," I chirped, "would you like something from the bar?"

He smiled at me until his wife noticed, and then said, "What a nice dress."

Trying to put a damper on his enthusiasm, I answered, "We all have the same one," and indicated the other waitresses with a tilt of my head.

"Well, it looks nicest on you," he purred.

An uneasy silence ensued in which I made a point of not answering.

If I were really like my Papa Eddy, I was thinking, I would be wearing a three-piece suit with a gold watch chain laced through the vest, not a clingy peacock-blue uniform cut a little too low at the neckline, and a white French-maid-style apron tied at the back with a big bow, meant to be feminine. Meant to be servile. Meant to be submissive, second-class.

I instinctively covered my exposed neck with my hand. Then I reached for my dupe pad in the pocket of that apron.

"Table 23," I wrote, avoiding his stare.

The look on his wife's face was pure, unadulterated hostility. She obviously had a bone to pick with him, but I was an easier target.

"Tell us the specials," she hissed.

"Sliced duck in coriander honey sauce with a spiced melon chutney," I began, wondering just how difficult this table was going to be, "and a—"

"Where are the ducks with melon chutney from?" interrupted the lady with a glare.

I took a deep breath. I would have bet all my tips that night that she didn't care if the ducks were from Timbuktu or New Jersey. What she had a craving for was goat. Scapegoat.

"Long Island," I said calmly.

"Let the pretty lady continue," said her husband. I could tell he got off on turning up the heat under her pot.

Undaunted, she challenged me again. "I didn't know you could make chutney from melon."

"Oh, sure," I said. "Traditionally it's made with raisins, but you can make chutney from any fruit or vegetable, sugar, spices, and vinegar."

Her husband couldn't resist putting the flame on high.

"See?" he gloated. "If you cooked once in a while, you would know that." His wife's jaw tensed visibly.

"We also have a fish special tonight," I continued in a light voice, "and it's—"

"Is the duck sautéed or what?" The lady at Table 23 loudly interrupted my recitation of the specials again.

Bistro Redux was packed, and I could tell already that this table was going to ruin my system of timing. Didn't she know that I was as annoyed with her husband as she was? Let's get hubby, here, out of the way, I felt like saying to her, and then we'll have a nice chat, you and me, about women and repressed anger.

Instead, I answered her politely, as I was trained to do.

"It's roasted. The pan is deglazed with wine and stock. Then the sauce is finished with butter."

"Can I get the duck without the chutney?" she queried.

"No, I'm sorry." I had specific instructions from the temperamental chef not to alter the specials at all, in any way. No sauce on the side, no substitutions, no nothing. These were his creations, his art. I could understand this.

"Some people want to change everything," her husband said, turning sideways in his chair so that he faced me. He crossed his legs and his ankle brushed my calf. I moved away a little.

"Go and ask the chef," she instructed me flatly. "I can't believe that."

I knew arguing with her was pointless. And I knew going to the manager was pointless also. He was busy and hated to be bothered, and he saw it as a sign of weakness if a waitperson couldn't handle a difficult customer. So I walked directly to the kitchen, painfully aware of the diners who had just been seated in my station and were waiting for me. Just inside the kitchen door, I leaned against the wall and paused twenty or thirty seconds. I knew she would be watching to see that I actually went inside the kitchen.

"What's wrong?" the chef barked at me. The chef wasn't a large man but fearsome. This bark was like a nervous small dog's bark, a ferocious yip with menacing sharp fangs.

"Nothing," I said, knowing full well the rules, and knowing full well what his reaction would be to any request like the lady's at Table 23.

"Then get out of my fucking kitchen!" he yelled.

I stumbled in my hurry to get out of the kitchen, and my apron bow got caught in the swinging doors, untying itself. As it dropped, I helplessly watched everything in my pockets scatter over the tile floor, causing havoc in the flow of traffic in and out of the busy kitchen. I cursed the apron as I struggled to pick up my pens, dupe pad and corkscrew, my lipstick and matchbooks, all the while trying to hold the low-cut top of my dress closed so that the voyeuristic customers nearby couldn't see down inside.

Now what? I thought ruefully as I headed back to Table 23, flushed and perspiring, clutching my apron with one hand and trying to smooth out my clinging dress with the other.

Let it also be known that the male waiters in this same establishment wore crisp white button-down shirts, uncompromising black pants, and long ties. But Papa Eddy would have thought this was the way it should be, because men always wore the pants in 1927, when he started his truck parts business, right? Wrong. I can tell you who wore the pants in Papa Eddy's family: Grandma Selma.

Beautiful and bleached blond with blue eyes, big breasts, and big red lips. Everyone always says that exactly what Grandma Selma is thinking comes out of her mouth without a second's hesitation in between. Even though she hasn't worked in decades, that red mouth can still give orders and opinions just like a man in charge. "Strong" barely describes the will of a woman who can get herself in trouble with her mouth and then make you love that mouth with all your heart for its bright red honesty and chutzpah.

Grandma was the reason Papa started the family business to begin with. Before that he had been a truck driver and mechanic for people who brought liquor into the United States illegally. Bootleggers. My family doesn't like to say "bootleggers," but I love saying it. It sounds so wild, so romantic, so James Cagney. Everything fades to black and white, and there's Papa in his fedora, driving his big new car down Prince Street, in the poor section of Newark, where he came from, showing off. A car too big and too new for a nice boy who fixed trucks, Selma's mother thought, convinced that Papa was up to no good. Even the grape farmers of Walnut Creek, California, had given up their lucrative wine-making crop for walnuts when Prohibition came. If Eddy wanted to be with Selma, he'd have to trade grapes for walnuts as well. Selma would ride in Papa's Cadillac, but she wasn't going to be the wife of a bandit. She refused to marry Papa until he went legit. And that's how Ring Bros. Truck Parts was formed. U.S. Highway 1, Elizabeth, New Jersey.

As soon as Papa Eddy arrived at our house for holidays or sat down with a menu at a restaurant, the first thing he would say was "What's for dessert?" My mother always tried to make sure she had something fresh-baked for him, otherwise he would be

content to slurp fruit compote that Grandma Selma made for him especially.

The women in my family all cooked and the men in my family all didn't. However, none of the women had jobs while I was growing up. Unless you count cooking, shopping, cleaning, and raising children as a job. None of the women were artists either. Unless you count sewing, knitting, crocheting, embroidering, tatting, and inventing recipes. Grandma Selma may be confused about how I grew up to be a working artist, but sometimes I think I know exactly how I turned out to be the way I am.

Out of my mother's six pregnancies, four of us survived; girl, boy, girl, boy, from oldest to youngest, the girls with a space between our front teeth and noses that looked as though they had been slightly flattened with a palm right before they set, just like our father's. We also inherited our mother's distinctive dark eyebrows. The two middle kids, my big brother and I, were born fair with light eyes and our older sister and younger brother both dark-haired with chocolate-brown eyes. "Like bookends," our mother used to say. As my big brother and I grew up, our hair turned darker brown, seeming to even things out, but we kept our hazel eyes. In the summer we burned to intense pink while the other two slowly turned an olive-tinted bronze.

My mother's sister, our Aunt Norma, had four kids as well, two boys and two girls, two dark and two fair. For a while she and my mother were referred to in the neighborhood as "those pregnant sisters," and the eight kids were dubbed "interchangeable." When we were all together, which was often since we lived only a few blocks from each other, the feeling was of being one huge fertile family that would multiply ad infinitum like a giant cell endlessly dividing. In fact, all of my cousins and siblings have grown up and had kids of their own, increasing our village to a virtual kingdom of family.

Which doesn't explain how I ended up single for so long, choosing to live alone without children when I came from a family as rich as dried fruit, plumping in a jar filled with warmth. No, my wariness had more to do with the lemon peel, without which Grandma always said the compote would be too sweet. Maybe that's why I could never imagine making compote. I would stand in my kitchen, all their hands on my hands, eager to guide me, a clean jar and a knife on the counter in front of me. But then I would stop. How much fruit to how much lemon? How much water?

I never wrote it down.

There are no amounts.

You just do it by eye.

By feel.

By taste.

Here, let us show you.

But I didn't trust them. All I could imagine was a suffocating jar full of bitterness, without balance, with a moldy lid as heavy as a tombstone. Like the daughters of seers who worry whether or not they have the sight, I wasn't sure if I had the same touch for family life as well as baking. I would abruptly pull my hands away from theirs, shove the compote jar into the back of a messy kitchen shelf, and stubbornly refuse to listen.

Dottie?

That would be Grandma Selma's voice calling my mother as she burst through the front door on holidays.

Selma would breeze through the house, leaving red lips on all our cheeks, admonishing this one for being ugly and that one for getting fat. Then she would put the tin can of mandelbrot and the mason jar of compote on the Formica countertop, throw on a flowered, ruffled apron of my mother's, and join the other women in the kitchen. She would greet me by stopping short in front of me with a decisive clop from her high-heeled shoes in her classic pose:

hands on hips, feet planted shoulder-width apart, a short, top-heavy Jewish grandmother as intimidating as a Sherman tank. I would keep my distance, bracing myself for her usual scathing opinions about my clothes, my current boyfriend, the rest of my life, and the rest of the family.

What kinda shmata do you have on?

It's the style, Grandma.

Style, my tuchas.

Then she would disarm me with a smile, her arms outstretched.

Get ovah heah and give me a kiss, you stinkah.

In my mother's suburban New Jersey dining room, in the twelve-room colonial house on an acre of green lawn and willow trees, on a street of other large homes and swing sets, in a county of horse farms and good schools near the exclusive seashore, I listened to Grandma tell stories about the Depression, about Papa Eddy escaping the three small rooms of his mother's railroad apartment on Willoughby Street, hopelessly shut off from the world by the thick milk of frosted glass in the heavy front door. About his mother, Bella Ring, sneaking out each day to make ends meet since Eddy's nogoodnik father, Nathan, had left them for another woman.

A fat shiksa with a big fancy house in Connecticut.

It was Grandma Selma who had discovered her mother-in-law's secret, stopping by the caterer's one day and finding Bella Ring in a tattered housedress, up to her elbows in chicken feathers and congealed schmaltz. The shame of it. Papa Eddy wanted to take a turpentine-soaked rag and erase this painting of his childhood poverty.

Eddy and his brother made Bella quit the caterer's and sent her back home, promising her that the only place she would have to go for money in the future was to the kitchens of her sons. Grandma

Selma showed off her jewelry, the extravagant bracelet she wore that spelled out her name in glittering diamond letters draped on her soft wrist, her hands with their long, polished fingernails. Selma's childhood home hadn't been much different from Papa's, as poor as a peasant's. But that story would be more important to me later. All I knew when I was little was that Papa Eddy's riches weren't all the kind that sparkled on Grandma Selma's ears and wrists.

C'mere, you dirty rotten little tomata can.

That's how Papa Eddy would get me to come over and sit on his knee.

Who hit Nelly in the belly with a fluke?

I'd giggle, already knowing the joke. Then we'd shout the rest together.

The same guy who hit Ed with a flounder!

Even though it barely made sense, it was funny, so funny. Then Papa would let me look at the tiny book made of gold he wore at the end of the chain that hung from his watch to his belt. Inside small gold frames that turned like the pages of a real book were photographic portraits of all four of us grandchildren. I never tired of looking at this little book, hiding in Papa's pocket with the crinkly, empty candy wrappers.

Papa carries that because he loves you.

Once I had my apron tied tightly around my waist again, I had only the length of the dining room floor between the kitchen doors and Table 23 to think of an excuse to give the lady about why she couldn't have duck without chutney. I walked slowly, pretending to arrange the things in my pockets that had dropped, and thought fast. Upon my arrival, I cheerfully told the lady that although the chef was very sorry that she didn't like chutney, he really believed strongly that it was an integral part of the dish and did not wish to serve the duck without it. However, he recommended the game hen on the menu highly and would prepare it any way she liked.

"I hate chutney," she said sourly, "and I don't want game hen. I want duck."

Her husband smirked at me.

"Do you think all women are so picky about what they eat?" he said, lowering his eyelids in an attempt to appear seductive.

The lady let out an exasperated breath. "I really can't believe this," she said.

"I can get you the duck without the chutney," I suddenly blurted out. I just wanted to end this as quickly as possible. My station was full now, and I could see hands starting to lift to get my attention. The manager had told us many times, "No one waves for a waitperson at Bistro Redux. They should never have to."

I had no idea how I was going to get the chutney off that plate.

I warned the lady at Table 23 that the duck took fifteen minutes to prepare. She ordered it anyway. I wasn't surprised when she flagged me down in exactly sixteen minutes to complain.

"I'll check with the chef to see what's holding up your dinner," I lied again, and then started walking toward the kitchen, wondering what excuse I would give the chef this time for offending him with my appearance. Luckily, just as I was about to enter the kitchen doors, the waiter carrying the dinners for Table 23 on his tray emerged.

"Wait, give me that," I pleaded when I intercepted him.

Puzzled, but glad to have two less dinners to deliver, he said, "Sure," and hurried back into the kitchen to pick up more plates.

There was a table just outside and to the left of the kitchen doors that we called the waiters' station. It had all our service equipment on it—side plates, doilies and condiments, whatever we needed during the night. All the waitstaff liked to drink tea or coffee during service, so we kept our ceramic teapots and cups there too, next to a big coffee machine. I beckoned to Tom, another waiter, and enlisted him to help me. Tom was more than just another waiter, actually, he was my partner in crime, a sympathetic listener, another artist, a friend. He stood at my side to block the view from the kitchen, to the right. The rest of the waiters' station and the coffee machine blocked any view from the left. I stood with my back to the dining room, facing a wall, and scraped the chutney from the plate into a clean teapot we had placed on the station just for this purpose. Tom clamped on the lid just as the chef peeked out of the kitchen to look around briefly before he went back inside.

"There," said Tom, "just move the duck over a little so you can't tell the chutney was there."

"Thanks, Tom," I said, "I owe you one."

"Your firstborn son in slavery for life will do fine," he kidded, and then stopped another waitress from trying to pour from the chutney-filled teapot into her cup. We both giggled.

"You two have a strange sense of humor," she said as she walked away. I covered my mouth with my hand, stifling laughter. Tom rolled his eyes.

"Go deliver the plate," he said soberly.

"Thank you very, very much for getting that the way my wife likes it. That was very sweet of you," cooed the man at Table 23 when I set the duck down on the table.

"Don't thank her until I taste it," spat out the lady.

My blood boiled. Some people have no class, I thought. More and more, I wished I could be home, slurping compote right out of the jar instead of serving chutney on fancy china to pseudo royalty in a restaurant. There was no dish as rustic and simple as compote at Bistro Redux. And no slurping.

Just then another wave of diners came into the restaurant, filling all our tables again and throwing us into another round of beat-the-clock and human-punching-bag, sparring with the touchy, demanding customers. Table 23 continued putting me through my paces too—water, no ice, a matchbook under the leg of the table to stop an imperceptible wobbling, balsamic vinegar from the basement storeroom for her salad, not the red wine vinegar that was already in the cruets, and the constant flirtation of that arrogant man.

When things calmed down a little, I stopped at the waiters' station and began to sort through the checks left in my pocket. Just then, the lady from Table 23 passed by me on her way to the rest room. I made the mistake of looking toward her table, and her husband gestured for me to come over.

"Here's my card," he offered, "I'm a film director. You're an actress, right?"

"No, I'm an artist."

He hesitated for a mere second, then recovered with a dazzling if insincere smile. "Perfect. I have a friend who owns an art gallery. Give me a call and I'll hook you up." He slipped the card into the pocket of my apron with practiced stealth.

Sure, I thought, and if I told you I was an astronaut, you'd have a friend who owned the moon.

Sometime later I realized that the chutney-filled teapot must have found its way safely to the dishwasher, because it was gone when I finally had time to look for it. Table 23 paid their bill and left me a big tip. Although I was thinking that couples therapy would have been a better use of their money than going out for expensive dinners. Oh, well, to each their own. And gratefully, one more time, I avoided the thieves that often prey on waitresses when they come out of restaurants late at night and made it home safely with my cash stuffed in my patent leather boot.

How long could I go on like this, I brooded at home as I tore up the offensive card from my apron pocket and angrily threw it in the trash. My rage was hotter than the scorching knife in a steaming compote jar, my life too sour with a heavy-handed excess of lemon peel. I have to get things into balance, I vowed. Life's too short. Unfortunately, it was Papa Eddy who taught me that.

When Papa died suddenly, I was fifteen, and the little gold book and the watch chain were handed down to my father. Years later, I would go into my father's dressing room, where he kept the book, to look at it and think about Papa. Papa, who had been so alive, then had put his head back in the passenger seat of his new Cadillac while Grandma was driving, and just closed his eyes. It was as if he had vanished into the air, leaving his custom-made pants, shirt, suspenders, and hat, the real gold tie pin and cuff links he was so proud of and his blue sapphire pinkie ring bodiless, in a heap right where he sat. The gold book lay in my hands like a prop from a classic film, imbued with the wild fame of its character. Everybody always said Papa looked exactly like George Burns. Maybe those tiny portraits were also part of the reason I had become an artist. But Papa had handed down more than his book.

Sometimes at Bistro Redux I imagined he was seated at one of my tables, scolding me. He wore his old suit, his face obscured by puffs of smoke and a child's blurry memory. How odd he looked in the bistro, so out-of-date.

Why are you working? How old are you now?

Thirty-two, Papa.

A woman your age should be married, with children.

Papa, I'm an artist now. And I work here so I can afford my own apartment in the city, and have daytime hours free to paint.

But that's where my imagination ends. I have no idea what Papa would think of my life now. I have no idea if I would confess to him that I didn't even know if I was capable of staying in a relationship, let alone being married or bringing up children. He had died in debt, keeping Grandma in the style she was used to and living to the end the myth of male provider. Would he do it all over again the same way?

"In the famine year of 1663," Waverly Root's compendium *Food* tells us, "peasants in the Dauphiné, after eating their walnuts, ground up the shells together with acorns to make what could not have been particularly palatable bread." Eureka, Ehrhardt, Payne, Concord, Franquette, and Grove—names like war heroes or famous bourgeois families—these walnuts were most likely cultivated for the kitchens of the rich. Wild walnuts, though, were free to any forager and fed the rankest poor. At Bistro Redux, despite the hassles, the money was good. I could afford as many overpriced cream-colored, plump English walnuts as I could eat. In my heart, though, I was starving, as if I were a miserable peasant in a servant's dress with a belly full of indigestible acorn and wild-walnut-shell bread.

I was damned tired of that dress. And the one I had to wear at Bistro Redux too—especially the obsession with appearance that that dress encouraged. The who-had-the-skinniest-waist contest. That dress was like a sausage casing, ready to pop. If I gained half a pound, it knew. To make matters worse, we were required to pay fifty dollars for it. It was like making slaves pay for their shackles. My alter ego, that primal, raw, intuitive woman I had started drawing a lot lately, seemed to have a skin that burned and chafed inside this dress, like a lawless animal, all teeth and claws, in a cage. I longed for my grandfather's roomy suit, to sit with my legs strad-dling the back of a chair, smudging my lipstick with a big cigar, play-ing poker.

Papa Eddy taught me how to play. I was just tall enough to see the men's thick hands dealing and passing out chips over the top of the table. They'd be talking business, politics. Papa would lift me into his lap, give me a hand, and patiently explain each card. Aces were higher than kings and queens, even the one-armed jacks and the suicide king. And deuces. Deuces were wild. Papa taught me how to make a bridge like a pro while shuffling. How to ante up, see, raise. How to bluff and keep a poker face. We won a lot.

I just wished I could keep my poker face when the chef or manager at Bistro Redux cursed at me. I would forget my lip-stick, which was required, or refuse to press my apron with pol-luting commercial starch. The other waitresses' smooth, stiff bows made mine look undignified. I would kid with the other waitresses, miming a search through the classified section of a newspaper.

"Person wanted for demanding job, limited benefits. Must work in dimly lit, smoky, noisy, high-pressure environment. Ten-hour shifts without breaks. Heavy physical work. Demeaning, psycholog-ically abusive atmosphere."

"Me! Me! I want that job! I saw it first!" we'd tease each other, laughing. But it wasn't funny.

Even though waiting tables afforded me the time I needed to create, I began to wonder if there was something I could do for money that would be less demeaning and more interesting for me. I was not the cheerful waitperson I once was. All my nails were broken. The images in my drawings were getting increasingly angry and disturbing. Earlier in the year I had abandoned the conven-tional small-town pictures I had been working on for years and fin-

ished a series of portraits depicting my subjects surrounded by anguished, screaming faces. My latest pieces were sculptures made of
found objects—street garbage. I'd finally become urban. I had so
much junk I'd picked up on the street in my apartment that I could
barely walk through my living room, which doubled as my studio.
At night, silhouetted against the open windows, the sculptures
twirled slowly on their fishing lines while my cat played with the
loose strings at their edges. They hung from the ceiling like mari-
onettes. But I was the one that felt like a puppet, woodenly saying
my lines over and over. I would wake up in a sweat more nights
than not from waitress-gone-crazy nightmares. It was restaurant
hell. And my bow was limp.

Grandma Selma's shortie apron ties in the back with a bow. But
when she's in her kitchen baking, no one is concerned with the condition of the bow. She's in there baking traditional recipes handed
down from generations of women, not all of them family, not all of
them professional bakers. The only thing they have in common is
that for every one of them, baking is as much a part of life as birth
and death. In between, you bake.

Grandma Selma would bake in her bra. After all, the kitchen
is hot. If a member of the family stopped by, she'd peek around
the door and say "Oh, it's just you," let us in, apologize for her
"bandeau," and stuff a dish towel in the front of it in a halfhearted
effort to be modest. The towel flapped over the front, drawing
even more attention to her voluptuous chest and heavy, soft
arms. To cover her lace-trimmed half-slip, she tied her shortie
apron around her waist. The lace trim hung below the bottom of
the apron. Her pedicured feet clicked around the kitchen in high-
heeled slippers.

Grandma emptied the brown paper bags of ocher-, honey-, and molasses-colored dried fruits by turning them upside down right into her compote jar. She reached in to gently mix the tiny pillows of soft dried apricots, prunes, peaches, and pears. Carefully, she would place a long, gleaming silver knife in the jar, letting it lean against the jar's lip, to absorb the heat of the boiling water she was about to pour over the fruit and prevent the glass from getting too hot and cracking. Then she would lift the spitting, shrieking kettle from her stove and pour a cloud of hissing water into the jar. A shroud of mist would envelop the jar, obscuring its contents completely.

When Grandma worked in her kitchen, she would pile all her expensive rings and bracelets on the counter, where they glittered with impudence. Papa couldn't really pay for them, but he and Selma lived as though they could, to show the world that he had "made it," that the raucous peasants had risen to genteel royalty. I forgive this lie. Papa was, and Grandma is, a fantastic person, magically unique—priceless. Slowly, the steam would disappear from the compote jar as the water cooled and the glass would become crystal-clear again. The compote would be perfectly visible, the mysterious fog evaporated. There would be no more lies. I was a poor, struggling artist who worked as a waitress, and everyone knew it. I wasn't ashamed, just desperate for a change.

It wasn't hard to decide what I would do if I chose a different job. I had been taught to bake when I was very young, just like any other basic skill, like tying my shoes. And I loved it. It was one of the few times I could get my mother's undivided, if exhausted, attention. What if it took another eight years to convince the art world that I was deserving of its patronage? I'd had numerous exhibitions and sold a lot of my work, won a few awards, and even had some small reviews, but the money wasn't enough yet to live on. I had to find something that I would enjoy to survive. Maybe I could move into the professional kitchen.

While in California during an artist's residency the following summer, I spent my days painting in an enormous barn converted to a studio and my nights baking cheesecakes, pear Tartes Tatins, and lemon tarts with the chef, Milo. While Milo and I whisked the butter and sugar into the lemon curd, I felt as sour as the lemons about returning to New York City and Bistro Redux. One night Milo, who had been listening to my complaints, turned to me and said, "You know, Nancy, you're a pretty competent baker. Why don't you bake for money instead of waiting tables?"

It seemed perfectly reasonable—he was simply validating an idea I'd had myself—but I still didn't think much about it at the time. Upon my return to New York, the relationship I'd started with a particularly unavailable saxophone player ended, not surprisingly, but abruptly, and slides of my sculptures were rejected from every art exhibition jury I sent them to. That does it, I thought, I've got to do something else or I'll crack like an egg on the edge of my frustration. Milo's encouraging words rang in my ears.

When I saw an ad in *The New York Times* for a pastry assistant at a prominent Manhattan restaurant, however, I got cold feet. How can I apply with no formal training and no restaurant kitchen experience? But part of me thought that what was a long shot might also be possible. So with a little of Grandma Selma's chutzpah, and Papa Eddy's wild deuces, I sent a résumé and cover letter to the box number accompanying the ad.

Grandma Selma would cut a sliver of lemon peel with a sharp paring knife from a fat yellow lemon and drop it into her compote jar. It would land on the soft fruit with a weightless bounce, as light as a feather. Then she would push it into the fruit with a wooden spoon and stir the compote a little so that the flavors would start to mingle and intensify. She would twist the lid on the top of the jar tightly and place the jar in the refrigerator. That's all. No amount of peeking in the jar, or stirring, or poking the fruit around will make compote come to full flavor any faster. You just have to wait.

Papa Eddy's Favorite Compote

1 pound mixed dried fruit (pears, peaches,
    apricots, and prunes, or others)
2 cups boiling water
1 piece of lemon peel, approximately ½ inch wide
    and 2 inches long

Make the compote: Place a knife inside a one-quart glass mason jar or other quart-sized jar with a tight-fitting lid. Add the dried fruit to the jar and boil the water. Pour boiling water over the fruit and cool to room temperature. Add the lemon peel. Cover the jar tightly and refrigerate 24 to 48 hours before serving.

Variation: In a medium soup pot, place $^1/_2$ cup each dried figs, dried cherries, raisins, currants, and prunes. The figs, if they are very large, can be quartered. Add one orange, unpeeled, seeded, and sliced very thinly, 1 cinnamon stick, $^1/_2$ cup honey, 1 tablespoon lemon juice, $1^1/_2$ cups cranberry juice, and $^1/_2$ cup red wine. Bring to a boil, and steep at room temperature until cool. Refrigerate and serve cold.

Note: There are hundreds of recipes for Jewish compote. Papa liked his compote plain and simple. An easy way to spice it up is to add some sugar and a cinnamon stick to the jar, but I have also included my version of this classic dish for those who like a dessert with a more complex flavor.

Apprentice

Three

"... It is recorded that St. Agatha crossed the Mediterranean
from Catania to Callipolis in a walnut shell."

BIZARRE PLANTS,

WILLIAM EMBODEN,

1974

When setup for service at Bistro Redux required that one of the waitstaff go into the basement kitchen to fetch a fresh carton of coffee filters or a new jar of mustard, I always volunteered. Going down there provided an opportunity to pass by the pastry chef's station. I loved to peek into Sophia's little bakery, where she worked surrounded by all the wonderful things I so coveted: bins overflowing with soft flour and sparkling sugar, thick bricks of fragrant chocolate, and piles of shining, professional-quality equipment.

On one of these trips to the basement storeroom, I stopped to lean on Sophia's table and chat with her. I happily breathed in the heady scent of buttery, freshly rolled dough she had draped over the marble-topped table like a linen runner. Sophia returned her rolling pin to the center of a bouquet of wooden spoons and tools in a ceramic jar, then counted the fluted black tart pans she had laid out in a row like china place settings. She looked up at my rapt expression, smiled, and shook her head.

"Look at you," she teased. "You're like a poor kid with her nose pressed to the toy-store window."

"It's true. I wish I were down here baking with you," I confided. Our mutual love of pastry making had made us fast friends.

"Don't be so sure," Sophia said with a laugh, stopping what she was doing to retie the black-and-white bandanna she wore over her long, dark curls. "Baking one cake at home is a whole lot different than baking dozens in a restaurant." She sighed deeply, then fixed me with her amber eyes. "Be careful what you wish for."

New York Times Box T533
New York, NY 10108
September 17, 1989

To whom it may concern,

Please read this letter if you are willing to train someone for the pastry position you advertise in *The New York Times,* Sunday, September 17.

Although I have no formal education in pastry, my great-grandmother owned a bakery and she taught all the generations of my family to bake. Baking has always been a part of my life. I am an enthusiastic and fast learner.

I am also a fine artist (painter) and have been painting and working in restaurants in New York City for the past eight years. My artist's résumé is enclosed if you would like to see it.

Please call me for an interview at your earliest convenience. I look forward to hearing from you.

Sincerely,
Nancy Ring

There is no Yiddish equivalent for the expression "out of the frying pan into the fire." Nevertheless, Great-Grandma Esther Hanna had seen many frying pans and many fires. Like the great fire of 1895, during which she gave birth to my grandfather, Max. Esther worried plenty about Max after that fire too, because no sooner would he reach the age of seven, than the Russian czar would want to conscript him and all boys his age into the Russian Army. Esther Hanna and Great-Grandpa Jacob had seven sons and one daughter, and they had no intention of giving up all those boys after their seventh birthdays. There would be no escaping to America—the quotas restricting the number of immigrants were filled for at least the next two years. There might have been no hope for Esther's boys, except for Baron Maurice De Hirsch, the rich Jewish philanthropist who donated most of his fortune to help Jews escape Europe. A friend of Jacob's told him that the baron had bought farms all over the world, and that his organization had an office in Slonim now, where Jacob and Esther lived on the border of Russia and Poland. So Jacob arranged a meeting with the baron's people.

Jacob knew full well the stature of this generous baron and humbly removed his hat before he shook hands with the representative before him. The representative told him that if Jacob accepted farming land from the baron's association, his family could work its way to the United States. But the only land that was available immediately was in South America.

Jacob said, "I'll take it."

Taiglach is a Jewish dessert that is traditionally made for happy occasions like Rosh Hashanah, the Jewish New Year. I like to think that Esther Hanna baked her famous taiglach to celebrate Jacob's successful meeting with the baron's people, but she probably didn't have time. She and Jacob and their eight children were offered a farm in Argentina, and if they wanted it, they had to pack up a lifetime and leave Slonim in one week.

Esther Hanna was a baker. Apprenticed to a master baker at the age of fourteen, she rose quickly through the ranks of the competitive bakery and soon established her own business. She was a good catch for the widower, Jacob. She knew how to organize, work efficiently, and make do in a pinch. So that's how she managed to pack up her seven boys, her daughter, and her husband, her tart pans and rolling pins and cookie cutters and knives, and her furniture and mirrors and curtains—the baron's people had told them to take everything they owned even if it was expensive to ship because things were so much more expensive to buy where they were going. Yes, that's how she managed to do all that in a week. At least she didn't have to pack her recipes; Esther's recipes were in her head. Measured in pinches and drops and just so much of this and that. She baked by feel. By instinct. And she had to trust that instinct now because it was all she had despite all the things she brought with her, because really, what does a baker know about farming in a remote part of Argentina named "Mosesville" that did not even appear on a map? Nothing. She knows nothing.

So Esther Hanna learned to speak Spanish, adding it to the Polish, Russian, and Yiddish she already knew, and she learned to make rooms in a cold, stone, one-story building without inner walls by hanging her living room curtains from the ceilings. And she learned to harness huge oxen to plow, to milk unruly cows, and how to pray not just for health and wealth and pretty brides for her sons, but for rain and sweet golden corn to sell. To pray for the immigration quotas to open up. For tickets. To America. Life on a farm ain't no step up from a frying pan.

At my interview for the pastry assistant's position, I sat across from one of the most famous chefs in the world in one of the world's most renowned restaurants. But at the time I didn't know that. In fact, I didn't know the names of any of the celebrity chefs. I didn't even know there was such a thing as a celebrity chef. But maybe that's why this chef liked me so much. Later, my friends in the know cringed in horror as I described asking this important man where he went to school and how long he had been cooking. What did I know? I knew Picasso, Rembrandt, Vermeer. I would have trembled like a rock 'n' roll groupie at the chance to meet Georgia O'Keeffe or Louise Nevelson. I had no idea that this chef received hundreds of résumés a week from hopeful apprentices all over the globe. I was just dutifully following the advice of my successful older brother, who told me that a good interview technique is to ask the interviewer something about himself.

My famous chef smiled a wry smile as he politely answered my questions. And I didn't get the job easily. I had to call every other day for three weeks to reach him after two interviews and working a full day for free. Finally, I was called in for one more interview with the esteemed personage of my famous chef.

"I'm going to give you this position," he said, "because I believe you'll be a good person to have in my kitchen."

Happiness, usually so elusive, surged through me with the force of steam through a teakettle's whistle. And I even got the extra amount of money I had asked for. Not that it was much. I wonder now if I would have bubbled so enthusiastically if I'd known anything about the task that lay ahead of me.

"How many, miss?"

I forgave him. I didn't expect him to call me Ms. Besides, maybe he was old-fashioned and noticed my ringless left hand holding my shopping list. "Ma'am" would be worse and make me feel old, and "lady" is almost derogatory these days. Anyway, I was buying nuts from him, not names, and there were a lot of people behind me on line, so I decided it was better not to argue the point. Honey, powdered ginger, fresh eggs . . . The only thing not crossed out on my list was the walnuts I needed to bake taiglach in celebration of getting my new job.

"I'll take a pound," I said.

The shopkeeper reached for a stiff white paper bag, snapped it open with one practiced, concise motion, a jerk of his arm as confident as a conductor leading with a baton, and began to fill it with nuts.

Walnut. Genus *Juglans*. Jove's nut, Jupiter's acorn. Fit for the gods. Nut par excellence, *nux persica, nux regia*, royal nut. A botanist will tell you that walnuts are not strictly nuts, since they are the large seeds of a drupe—a sticky, fleshy green husk—rather than those of a hard, dry casing. Unfortunately, a botanist doesn't price them. Nuts are expensive. Even during the Depression walnuts could fetch a dollar a pound. I flinched at the price, then remembered that walnuts also mean toffee, fudge, cakes, and ice cream, having been preferred by bakers since ancient times for their ability to retain their distinctive flavor after cooking. I accepted the overpriced bag of nuts without complaint.

The Yiddish word *taiglach,* if translated literally, means "little bits of dough." Small balls of pastry are cooked in a gingered honey syrup with walnuts until golden. It is closely related to the Neapolitan *chiacchiere,* literally "chatters," and the French *croquembouche,* meaning "crunches in the mouth." Small pieces of dough, whether cream-filled and piled into tall pyramids, like the French, or baked or fried and studded with candied fruit and colored sprinkles like the Neapolitan, are glued together with a golden caramel. Similarly, my great-grandmother and I were not born in the same country. But I knew in my heart that we were essentially the same.

I was born to bake, and of this I had no doubt. What I didn't know was whether or not I was born to bake in any other kitchen than my own.

In the beginning I felt that somehow Great-Grandma Esther had reached through time to help me get a new job where I would be happier. For one thing, I liked my new uniform. Both male and female chefs always wear the same roomy white coat and baggy hound's-tooth pants. With my big sleeves loosely rolled, and up to my elbows in flour and cookbooks, I heaved an enormous sigh of relief. Relief from the rut I had been in for eight years as a waitress, relief from the boredom, the pretending, the dress. In the kitchen I could be myself. I didn't have to wear makeup. I was being judged for my work, not my bow. That comfortable unisex chef's uniform seemed to even out the competition once and for all.

Or so I thought. All of a sudden I became very aware of my small size and limited strength.

"You need to work out," my new boss, Arana, advised me, giving me the hand exerciser she kept in her purse.

"Just use it whenever you have the chance," she said, "you know, while you're watching TV, or sitting in a bar, or riding the subway."

Arana demonstrated for me casually as we sat after work at the elegant bar of LaCoupe, throwing her thick mane of wavy black hair behind her shoulder to show off her pulsing bicep. It bulged conspicuously beneath the cut-off sleeve of her denim jacket. It was then that I noticed for the first time the long, curved scar that underlined her bicep, and wondered in what battle she had earned it. Because she never mentioned it and I was too shy to ask, its mystery only heightened my awe of her.

I could tell by the amused look in her mint-green eyes that she thoroughly enjoyed the stares of the suits and simple-black-dresses-with-pearls around her. I was inspired. I had a new role model and she was a Woman Chef. Never mind all those women artists I had been admiring my whole life. Here was a woman who could press steeped milk from nuts through cheesecloth with her bare hands, a woman who could lift huge metal bowls of batters and dough, a woman who could carry fifty-pound buckets of peeled Bosc pears, a woman who could organize, manage, and be in charge. And who could cook too.

I felt as if the executive chef at my new job had given me a passport to a new life—a life paved with hard work, but better and freer. I sat on the subway on my way to and from work squeezing my hand exerciser, my nose in a pastry book, completely engrossed.

Footnote. Goodman, pages 295–96, 299. "New nuts, picked before St. John's Day (24 June) were peeled, pricked, and set to soak in water for nine days, the water changed each day. They were drained and dried and the prick holes filled with tiny scraps of ginger and cloves. After, they were boiled in honey and the whole sweet, sticky, fragrant mixture was put in a pot and stored for some very special and very lucky guest." So reads a medieval recipe for "nut sweetmeat" attributed to the Goodman of Paris by Bridget Ann Henisch in her book *Fast and Feast*. Sounds an awful lot like taiglach, I mused when I arrived home with my walnuts and prepared to bake.

Nut sweet-who?

Esther Hanna didn't know from medieval Paris.

My handwritten copy of Esther's taiglach recipe is two pages long, including every detailed instruction that my mother taught me. Still, there are things that can't be explained, that require intuition, the combined memory of a family of bakers—feel.

Add flour to the dough until it can be handled but isn't too dry.

Cook the syrup to just the right shade of caramel, not too dark, but not too light either.

What do you mean, how much ginger? There is no how much.

You do it to taste.

You know.

Yes, I do know, because they know and because they had gathered around me in my kitchen again as I reached for my wooden pastry board and laid it on the counter, imagining the glistening square of taiglach cooling under wax paper, the peppery scent of ginger hanging in the air. All the hands smoothed away a few stray crumbs when I did, and I felt the urge again to pull my hands away, but Esther's hands lingered over mine, insisting I keep listening, moving back and forth over the table, searching the past like turning pages in a cookbook. A baker must have a good imagination and plenty of ambition. I know Grandma Esther did when she was given land in Argentina as smooth and bare as the surface of my pastry board.

Esther's new farm was completely unplanted, without even trees. It would take more than imagination to sow it. And her only ambition at that moment was to work her way to America. And I mean work. Aside from farming corn and potatoes, she had to bake bread each day and sew clothes for eight growing children, with the nearest town eight miles away. And the nearest water.

Grandpa Jacob dug one hundred wells on their land and brought up salt water one hundred times. No farm anywhere around them had clear water. So they had a wagon built with a barrel on top, and three of the boys traveled sixteen miles round trip every day to draw water by hand from a well in town. Jacob fixed it so that if it rained, the rainwater would run down the metal roof and fill a tub. But each morning it didn't rain, the boys would be away five hours. At least they could stop at the kosher market and buy flour and meat while they were away getting the water.

One day Esther had no wood left to burn for her baking and cooking. What little could be found on the bare farm was already burned, the last of it smoldered in the hearth. She couldn't burn the furniture—they would need to sell that for extra money when they left. What could she do? she wondered as the loaves of bread sat rising on a beam near the roof in the warmest spot of the kitchen. She looked out the window. Not the cart or the plow—they needed those even more than the furniture. Esther wasn't one to despair. She walked outside into the midday heat and looked around. There must be something, something.

Great-Grandma Esther believed that food was love.

In a restaurant kitchen, however, food is work.

As the second pastry assistant, I mostly worked at night, plating desserts for dinner service. The huge restaurant filled to capacity with impatient customers, and it was my job to get the pastries out to them as quickly as possible. The plates were elaborate, some with two or three garnishes and just as many sauces. The chef I worked for is known as an artist with food, and all his presentations are like paintings. I could easily appreciate food as artistry. The elaborate dishes were as beautiful as art created during the High Renaissance. What I wasn't so sure about was the High Pressure.

I worked in a tiny space within the huge kitchen. I'd have cakes directly behind me, sauces and garnishes and plates in front of me, and immediately to my left, ice creams, nuts, and fruits. The orders would come in on a little computer, like machine-gun fire: five banana sundaes, four crème brûlées, six chocolate cakes, three sorbets, and I would whirl around in a circle, cutting and squirting and scooping, spatulas and plates and doilies flying, with more and more orders firing in and waiters yelling things at me like "Where's my sundae without nuts for the little girl at Table 12?" or "You forgot the lemon peel for the owner's friends!" or "This is supposed to be chocolate sorbet for the rush order, not raspberry!" I got into a screaming match one night with a haughty waiter named Billy. When I was a waitress, I was quick to criticize or blame the cooks for mistakes or accidents, just like Billy. Now I knew how hot it was in the kitchen. The executive chef stepped between us, took me aside, and calmly advised me.

"Don't fight with them. I know exactly how you feel. They drive us all crazy when it's busy, especially that one," he said, giving the back of Billy's crew cut an angry glance. "Unfortunately, he's an excellent waiter. Just say, 'What do you need?' That's all you need to discuss with them. Not the details of why the lady in green at Table 17 hates hazelnuts. Just ask them until they tell you, '*What do you need?*'"

With my head spinning, I drew a deep breath and tried to absorb this sage advice. With five nights of this hell each week and only one day of actual baking with the pastry chef, I was quickly getting burnt out. On top of everything else, another claustrophobic relationship with a man wasn't working. I would wake up in the mornings with a headache and sit on the floor of my studio trying to draw. All I could manage to make were tiny, crowded boxes filled with diabolical-looking paper dolls that had titles like "Jealousy" or "Snake Garden."

Larousse Gastronomique argues that some historians attribute the recipe for flaky pastry to the seventeenth-century painter Claude Gelée, who apprenticed as a pastry cook. Others say it is the creation of a renowned pastry chef, Feuillet. Larousse explains: ". . . It certainly seems more logical to attribute this invention to a pastrycook than to a painter, but there is no reliable documentary evidence to support this view." With my painting barely touched in months, and clocking out of work at 1:30 in the morning covered from head to foot with chocolate and dough, I'd put my money on the painters. My artwork was definitely on the back burner. All I could hope was that just as the ginger slowly infused the syrup while I baked taiglach, the painter in me would steep in my experience as a chef, making my art richer in the future.

The sun was high in the sky. Esther walked out onto her land in Mosesville, Argentina, and surveyed the terrain. She was tired. All the hard work was catching up with her. She rubbed her aching eyes and squinted into the sun. There was no wood to burn as far as she could see, only the grazing cows, swatting flies with their tails. Esther turned away from the dusty breeze blowing the stench of cow dung into her face. She angrily kicked a piece of dung out of her path. It broke in two, dry and brittle from lying in the sun. Dry and brittle. Esther suddenly had an idea. She pushed the dried dung into a can with a stone and ran into the kitchen with it, placing it gingerly on top of the few remaining coals smoldering in the hearth. It burned. But her elation immediately turned to sickening disgust. Cow's dung, of all things. In her kitchen, of all places.

Esther was Orthodox and kept a kosher kitchen. With every task, no matter how small, she remembered God by following the rituals to the letter. The cow's dung was an insult to all that—to the crumbs she brushed away with a feather on Pesach, to the hand-embroidered cloth she covered the matzos with before she blessed them. Exhausted, angry tears started into her eyes. How do you raise a family in such a place? she cried to herself. But pride was no match for eight hungry children who depended on her, and who looked to her for an example. If she gave up, they would all give up too. Besides, the breads were overproofing beneath the hot metal roof. So Esther summoned her nerve and rose, wiped away her tears, and went back outside to rake all the cow's dung into the sun and let it dry.

Esther stood in the orange glow of the fire, watching the challah bake, comforted and soothed by its fresh smell. But as she watched, she worried. When would the quotas open allowing them to leave Argentina? How much longer would they have to wait? It had already been three years. How much longer could they wait? What if the next time she ran out of something there was nothing to take its place? She had learned a lot of things from the master baker in Slonim, but no one had taught her how to wait so long or how to continue to hope while she waited.

As it turned out, Larousse reports, early documents prove that flaky pastry was known not only in the Middle Ages, but in ancient Greece as well, long before the birth of Claude Gelée. Larousse's recipe for flaky dough requires 3¾ cups of flour, 1½ teaspoons of salt, and 1¼ to 1½ cups of water, depending on the moisture content of the flour. There are eight detailed photographs illustrating how to handle the dough. Its chemistry and physics. Its myth and history and storytelling handed down through generations. Great-Grandma Esther Hanna's taiglach is just as complicated and requires as much careful attention as flaky pastry.

Esther's niece, my cousin Minnie, eventually took all the ingredients from Esther's hands as she was baking and measured them in cups and spoons and wrote them down. Then she translated Esther's directions from the Yiddish so everybody could understand them. Not that it was any more scientific that way. In Esther's taiglach recipe she instructs us to roll dough to the thickness of a jumbo pencil, or walk on a bag of walnuts wrapped in a towel to crush them instead of chopping the nuts with a knife. So the pieces are small, but not too small.

I can tell exactly what Esther was like from her recipes. She was a purist; *use only an unpolished cutting board, natural wood.* And economical, of course; *the honey need not be the expensive grade.* I have a Cuisinart now, and a space-age cutting board made of a nonstick miracle substance. But I still follow the recipe as Esther dictates. I like listening to her. And I like to imagine—if I let myself imagine—my own great-granddaughter in her kitchen with this recipe, walking on walnuts. So the pieces are small. But not too small.

The English word *walnut* derives from the Old English *walhhnuta* as well as from the German *Wallnuss,* or *Welsche Nuss*—*welsche* meaning "foreign," because walnuts were imported.

So were we.

At last Esther and her family were able to purchase visas allowing emigration from Argentina to America. And on February 4, 1904, after selling everything they owned, they boarded the S.S. *Tintoretto* in Buenos Aires and sailed to New York. The passenger list of their ship names each of them and records their ages, sex, marital status, occupation, nationality, race, last residence, destination, contact person in the States, whether they could read and write, and the amount of money they had in their possession at the time they sailed. Five dollars, and I quote, "for the whole family." Still, when they arrived in New York harbor, there was one more sacrifice to make—their name.

My mother tells me that the original version of Esther Hanna's last name sounded almost exactly like the Russian word for "charming," but she can't pronounce it for me anymore. The Americans changed it on Ellis Island, and it was long ago forgotten.

Many walnut trees have sprouted where rodents have buried the nuts for winter food and then never retrieved them. Some forgotten nuts are also carried long distances by floods, which partly explains how walnuts now grow from western Massachusetts to Minnesota, in Connecticut, amid the honey locust and red cedar in the limestone soils of Kentucky, Tennessee, and western Missouri, in a path southward to Florida, in the valley of the San Antonio River in Texas, in California, across the sea in China and the Himalayas, in the adjoining areas of the former USSR, in Iran and Afghanistan, in a swath across the Balkan Peninsula, in Italy and France, in the mountains of Poland, and as far north as Sweden. Often the walnut tree is surrounded by white ash, beech, maple, black cherry, oak, and hickory, or found along stream banks, or thriving in sheltered valleys and on mountain slopes, wherever the soil is rich, fat, and black, wherever their branches can grow large and spreading and their roots can grow deep. Great-Grandma Esther and her family were not to be forgotten, barely surviving in the dry, sandy soil of Argentina. The ocean bore their ship as easily as a walnut carried in a strong flood. All they needed to find out now was whether or not they had been planted in a fertile place where their thirsty roots could dig down.

When the caramel for my taiglach was just the right shade of golden brown, I spread a light film of ice water over my pastry board and quickly poured the molten taiglach onto the board. Then I dipped my warm hands into the icy water again and again to smooth the hot taiglach into a rectangle without burning myself. I covered it with wax paper and carried it to a cool, shaded place in my apartment so that it could set before I cut it.

So many of Great-Grandma Esther's recipes, like taiglach, have methods, like boiling pastry in honey syrup, that echo the cooking of other lands, other cultures. The recipes are as worldly and well traveled as the trunks and suitcases that Esther and her family carried with them. So many recipes, in so many hands, the hands of Jews who had to flee in droves, in shiploads and wagon loads, by the tens of thousands. From Spain, after the expulsion of 1493, to Portugal and South America, and some farther east, to Greece, arriving with their cooking pots and recipes in the thick walnut groves of Italy and Turkey. Or later, in the Carpathian Mountains of Poland, where the partisans camped beneath a towering welter of walnut branches. Perhaps taiglach was made for the very first time from one of those well-traveled recipes for pastry, baked one day in the shade of a walnut tree near a pot of boiling honey syrup in Greece. Perhaps. What's certain is that the recipes were changed by the cuisines of their new homes as surely as boiling honey takes on the flavor of a teaspoon of ginger. And perhaps Great-Grandma Esther's recipes were changed the same way, in America, when she cut her taiglach into bars, just like the popular American bar cookies, instead of forming them into the large rings or balls the Jewish bakeries displayed in their windows. Perhaps. What's certain is that America would change more than Esther's recipes.

Great-Grandma Esther Hanna and I both made it to our "foreign" destinations—she to New York City, and me to a three-star restaurant kitchen—at nearly the same moment in our lives. Esther was very close to my age when she sailed on the *Tintoretto*. Too bad, though, that Esther couldn't see me in the future as clearly as

I can see her in the past across the ocean of nearly one hundred years. She could have warned me if my fate in the kitchen was to be the same as hers in America. Because the trick now wasn't the choppy passage to a new world, which we had both navigated without mishap, but the survival of our dreams—dreams as vulnerable as a taiglach recipe baked in a new country—now that we had arrived.

Great-Grandma Esther Hanna's Taiglah *

4 extra-large eggs, separated
4 tablespoons vegetable oil
1 level teaspoon ground ginger (for dough)
Approximately 1½ to 2 cups all-purpose flour
12 ounces honey (need not be expensive grade)
1 teaspoon ground ginger (for syrup) plus extra for sprinkling
½ cup sugar
6-ounce bag of shelled walnuts
6 or 7 vanilla wafer cookies

*As dictated to me by my mother, Esther Hanna's granddaughter, while she baked.

Prepare the dough balls: *Preheat oven to 425 degrees. Lightly oil two cookie sheets and set aside. Beat together yolks, oil, and 1 teaspoon of the ginger. Beat egg whites until they form stiff peaks. Fold egg whites into yolk mixture. Add flour to egg mixture, $^1/_2$ cup at a time, folding until a sticky dough forms that can be handled with floured hands. Flour a board, and sprinkle the dough with extra flour. Pull off medium-size pieces of dough one at a time, and elongate each piece by rolling with palms and fingers to the size of a thick jumbo pencil, at least $^5/_8$ inch wide. Flour a knife and cut dough logs into marble-size pieces about $^3/_4$ inches long. Gently place each piece of dough on the baking sheet. Space the dough $^1/_2$ inch apart. Bake 8 to 10 minutes, until dough is golden, puffed up, and dry inside. Cool.*

Prepare the syrup: *After dough cools, pour honey, remaining teaspoon of ginger, and sugar into a medium-size soup pot, stir, and bring to a boil.*

Cook the taiglach: *Wrap walnut bag in a towel and walk on it briefly to get small pieces. Add baked dough and walnuts to hot honey syrup and stir to coat. Cook walnut/taiglach mixture over medium-low heat, stirring occasionally from the bottom of the mixture up, 15 minutes or more. Mixture will bubble. Taiglach is ready for the next step of the recipe when it is dark golden brown.*

Form the taiglach: *Have a clean, unpolished natural wood board ready, and the extra ginger. Put ice water in a bowl and set nearby. Rub cold water on wooden board in a light film. When taiglach is ready, scrape it from pot onto wet surface. Taiglach is extremely hot and must be handled quickly before it sets. Put hands into ice water until they are wet and cold. Push taiglach down while returning hands to ice water as necessary, until a rectangle is formed, approximately 1 inch thick. Any size rectangle is fine. Square off the corners. Sprinkle with more ground ginger while hot, to taste. Cover lightly with wax paper and let cool until solid, in a cool, shady place, no sun.*

Finish the taiglach: *Crush vanilla wafers between sheets of wax paper with a rolling pin. Cut cooled taiglach into bars. Dip bottoms of bars into cookie crumbs and store in a cool, dry place in an airtight container. Do not refrigerate. Yields approximately two dozen two-inch squares.*

Four

*"The walnut is a melancholy tree, for in parts of the old world,
as you walk beneath it of an evening, you may hear
the servants of the devil whispering, snickering,
and gibbering in its branches."*

MYTHS AND LEGENDS OF FLOWERS, TREES, FRUITS, AND PLANTS

IN ALL AGES AND IN ALL CLIMES,

CHARLES M. SKINNER,

1911

*lam.* Arana's chocolate-smeared hand slapped a piece
of paper down on our crowded worktable, amid the
cutting boards strewn with flour, the metal containers full of knives and spoons and spatulas, and the
square plastic containers of half-finished strudel fillings and sorbets.
I was adding my name to the list of employees attending the staff
Christmas party the following night, and the table and everything
on it rocked, distorting my signature. I gasped. What was that, an
earthquake? No, it was a recipe, which was nearly the same thing at

LaCoupe, where every task was so huge, it had the potential to level the kitchen. I tentatively reached across a sheet pan of reindeer sugar cookies and slid the recipe from under Arana's hand.

"What is it?" I asked, not without some trepidation.

The cook who had asked me to sign the party list shoved a chef's hat in my face and gestured for me to pick a name from the hat for the grab-bag gift-giving at the party.

"It's the crème brûlée," Arana announced. "I need you to make them as soon as you're done piping red icing noses onto all those Rudolphs. We're completely out and we need them for tonight." Then she abruptly turned and hurried back to the walk-in refrigerator, where she was rolling chocolate truffles away from the heat of the kitchen.

I opened the notebook where I kept instructions on all the recipes I had learned so far, which were many and detailed. Crème brûlée, crème brûlée . . . here it was, a page of dense scribbling, arrows, crossings-out, and drawings. Everything I learned I learned in a hurry. LaCoupe was so popular that Arana could barely keep up with the production of desserts, even with two assistants. One of those assistants was me, inexperienced and slow. While I was being taught most of the recipes, there was barely time to think, let alone take notes. It had been fairly easy to learn biscotti, which were so much like Grandma Selma's mandelbrot, or work with phyllo dough, which was exactly like Great-Grandma Esther's strudel dough. An elegant custard like crème brûlée, though, bore little resemblance to my grandmother's rustic custard for noodle pudding. Besides, I felt vulnerable in the big kitchen, surrounded by mostly male cooks who were not only ten years younger than I but also hotshot culinary school graduates. I looked up. The executive chef was watching me like a beady-eyed hawk, as usual.

I'd seen Arana make crème brûlée only once. Sweat formed on my top lip as I stared at her copy of the recipe. Only amounts of ingredients were listed, no methods or explanations. I suddenly re-membered that feeling I would get during hide-and-seek as a child, so scared I thought I might wet my pants right before getting found. I've got to get her to show this to me one more time, I thought. I don't think I'm ready to do this by myself yet.

"You've got to do this on your own," Arana growled at me when I came into the walk-in refrigerator to ask her for help. "We're too busy for me to baby-sit you anymore."

"I really don't feel confident yet about this," I tried to excuse myself.

One of the other women chefs, Wendy, was in the walk-in lift-ing a huge bucket of peeled carrots.

"Crème brûlée is such a beginner's recipe," she sneered, looking disgusted.

"Just get out of here and do it," said Arana, annoyed. "I do not have the time to help you, *period!*" She looked at me sympathetically, but her tone of voice let me know that she meant what she said.

Sheepishly, I said, "Okay, but I need to borrow your timer again, if it's all right."

I'd had to buy several costly knives when I got the position, and I didn't have the extra money yet to buy an expensive timer. The pastry chef had a sleek digital timer that had a clock in it as well.

"Fine," she said, "borrow the timer. Just get your butt in gear."

As I anxiously walked out of the fridge back to the crème brûlée recipe, I heard the tinny popping sound of a metal can being pumped as Arana squirted walnut oil into her melted white choco-late to thin it. Walnut oil was also smeared on the inky smocks of engravers, who considered it essential for printing engravings in seventeenth- and eighteenth-century Paris. There was also walnut oil in van Eyck's paint, on the Venetian painters' canvases, and on the tip of Caravaggio's brushes to help dry the paint faster. If wal-nuts could work in both pastry and art, I decided, so could I.

~⌒~

Crème brûlée, literally "burnt cream," is an egg-rich vanilla-sweetened custard served with a layer of brittle caramel on top as thin as a sheet of glass. The English boast that they created it first, since it was served at King's College, Cambridge, for special occasions at least two hundred years ago. Because of its similarity to the Spanish custard crema Catalana, though, the Catalans also claim to be the dessert's inventors. Britain seems to have the weight of documentation on its side, however, since burnt cream is included in a seventeenth-century recipe collection from Dorset. In the kitchen of LaCoupe, I was as much at a loss to produce my baking credentials as crema Catalana, looking for all the world like the real thing, but without papers to offer as proof.

It's funny how women do most of the cooking in the home, but in the workplace it's mostly men—men with degrees in cooking who love to lord that fact over self-taught women. I had a degree, also, but it was in art. So I had followed the advice of friends and enrolled in part-time pastry school as soon as I knew I had an interview for a pastry position, believing it would help me get the job. It did. But real life soon made it obvious that school wasn't worth the amount it was putting me in debt.

In school we made small amounts of pastry on pristine, state-of-the-art equipment, baby-sat by an experienced teacher who made sure we succeeded with each recipe. At work we made giant quantities of cakes, sauces, batters, and dough on old equipment with missing parts. It was often unclear whether I was controlling the dough, as big as a battleship, or the dough was controlling me. We usually had to substitute an ingredient or a different size bowl or pot for the one we couldn't find or didn't have, and half the time, as with the crème brûlée, Arana was too busy to stay with me every step of the way. Besides, no amount of schooling can help a woman in a man's domain. That takes a kind of nerve. So I quit school. Besides, it was Great-Grandma Esther's intuition that was guiding me now, and that was free.

Whisk, ladle, large bowl, chinois. Arana always told me, with every new recipe, to get my equipment first. I scanned the scribbled instructions in my notebook. No—whisk, ladle, large bowl, *measuring cup*, chinois. Oh, forget it, I thought. I had a liquid to cook, correct? The recipe began: "Bring cream, vanilla beans, and one cup of sugar to scald. Remove from heat and steep for two hours." What I needed first was a pot. I hurried across the kitchen, big enough to be an airplane hangar but crowded with cooks in the midst of every conceivable project, dodging a sheet pan perched on a shoulder here, a crate being hoisted onto a table there. Pots, pots, pots. I was standing in front of the pot shelf, where they should have been, but every single one was in use or in the sink. I ran to the dishwasher.

"José," I pleaded, "please, uh, *por favor, limpia esto ahora. Y no lo ponga alli.*" I pointed at the pot shelf. *"Gracias. Muchas gracias."* I knew if the pot went back on the shelf, it would disappear in a minute.

Luckily, I'd also inherited some of Great-Grandma Esther's ease with languages. A restaurant kitchen in New York City probably requires as much Spanish as Argentina. I raced back across the kitchen to get cream and vanilla beans, and measure out the sugar that would go into the pot, while glancing over my shoulder at José, to make sure he understood me. That's when I ran smack into Dean, another cook, carrying a huge tray of salmon fillets. Beautiful and terrible, the glowing orange fish skidded across the slate-gray tile floor of the kitchen like a fluorescent waterfall churning down into a slick, dark sea.

"Goddammit, Nancy!" complained Dean as we scurried around on the kitchen floor, picking up the salmon fillets. "Watch what you're doing!"

"I'm sorry, Dean," I said, knowing my apology was worthless compared to the arduous task of rinsing and drying all the fillets.

"Do you want me to wash them for you?" I offered.

"No, no, it's okay," he said. Dean was nice to me. He was like a big teddy bear, a teddy bear with a beer belly and frizzy red hair. "You've got enough to do," he reminded me.

A porter carrying a tray of martini glasses nearly tripped over us and swore, and then one of the cooks slipped on a fillet and dropped some empty bowls he was carrying.

"Nice going!" the cook yelled at me.

"Just pay attention," said Dean gently but firmly. "You're pissing everybody off."

I walked quickly but carefully to the refrigerator, where Arana was still working, and piled nine quarts of cream into my arms, balancing the bag of vanilla beans on top. Arana made small talk, as if she were trying to let me know she wasn't really mad at me.

"What are you going to wear to the Christmas party?" she asked.

"I don't know," I answered honestly, "I haven't had time to think about it, really. What are you wearing?"

"Just wait and see!" She laughed. Her eyes glowed like a cat's with mischief.

I smiled appreciatively. Everyone at work knew that Arana was flamboyant. When things got tough, she would stand up on the worktables and do her imitation of Janis Joplin singing "Piece of My Heart" at the top of her lungs. She had an amazing voice, powerful and throaty, but swore up and down she had never sung professionally. Her opinions, on everything from sex (which seemed to be her favorite subject) to law, were scathingly funny. And she never hesitated to opine, in a loud voice, reducing everyone around her to delirious laughter. Feminist to the core, it irked her no end that her name wasn't on the dessert menu yet after two years in the pastry department. The executive chef received all the credit. I don't know if that had anything to do with why she showed up to work hung over occasionally, but when she did, I just tried to ignore it.

I looked at her in the walk-in, rolling her truffles—her strong, muscular forearms and hands covered with chocolate, a strand of her dark hair, escaped from the topknot she wore at work, hanging down on her smooth forehead, and her starched apron smeared with cocoa handprints. With her eyes lowered in quiet concentration, her face was as delicate and serene as a portrait of a virgin from a Renaissance painting.

"They should put your *picture* on the menus," I teased her.

"Wait," she said, popping a truffle into her mouth. "Okay, now you can take my picture."

She chewed the truffle, then grinned broadly at me, chocolate lips, tongue, and teeth. I cracked up, at once repulsed and appreciative of her irreverence.

"Now, get the hell out of here and get your ass to work!" she yelled, her chocolate mouth still grinning.

Arana may have had a virgin's face, but her mouth was pure harlot.

I could feel the smile wipe right off my face the minute I stepped out of the walk-in, however, when I saw José absentmindedly put my clean pot on the pot shelf. I piled the quarts of cream and vanilla beans on my worktable and hurried across the kitchen to try to save my precious pot.

Esther Hanna knew that hard work was nothing to fear. Work wasn't a grind or a dead end. It was a beginning, a ticket to a better place. Like America. A place where they believed in freedom for everyone. And education. Her son, Max, had been only four when his family left Russia. So it was with much pride and a mother's high expectations that Max was proudly enrolled in school for the first time in his life in America, the land of opportunity. Class 1A of the first grade. It was September 1904. He was eight years old.

Max did well in school, testing eighty-second out of thirty-five hundred boys in the exams for vocational school admittance. And he excelled there. But this was during a recession, and Papa Jacob didn't always get paid on time by the customers who hired his construction company. Esther had to borrow a quarter each day from the neighbors so Max could take two buses and a subway to get to school, buy lunch, and return home. Max hated hearing Esther asking for the quarter in the hallway of their tenement building. Some days he would hitchhike to and from school just so he wouldn't have to bear the sound of her begging on his behalf. The quarter seemed to shine with insolence, burning Max's leg inside his pocket with the fire of shame. The neighbors didn't mind lending Esther the quarter, proud as they were of little Max, grown up so big and handsome and smart. But Max minded.

One day he came home and told his mother that a new school had been built nearer home. Great-Grandma Esther was probably feeling grateful for small favors when Max said he'd be able to walk to the new school, saving the evil quarter. Esther would have to come with Max to the Board of Education office to sign papers allowing him to transfer to the new school. Esther spoke no English at this time. Max would tell her what to say and do when they got there.

Walnut trees were once believed to harbor evil spirits in their branches. If one walked beneath them, it was possible to hear the spirits and be inspired to behave in an obscene or hostile way. The old stories allege that in Benevento, Italy, under siege by Emperor Constantius, Saint Barbatus blamed the perversity of the populace on the local black walnut tree. Barbatus claimed that the tree was the source of the scandals, had it cut down, sprinkled holy water on the serpent that tried to escape from the tree trunk as it fell and revealed Satan. Maybe Max walked under a black walnut tree before he arrived at the Board of Education with Esther.

"Come with me."

Arana caught up with me as I hurried across the kitchen to get my pot. She had to change into a clean uniform for a meeting with the chef to be held upstairs in the dining room, and she pulled me into the cooks' locker room to talk while she changed.

"Arana, I'm right in the middle of making the crème brûlée you said you needed," I told her anxiously, "and I have to get my—"

"I'm late and I need you for a minute right now before I go upstairs to this meeting," she interrupted, and began pulling notes for the spring menu we had worked on together out of her locker. She held the notes in her mouth while shrugging out of her dirty chef's coat, all the while speaking through her clenched teeth. "Tell m' again the deshcription of the shundae you want to shubmit t' da chef."

I edged my way to the locker-room door and squinted across the kitchen at my pot. It sat there as vulnerable as a baby chick in a roomful of hungry hawks. Arana yanked me back into the locker room to get my attention on the menu again.

We shared a locker room with the men and it was supposed to be understood that the men would wait while we changed and vice versa, but the cooks always tried to peek. They were constantly threatening to come in while the women changed, or trying to walk in "accidentally" so they could see us. A bunch of the cooks were standing near the locker room while Arana changed, craning their necks in her direction and shouting catcalls at her. We tried to ignore them, but I could tell by the expression on Arana's face that she was getting angry.

"I'm gonna teach those guys a lesson," she abruptly said, shoving the menu notes into my hands. Defiance lit up her eyes almost more than mischief.

I watched as Arana peeled off the rest of her uniform and underwear and stood completely naked in the locker room. She wrapped her clean chef's coat around her like a robe, holding it closed with her hands.

"Watch this," she told me.

She waltzed out into the kitchen, stood in the middle of the room, opened her chef's coat, and flashed the cooks her beautiful naked body in all its glory. She smiled from ear to ear. Then the smile dissolved and she shouted at them, "There! Now you've seen it, all right? So shut up!"

The cooks were stunned speechless. Their mouths dropped open so wide, I thought they'd never close them again. Arana returned to the locker room, where I was standing immobilized by shock. Her face looked as cool as a porcelain sink. She put on her uniform, took the menu pages from my hands while giving me further instructions about work, then exited the locker room to thunderous applause. She strode up the stairs to the dining room, her head held high, triumphant. Several of the cooks bowed and I heard someone yell, "You're a goddess!"

For a minute I was afraid to leave the locker room. I didn't know how the cooks would react. But Arana's ploy had worked, taking the fun out of the cooks' hunting game by taking away the prey. I cautiously tiptoed out, realized with relief that the cooks were not even looking in my direction, and then ran across the kitchen in hot pursuit of my pot just as it was being picked up by another cook.

"Hold it, Josh," I said when I got to the pot shelf. There was a serious lack of equipment at LaCoupe, as at most restaurants. José was nowhere in sight. "That's my pot. I had José wash it for me."

"Nice try," said Josh, starting to walk away with the pot.

"No, really," I pleaded. "C'mon, Josh, have a heart. I'm in the weeds. I really did have it washed for me, honest."

Just then my guardian angel walked by and overheard the conversation.

"It's true," said Dean. "Give her the pot."

Josh looked mildly annoyed, but he stopped walking away. I couldn't help wondering if I was a guy, like Dean, whether Josh would have argued with me at all. Or a woman like Arana.

"Give her the pot, Josh, you jerk," Arana said, unexpectedly coming up behind us, and swiped the pot out of his hands. As she handed it to me and hurried off, she said, "Didn't I tell you always to get your equipment first?"

"I—I thought you were upstairs . . ." I stammered to Arana, who hurried off again, saying over her shoulder that her meeting was delayed. There was no use in explaining to her back, so I just begged for space on the stove—no small feat, as the stove was covered with stockpots and meats and vegetables being prepared for lunch, with four cooks crowded in the small space in front of them—opened up all nine quarts of cream, emptied them two at a time into the pot, split the vanilla beans down the center lengthwise, held them open and scraped them with the back of my paring knife onto a piece of parchment paper, scooped up the sugar with a metal measuring cup, and dumped it with the vanilla seeds into the pot.

Then I put the flame on high.

"Whose name did you pick to buy a Christmas present for at the party?" Dean asked me as I worked near him on the stove.

"I'm not telling," I said, smiling. "Who did you pick?"

"I'm not telling either," he replied, not a little smug.

I hadn't thought about it until then, and I wondered just who had picked whom.

"Who do you think got the chef?" I asked rhetorically, raising my eyebrows.

"I don't know," laughed Dean. "What do you think he got us?"

All week the chef had been hinting that he had a special gift for each of us.

"Ha!" I said. "Probably diapers!"

We both laughed.

Unfortunately, the stove was not within sight of my worktable, to which I had to return to continue the other things I had been do-ing before Arana asked me to make the crème brûlée.

"Don't let this boil over," I said to no one in particular.

Great-Grandma Esther sat in the Board of Education office with her hands neatly folded in her lap. Her son Max was with her, whom she had carried through the Argentinean back roads, whom she had learned to trust like she trusted the steady weight of the handle of her oldest chopping knife, whom she trusted like good black lace-up shoes, or like the thickness of her sturdy tea glass. This trusted son stood nearby.

"Do you wish your son to quit school and go to work, madam?" asked the superintendent.

"Mama," Max 'translated,' "the man says, do you want me to transfer to the new school closer to home."

Max motioned for Esther to say yes, nodding his round face, just like hers. His wide-set eyes, just like hers, were steel gray this morning, and his full mouth, just like hers, set in a firm, straight line.

"Yes," said Esther Hanna Kasofsky.

With a sigh, but no protest, knowing these were hard times, the superintendent pushed a contract toward her. "We just need your signature," he pointed, "there."

"Mama, sign where he tells you and I can start at the new school today."

Esther signed. Then Max took her home and that afternoon got a job in a taxicab factory. Two dollars a week for six days' work, with Saturdays off. And he could walk to work.

To make the caramel on crème brûlée, the professional baker sprinkles just the right amount of sugar onto the set, chilled custard, and then slowly torches the sugar until it is deeply colored and brittle but not burned. Using a torch to make the caramel takes a bit of practice and patience—the sugar must not be sprinkled too heavily or too lightly, the torch must be held at just the right angle and for just the right amount of time so that the caramel is sweet, not bitter, and not too thick.

Great-Grandma Esther and Great-Grandpa Jacob had been very patient. By the time they arrived in America, their plans were laid as carefully as grains of sugar on the surface of crème brûlée. They were certain that the future in America for their children would be just as sweet. But their crème brûlée was a caramel-covered dream of a dessert, of a reward for all their suffering. It was a painting of a perfect dessert, and not a real one. In order to eat a real crème brûlée, the caramel must be broken.

"Boiling over! Boiling over!"

I ran to the stove and turned off the flame under the pot.

"Thanks, you guys," I kidded the cooks near the stove. "I told you, 'don't let it boil over,' not 'tell me when it boils over.' "

"Hey, we're not being paid to watch your pot," one of them retorted, and gave me a too hard but playful slap on the back.

He was right, but I was irritated and not in the mood. "Cut it out," I said sharply.

"Oooh, watch out," he said loudly to everyone, "I think it's that time of the month." The cooks howled.

I don't even have to say what I was thinking then. As we were soon to discover, Arana had scored one point when she stripped for the cooks. They never bothered us in the locker room again. But the cooks lost no time trying to win back the advantage. Too bad I had to ask one of them to help me lift the pot off the stove and carry it to the pastry table. Humiliated, I swore to myself I would start lifting weights as soon as I could. Then I measured the cream again to see how much I had lost. Only two cups. I added that back in and returned to my other work, letting the liquid steep for the required two hours.

"Is that cream steeping?" asked Arana as she passed by, carrying strudels into the walk-in. "Good," she said when she saw the pot, "we used up the few that were left from yesterday at lunch." I felt the pressure climb up my neck. "Bake off half the batch when it's ready," she continued. "You'll need about thirty-five custard dishes, right?" She was testing me.

"Right," I answered hesitantly, looking over at the custard cups on the shelf beneath the stove and quickly counting in my head. Twenty or so. Damn. Back to the dishwasher. In Stark City, Missouri, a black walnut tree once produced the record annual yield of walnuts: five hundred and seventy-one pounds, which was estimated at 12,740 nuts. Too bad custard cups didn't grow on walnut trees.

The first week at the taxicab factory, Max got paid on Friday, after only four days of work. There were two crisp dollars in his envelope. Two dollars was the pay for six days, not four. Max approached his new boss immediately, as honest as he was proud.

"Mr. Goldman," he said, "I worked only four days. You paid me for six."

"You're worth it," Mr. Goldman replied simply.

Max worked so hard the next week that he got a raise, to $2.50 a week. Up until then he had kept his job a secret from Esther and Jacob, afraid how they would react. But with the salary he had earned in his fist, he ran all the way home, convinced that his parents would be so happy to see the money they needed so badly, they wouldn't mind how he had deceived his mother to take a job. He arrived at their apartment, completely out of breath from running from the factory and taking the three flights of stairs to their walk-up two at a time. He was so excited and clenched the money so tightly that he could barely open his fist. Esther watched, astounded, as Max slowly opened his trembling hand and four and a half dollars fell onto the oilcloth on her kitchen table. Great-

Grandma Esther took the sugar cube from between her front teeth where she held it while drinking tea from her glass.

"Where did you get that money?" she asked him, delighted and confused.

Jacob had entered the room by then, also, and looked at his boy, waiting for an answer.

"I'm not going to school!" Max blurted out, flushed and panting, "I'm working!"

Esther and Jacob looked at Max in dismay, suddenly deprived of their dream to see their boys finish school and have a better life in America. A dream that had kept them going in Argentina, that had put life back into their cramped fingers while they pulled stubborn potatoes from the hard ground, a dream that had eased the pain from their arms and backs as they hoisted huge bushels of corn, a dream that had urged them to sell everything they ever owned to buy visas and tickets and lose even their proper name, their history. The smiles and laughter Max had anticipated were not to appear. Instead, Max watched with an aching heart as both his parents hung their heads and wept.

Once, when I had despaired as a child, I tried to run away from home. I made it to the lonely, dark cul-de-sac at the end of our street before I realized that I knew of absolutely no place I could go where I could trust someone not to return me home immediately. Fear stopped me from going where I had never been without money, without even a suitcase. I was wearing a sleeveless cotton sundress and plastic beach shoes, and carrying my doll. I turned back, frustrated and powerless, and took refuge in my mother's kitchen.

We were pensive bakers that night, she with that worried expression that later became permanent when the lines above her nose and next to her eyebrows deepened, and me, pouting. There didn't seem to be any more of an alternative for me now other than staying in the kitchen at LaCoupe. I ached all over and I was still broke, with no overtime compensation. I despaired over my art studio, practically empty since I had started my new job. What would happen now to four years of art school and ten years of painting? Then again, time passed quickly while I was baking, unlike the minutes that had turned to hours while waitressing. Maybe the kitchen was still a good place to come back to.

"Do I pour the yolks into the cream or the cream into the yolks?" I asked the air around me when I stood ready to make the crème brûlée. I had the reheated cream in the pot on one side of me, and the yolks mixed with the rest of the sugar in a huge metal bowl on the other.

"First some of the hot cream goes into the yolks, to temper them," said Dean, behind me, "and then the warm yolks go back into the cream. Or you can just continue to pour all the cream into the yolks. It doesn't matter."

"I feel like the scarecrow in *The Wizard of Oz,*" I said, and crossed my arms over my chest, pointing my whisk at one wall and my measuring cup at the opposite wall.

"You have a brain," he chided me, "unlike the scarecrow. Use it."

"Thanks for the vote of confidence," I said. I needed that.

Squinting anxiously at my notes through the entire operation, I gently whisked the custard and poured it through a fine strainer into a metal container, letting the tiny vanilla seeds pass through. Then I washed off the hulls of the vanilla beans and put them aside to dry. We would use them later to make vanilla sugar.

After the crème brûlée was mixed, I began to pour it into the custard cups I had gathered from all over the kitchen and wiped out by hand (when will they invent a dishwasher that can get crème brûlée out of the corners of ceramic dishes?) and that I had arranged in the newest, flattest sheet pans I could find, another scavenger hunt and adventure in bartering. The sheet pans have to be flat so that the custards don't come out lopsided. With these treasures assembled, I had only to fill the cups, surround them with water to steam them, cover the trays to prevent the steam from escaping, and bake them in the oven, behind me. I filled thirty-two cups on two large sheet pans, burning the bubbles off the top of each one with a small torch so that the custards wouldn't be pockmarked, and stirring the mix from time to time so that the vanilla seeds wouldn't settle to the bottom, just as I had written in my notes. Then I ever so slowly picked up a large tray of sixteen cups, balanced it, and turned. The oven was only four feet away, but it seemed like miles with the custard sloshing gently in the cups. I held my breath and took a small, tentative step.

Suddenly I felt someone tap me on the shoulder.

"Scuze me!" said Antonio.

I stopped to see who it was just as the waiter, Billy, swung around the corner toward me carrying an exceptionally tall, shivering tower of salad swaying precariously back and forth on its plate, balanced on a tray.

"Watch out!" cried Billy. "I just want to get this ridiculous thing safely to the table without it falling over!"

I gasped and wobbled, surprised, but not set off balance.

"Please, miss," Antonio said politely, "I can use the peeler?"

"Sure, sure," I answered, "take it from my bag." I had a French peeler, with a shiny red handle and a sharp stainless swivel-top blade that could be adjusted for peeling in two directions. It cost only five dollars, but I knew to Antonio, with his porter's pay, a wife and two kids, English language night school, and whoever else he was supporting back home in his country, it must have seemed like it cost a fortune. He borrowed it nearly every day, since it made his work go much faster than the old dull peelers the restaurant had.

I centered myself again, and continued toward the oven. That's when I noticed I hadn't opened the oven doors.

"Idiot!" I scolded myself under my breath. There was no way I could open those doors without putting the tray back down and starting over.

Just then wonderful Dean, heroic Dean, fabulously special Dean, came around the corner. He shook his head, grinning, and opened the oven for me.

"What would you do without me?" he asked me.

"Scary thought," I answered, putting the tray in the oven.

I slid the tray onto the oven shelf and filled it with water from a pitcher until the cups were in a bath halfway up their sides, covered the tray with another sheet pan, and shut the oven door.

As I picked up the second tray of custards, the hand towel I kept tucked in the waist strings of my apron got caught underneath, between my hand and the tray, and when I tried to lift the tray, it jerked and spilled a third of the custard mix into the tray. Mortified, I looked around. Luckily, Arana and the executive chef were finally in their meeting upstairs. A couple of cooks nearby gave me amused looks, but nobody said anything. Blushing, I set the tray back down and began the task of lifting out the sixteen cups, one at a time, wiping the tray and the outside of the cups, and refilling the cups once again. Finally, I waddled to the oven with this tray and nervously set a timer. The crème brûlées are tricky. They have to be timed carefully or they can all be lost.

Smoke is pouring from the ovens. Something is burning. Something is wrong. Suddenly I'm running down Stanton Street on the Lower East Side, to Esther Hanna's redbrick building, the one with the stoop, next to the egg cream shop. I run up the three flights of stairs, take the intricate, old-fashioned key, and unlock the big wooden door, anticipating Esther's warm embrace, the blessing she will say, as she always said for the children, with her warm hand on my forehead, the smell of her cooking like a blanket wrapped around me. I run through the kitchen—maybe she is on the fire escape, pounding a rug with a righteous vengeance. No, not there. Maybe in the bedroom, making the high bed covered with goosedown pillows and quilt, or tasting her homemade honey wine, kept in a barrel by the door, the wine her boys discreetly sold to the neighbors during the Depression. Still, she's not there. Maybe in the dining room, playing her Victrola. She isn't there either. My heart pounds in desperation. I need her, I need her advice, her concern, her care. But she can't be there. She is gone, many years gone. And even if she were there by some miracle of time warping in on itself, she still wouldn't recognize me. She never knew me.

Great-Grandma Esther Hanna died before I was born. How do I know so much, then, about her house, her clothes, her thoughts, her life, her ability to help me overcome my feelings of despair? From the stories. The stories I longed to embrace, if only I could be sure that I wouldn't be trapped in that embrace.

My cousin's son, Aaron, tape-recorded my grandfather, Max, for a school project years before he died. It's difficult to listen to Max's gentle voice on the tape now, as his body lies deep in the cold earth miles and miles away. But I listen and listen well. That's how we got so many of the stories. Stories about people who weren't famous enough or historically important enough or powerful enough to end up in the books that every schoolchild studies.

When Great-Grandma Esther died, the community she lived in afforded her an honor that usually was given only to Orthodox rabbis at their funerals. The hearse carrying her coffin stopped in front of her synagogue. Her coffin was carried into the temple, where the holy men said prayers over her before she was returned to her trip to the cemetery. They did this because she was an important woman in the temple, having started a soup kitchen there for the hungry, having sheltered the homeless, and having lived a long, productive, and loving life.

That's famous.

When Great-Grandma Esther and little Max left Slonim with their family, it was 1899. Nearly one hundred years later, her great-granddaughter sits writing about the pull-chain toilet in her family's walk-up tenement apartment on Stanton Street, where Esther wore her rolled stockings with garters, listened to her hinged-top wooden wind-up Victrola, and had ice delivered for her icebox.

That's history.

And listening to Max's voice on the tape, tears flowing relentlessly down my face, I swear I can see every muscle straining in Max's arms as he and his brothers pull pure clean water up in a metal bucket from a brick well in Argentina, the coarse handmade rope burning their callused, reddened hands. As Max tells and tells, and they pull and pull, I can feel the heat, I can feel the beads of sweat on his forehead under his felt cap, I can feel his thirst, his will to survive, his perseverance, his hope. I'm armed with this story. This story is my shield. I carry this story in my body like a strong backbone, like a ringing voice, like a pair of wings.

That's power.

In Mosesville, Argentina, there is no monument to Esther Hanna Kasofsky. Go ahead. Try to find one. What you will find eventually, if you keep trying, is the name of the town she came from, Slonim, etched on the wall in the Holocaust Museum in Washington, D.C., where they have etched the names of all the towns that were completely or partially destroyed during World War II. We have no records, no birth certificates, nothing. What we have are the stories. And the recipes.

What I had yet to realize was that I was studying more than recipes at LaCoupe. The moment I put on my chef's coat, a door opened into my past that I could enter just by holding tight to Esther's apron strings. Behind that door was something I needed in the present, something that would keep all the recipes from the past from turning to dust the minute they hit the glare of my modern life. I just wouldn't know what that was until all the recipes had been followed.

The timer went off.

Crème brûlées take about forty minutes to set. One has to watch them carefully at the end, though, because there is only a minute's leeway between set and curdled. I could safely set a timer for twenty minutes, and then begin the checking and rechecking every two or three minutes.

I opened the oven doors and slowly lifted the sheet pan covering the first tray of crème brûlées. A cloud of steam wafted toward me, obscuring my view for a few seconds. Then I had an unpleasant surprise.

The entire first tray of brûlées was ruined—the surfaces of the custards as uneven and potholed as the surface of the moon. How could this be? Panic crawled up my back and raised the fine hair on my arms. I had been so careful setting the timer. I knew I had set it for only twenty minutes. I was sure of that. I looked at the oven temperature. It was correct, 325 degrees. I carried the tray to my table and quickly dug a spoon into a custard—curdled all the way through. For a horrified moment I was completely at a loss for an explanation. Then I realized—I had forgotten to take into account the fact that this tray went into the oven first. During the ten minutes it took me to clean up after my spill on the second tray, the first tray had been baking. I was so nervous, I didn't even think about the extra time going by. Some things I was destined to learn the hard way. Arana looked over my shoulder, exasperated, while I tried to explain.

"It's okay," she said. "You still have the other tray. Just keep your eye on it, *please*. Tomorrow we close early for the staff Christmas party, so we won't need so many anyway. I was just trying to get ahead, which would be nothing short of a miracle around here." I hung my head guiltily. "Don't look so upset," she added. "The chef loved your idea for the coffee and sambuca sundae on the spring menu."

I looked up, happy but shocked. Arana had asked me for input, but I never thought my ideas would be taken seriously.

"Maybe there's hope for you after all," she said.

At that moment I didn't entirely share Arana's optimism. It's not just that I worried whether I would ever learn to be organized like Arana, with a head full of tried-and-true recipes. The executive chef had told me, "When you're learning, it's just like elementary school all over again. Never be jealous of the kids who do things better. Instead, get close to the best kid and find out how she does it." I took his advice, following Arana around like a rookie apprentice tailing a master painter in the artists' guild during the Renaissance. I wasn't the first artist, nor would I be the last, to love the kitchen. One of Leonardo Da Vinci's many inventions was a spit with a propeller that turned the meat over the fire for his cook, Matrina, the only woman mentioned in his writing. The trouble was that I was starting to wonder who I was identifying with more lately—Matrina, receiving the sketches Leonardo made of what he wanted her to cook, or Leonardo, drawing. In the meantime, my dream to be an artist was boiling over on the stove.

At King's College in Cambridge two hundred years before, crème brûlée was served in sparkling crystal dishes, and a tiny, shining gold hammer was passed around to gently break the brittle glaze. Great-Grandma Esther and Great-Grandpa Jacob were not to be disappointed when the hammer fell on their dream. Max eventually became a success, owning his own busy construction business, just like his father's, and learning from architects on the job everything he might have learned in school.

Black walnut—despite its evil reputation as the devil's hiding place—is prized for its dark and beautiful wood. It doesn't warp or swell badly when wet and is easily worked with tools. A partial list of its uses includes countertops, railings, interior finishings, furniture, gun stocks, picture frames, coffins, switchboards, shingles, building materials of all kinds, carvings, and ornamental work. Even the old stumps and crooked logs are valuable for their beautiful grain, proving, just as Papa Max did, that much good can come from evil.

Nervously, I peered into the oven every two minutes, checking the remaining custards for the delicate smooth sheen and slight jiggle that indicated they were set. When the custards were safely on the rack, cooling, I cleared my head enough to decide what I would wear to the Christmas party.

The next day, Christmas Eve, the phone rang in the early evening before I left my apartment for the festivities. I wasn't surprised when it was one of the pastry chefs I had interviewed with before I took my job at LaCoupe; it was typical of a chef to be oblivious of the fact that he was calling on a holiday. LaCoupe was the extraordinary exception, closing the kitchen in order to throw the staff a party.

"Don't repeat this around," he confided, "but the truth is I'm not happy with the person I hired for this job. There's going to be an opening here soon. I came across your résumé and wondered if you had ever gotten any experience."

He was impressed when I told him who I was working for now. The job he offered was for baking with no plating and shorter daytime hours. I hesitated briefly before I replied.

Fate is something you believe in or you don't. Me, I like to leave it an enigma. But if it was fate that led Esther to America and Max to success, then maybe it was fate directing me in my decisions about my job.

"Look, it's Christmas Eve," I hedged, trying to remind him with my tone of voice that as impossible as it seemed in a restaurant kitchen, it was also an evening when some people weren't working. "Let me think about it and get back to you after the holiday."

As I hung up I couldn't help feeling as though the hand of fate were in fact reaching out to lift me from the boiling cauldron of LaCoupe. From somewhere inside me a voice whispered, *Grab it.*

Crème Brûlée *

5 tablespoons plus 1 teaspoon granulated white sugar

½ teaspoon vanilla extract

1 teaspoon dark rum

1 vanilla bean

1 pint heavy cream

1 tablespoon plus 1 teaspoon vanilla sugar (see note)

½ cup egg yolks (5 to 6 yolks)

Adapted from a recipe by Wayne H. Brachman

Note: *Vanilla sugar can be purchased at specialty stores. Or, to make it, store dried hulls of used vanilla beans in sugar, then process the mixture in a food processor fitted with a metal blade. Strain vanilla sugar to use. If vanilla sugar is unavailable, plain granulated sugar may be substituted.*

Prepare the crème brûlée: *Set oven to 325 degrees. Arrange eight $1/3$-cup capacity ovenproof ramekins inside a deep-sided baking pan. Place granulated white sugar, vanilla extract, and rum in a large mixing bowl. Whisk to combine. Split the vanilla bean in half lengthwise and scrape out the seeds. Place vanilla bean hull and seeds, cream, and vanilla sugar in a medium saucepan and bring to scald. Just before scald, add yolks to sugar/rum mixture and whisk to combine. Temper yolk mixture with scalded cream by pouring hot cream into yolks in a thin stream while whisking continuously. Mixture can be used immediately, or, if more vanilla flavor is desired, steep vanilla bean in hot cream for one hour. Strain mixture. Rinse out vanilla bean hull and set aside to dry for future use.*

Pour mixture into a pitcher and carefully remove bubbles from its surface with a spoon. Fill ramekins $3/4$ full. Once again ladle off any new bubbles that may have formed. Bubbles will cause the surface of the custards to become pockmarked. Fill baking pan with water to within a half inch of the lip of the ramekins and cover entire pan with aluminum foil. Do not touch the surface of the custards with foil.

Bake the crème brûlée: *Bake custards 30 minutes. Check for doneness and bake 10 minutes more if necessary. Custards are done when they are just set but the surface still lightly ripples when the pan holding the ramekins is gently agitated. Overbaking, even by a few minutes, will curdle the custards, so check them often, especially as the end of the baking time nears. After 40 minutes of baking, continue to bake custards in 3-to 5-minute intervals until done. Cool custards, uncovered, in pan. Remove from the pan and refrigerate until completely set.*

To serve: *Sprinkle granulated sugar over surface of custards and either torch the sugar with a gas torch or place them under a salamander. A broiler is not recommended, because in the time it takes to caramelize the sugar, the custard also gets hot. The caramel should be a medium-amber color and thin. A mixture of half brown sugar and half white sugar can be substituted as long as* *the brown sugar has been left out in a cool place to dry before it is used. Yields eight.*

Five ⟋

*"walnut brown n.: a light yellowish brown that is redder, lighter, and
stronger than khaki, paler and slightly yellower than
cinnamon, slightly redder and lighter than manila,
and stronger and slightly redder and lighter
than fallow and is the color of the
shell of the English walnut"*
WEBSTER'S THIRD NEW INTERNATIONAL DICTIONARY,

1981

aybe the champagne had put a veil like spun sugar
over everything I saw and heard that night, or maybe
I was so full of chestnut cake and cranberries that I
was groggy and not really paying attention. Maybe
the story just got stretched, or elaborated on, or even a little invented in the telling and retelling, and by the time I get through
telling, maybe it'll have changed a little bit more.

It was a Christmas party, remember. That crystalline kind of
cold outside that could crack the glaze right off the petits fours. A

black, black night without stars that smelled like snow, as wide open as an uplifted palm.

I wore my black suede dress. Upon entering the dining room of LaCoupe, I noticed that wrapped presents were already crowded on a table in the center of the room, so I added the gift I had brought with me to the pile. When we had picked names for gifts, I'd picked Antonio, and it was no problem deciding what to buy for him. I noticed a couple of presents with my name on them. Why did I have two? Everyone had picked one name. Pondering this, I picked up a glass of champagne and surveyed the room. La-Coupe had really gone all out for us, unlike other restaurants, where the holidays were just another burden on a tight budget. The dining room was magnificent, with high ceilings, and a *trompe l'oeil* mural of windows looking out on a wintry garden of pine trees and cobblestone paths. There were pine wreaths with red satin ribbons hung on all the walls, and a glowing electric menorah, small but significant, perched on a windowsill. Most of the guests surrounded a table heavy with catered food and were loading up colorful paper plates.

I walked the length of the table slowly, plate in hand, finding it difficult to decide what to take first from the platters of glistening terrines, roasts, puddings, and sauces. Ultimately what caught my fancy was a silver tray heaped with voluptuous, ostentatiously bright strawberries, exotic and almost obscenely luscious looking in the middle of the bleak city winter—a real treat. They must have been flown in from some warmer climate at great expense. As I took a big, hungry bite out of one, I realized I was directly across the table from the chef, who winked at me. I blushed self-consciously, embarrassed by my unbridled lust for strawberries. He, on the other hand, smiled back with the obvious satisfaction of a man whose costly gift has had the desired effect. He wore a rainbow-colored cap that made him look almost boyish, more casual than I had ever seen him. He turned away to greet another guest. Grateful to be out of his scrutiny, I joined the crowd. Amid the kissing on the cheeks and the oohing and aahing over cooks and porters in suits and ties and gowns instead of smeared kitchen whites, I noticed that Arana wasn't there yet. I spotted Dean coming toward me in extravagant top hat and tails.

"Madame," he said, bowing low and mimicking a cultured English accent, "I hahdly recognized you in yaw civvies." He kissed my hand, and stood up. "It was my father's wedding suit," he explained in his natural New York accent in response to my incredulous stare.

"How romantic," I said, my voice tinged with jealousy. After all my unsuccessful relationships with men running from commitment, even someone else's father's wedding clothes could remind me of my over-thirty-and-unmarried condition. I don't think it's a coincidence that in all the hours I spent training to be a pastry chef, I never learned how to construct a wedding cake.

Besides, my alter ego had a decidedly different opinion on the subject. As a woman artist and somewhat of a rebel, I enjoyed a certain ironic stance toward society, especially the institution of marriage. And yes, I confess that was me who took those solitary walks after my boyfriend and I had had yet another argument, to moon over the lace dresses in the window of the bridal shop on Madison and 77th Street. Call it brainwashing, call it indoctrination, but somehow the message of too many Barbie dolls dressed in wedding gowns and too many card games called Old Maid had insinuated its way into my desires. Sometimes I didn't know if I wanted to fulfill or forget them.

Dean knew the whole story, from our many heart-to-hearts. Seeing the look on my face, he asked, "Where's Arana?" tactfully changing the subject.

"She probably wants to make a grand entrance," I said.

"Well, I hope she shows up soon," Dean joked, "I've got to get these clothes back in the attic before my father notices they're missing."

Our conversation was interrupted by an announcement from the chef that he would now begin handing out the gifts. The crowd pressed around the gift table, which sat elevated on a makeshift platform as if on a little stage. The chef had taken his place next to the gift table, and as he called the name of each person who had a gift, that person walked up to the gift table and received it in front of the entire group at the party. The crowd was hollering and hooting as people opened up everything from extra-large green and red condoms to stuffed gorillas wearing chef's clothing and read the cards out loud. When the chef came to his own name, a voice called out for him to wait a moment. Everyone's head turned toward the bar and I heard someone whisper, "Billy picked the chef." Finally, with much ceremony, the waiter, Billy, emerged from his hiding place behind the bar carrying a tray that held a dinner plate upon which sat a gift tied with an enormous tower of curled gold and red ribbon.

The ribbon shivered and shook as he walked over to the chef. The chef grinned—thoroughly pleased as this obvious homage to his style was placed before him on a tray stand. Billy formally served the chef his gift with a white cloth folded over his arm and waited while the chef opened it.

Everyone was straining their neck and speculating out loud what it would turn out to be—a garter belt, a whip, a leather teddy. It was a big water gun, and full. The card rhymed, and the chef read it out loud, pointing the gun carelessly this way and that, while heads ducked and arms went up in defense. Finally, the chef squirted Billy right out of the room with it. Everyone was laughing, even Billy. Then the chef handed out presents for all of us, which were soft, thick, white LaCoupe sweatshirts. We all threw them on over our dress clothes, pulling pearls and ties out of the necks, smearing them with lipstick and perfume and chocolate.

When my name was called, I received a miniature baking set complete with tiny rolling pin and whisk from one of the cooks—things that each day were so large and unwieldy that to see them so magnificently small was an exquisite pleasure. I beamed at my bestower. Then the chef handed me my other present, the mysterious one, and I hastily ripped the paper and ribbon off a nice bottle of champagne. There was quiet in the room as I tore open the card.

I read out loud, "I would say that when you enjoy this gift, you should think of me, but you won't know who I am. Merry Christmas and Happy Chanukah from your secret friend." I heard the "ooh!" and could feel the heat in my face. As I headed back to my seat, I tried to catch Dean's eye, but he wouldn't look at me. Funny, I could never get him to admit that it was from him, even though I knew. That was just like him, though, never expecting thanks.

When the chef came to Arana's gift, he called her name a few times until everyone shouted to him that she wasn't there yet, so he went on to the next person. Antonio was in the process of tearing open the gift I had bought him, when we heard an enormous crashing sound near the door followed by the sound of glass rolling and breaking.

In the wake of the Christmas tree, which she must have toppled on her way in the door, was Arana. Not that the tree had been in a precarious place. Arana was just wearing something, well, *big*. Everyone turned and gasped simultaneously. One last Christmas ornament tappity-tapped down the step at Arana's foot and crashed lightly before her, bringing all eyes to the toe of her bright red spike-heeled shoe. There was a very pregnant pause before she spoke, during which time one's eyes had the chance to travel up the red fishnet stockings on her muscular calves and thighs to the very short hem of her flaming red skintight sequined dress, and then to the edge of what looked like a cape, but on second glance revealed itself to be a red-and-green tablecloth laid over a faux tabletop balanced across her shoulders like an enormous collar. The tablecloth parted in the center to show off her bulging breasts, barely stuffed into the top of the dress. On top of the "table" were laid three place settings, complete with wineglasses, plates, and utensils with bright green carefully folded napkins. On each plate was a piece of fruit tart. Her long, slender neck rose from the center of the tabletop, and on her head she wore a large Carmen Miranda–style hat laden with fruit, ribbons, and Christmas ornaments. Arana took a drag on a long red cigarette holder she held between fingers swathed in black gloves reaching above her elbows. The woman had thought of everything. Finally she spoke.

"Sorry I'm late, dolls."

She descended the steps, hips swaying, threatening to slide all the plates right off her whatever it was. Apparently, everything was glued on. Some porters swarmed around the tree, trying to right it, but they couldn't take their eyes off her. She walked straight up to the chef and placed herself directly in front of him. Arana was very tall, and in those heels she towered over the chef, who stood barely over five feet. Her breasts were nearly exactly level with his eyes. When I tell you the crowd was disintegrated in laughter, I mean it.

"Arana," the chef said in a tone somewhere between shock and appreciation. I swear, he blushed. Then he pulled himself together and addressed her in his typical oratorical fashion.

"Arana," he said, looking directly at her breasts. "This is a party, not a watermelon sale."

Knock-down, all-out, knee-slapping laughter. Somebody yelled, "Touché!"

"Hmmpf," said Arana, real Mae West style, "don't you know what I am?"

More hollering as the cooks tried to answer for the chef, most of it unprintable. I heard "cherry pie" and "broken cherry."

"No, I don't," he laughed.

Arana stood with her hands on her hips, glaring at the crowd until they quieted a little. Then, when she was sure they would all hear her, she turned back to the chef, enjoying her captive and her audience.

"Would you like a bite?" she smirked. "I'm the tart of the day."

Then she took off the hat and the giant collar, slipping it over her head, revealing the rest of her dress, which was nothing more than the halter strap holding it up. Her back was bare to below her waist. The scar encircling her arm exaggerated the pulse of her bicep as she ripped one of the plates off her costume and held it up for the chef.

"Boys," she addressed the cooks while keeping her eyes glued to the chef's, "bring the chef a fork."

Somebody passed Arana a fork, and she took a piece of the tart and seductively fed it to the chef, while the cooks nearly went out of their minds yelling and stomping their feet. I liked the way he never took his eyes off her. Maybe I was feeling unplugged in general, but the look on his face made something sting in the center of my chest, something with loose wires, something hungry. I liked the look in those eyes. That smoky look, amused but full of dark mischief. I never saw it again. That's the trouble with out-of-season strawberries, even beautiful ones. They put on a good show, but they don't taste very good.

Papa Max wouldn't have thought much of the food they served for the Christmas party at LaCoupe. What good did it do to fly in fancy strawberries, even if they were delicious, without rhubarb? Strawberries and rhubarb, made into a pie or compote or crisp, was one of Papa's favorite desserts. The sight of a fresh strawberry-rhubarb pie shining through the cellophane window in its bakery box on

Papa's kitchen counter always heralded the end of winter and the beginning of spring for me. Yes, it's true, Grandma bought the pie and didn't bake it herself. Strawberry-rhubarb pie is a particularly American dessert, one that wasn't in Grandma's Eastern European repertoire. Maybe that's why Papa Max embraced it so heartily—in the same way he embraced his new homeland. Maybe that's also why I made it my business to learn how to make it—to please Papa's palate as well as his patriotism. For Papa Max, strawberries and rhubarb heralded the start of his new calendar as well as spring; the Hebrew calendar begins with the month of Nisan, which falls in March to April.

Most people don't know that rhubarb got its name—*Rheum rhaponticum*—from the sea; rhubarb once grew on the banks of the river formerly called Rha, which flowed into the *pontus*—the sea. Papa Max probably didn't know it either, but I imagine that might be one of the other reasons he instinctively loved it so much.

No one in the family can think of Papa Max without thinking of the sea. He always dressed in pastel colors, as subtle as the shells he collected, with his round face and sensitive bald head protected by a white cap, brilliant in the sunlight. Even in his eighties, his face barely showed a wrinkle, like beach glass smoothed by the restless ocean. His hazel eyes changed color in empathy with the moody sea. And he had a disposition like a summer day, even tempered, kind, giving, and sweet. I do not romanticize him. If anyone believes that I still see him through the eyes of a biased, loving grandchild, then let that person ask anyone who ever knew Papa to tell what he was like. The answers will all attest to the truthfulness of my description. If Papa was, in fact, one oyster among millions, then he was the one with the pearl in it.

I can just picture Papa at LaCoupe's Christmas party, politely trading in his glass of champagne for a bottle of beer and then turning away from the platters of nouvelle treats on the buffet table, disappointed. No fried smelts? No boiled crabs? Outside the frosted picture windows of LaCoupe, the slate winter sky would suddenly melt to pale blue spring. The next thing I knew I'd be in the back of a Buick, with Papa at the wheel driving to the beach near our home in New Jersey in search of the seafood stands sprinkled along the wharves. We would sit outside, plastic lobster bibs tied around our necks, the wet, salty ocean air in our nostrils as intoxicating as a head of foam on a beer, and dig into a big bucket of piping hot steamer clams or cardboard cups of thick chowder. To this day, eating seafood outside on a wharf immediately brings me back to the altar of my childhood by the sea—the unctuous yellow butter clarifying in a cast-iron pot, the lobsters blushing furiously in their steaming cauldrons, and the lapping sound of the water as it gently licked and kissed the pier good night beneath a serenade of calling gulls.

Papa taught me the names of all the shells and the times of the tides. He taught me the sailor's rhyme, "Red at morning, sailor's take warning. Red at night, sailor's delight." And he taught me how to fish.

Papa was practical, which may have been why he ended up a businessman when he had a fisherman's heart. His construction company was his job and fishing was his art. As he taught me how to secure my bait, he was the most patient, caring teacher I've ever known. Anyone who can convince an eight-year-old girl, a girl who is at a stage in life when just about everything in the world is "icky," to impale a worm on a hook without flinching deserves a medal and the deepest respect. I would follow Papa anywhere, even into the shadows of Steve's Bait Shop in West End, New Jersey.

Steve's Bait Shop was a work of art. As soon as you walked through a wooden door on which hung a bell that announced visitors with a magical tinkling, you entered another world. A world of rods and lines, hooks and boots and flies. Not insect flies, but the hooks called flies that were made to resemble insects, carefully hand constructed of feathers and threads and beads. They hung in glass cases, mysterious and strange to a child's eye. In retrospect, they remind me suspiciously of my sculptures. In any case, Papa knew all the men in the shop, so that even a place like this, full of sharp and forbidding objects, seemed friendly and warm. But the flies were for freshwater fishing. We needed bait for fishing in the ocean.

They say that a bucket of water, stained dark overnight with the dye of mashed walnut hulls and poured over some night crawlers' favorite spot, is all a fisherman needs to get the big worms to wriggle up. Papa didn't follow that recipe, nor the one preferred by some native people that said walnut leaves thrown into the water will poison the fish and make them easier to net. Instead, a Chinese takeout container of worms from Steve's Bait Shop was safely stashed in my mother's refrigerator. That night, with the red sky glowing reassuringly beyond the pink-and-white-checked curtains on my bedroom window, I fell asleep eagerly anticipating the next bright morning on the jetty with Papa.

Papa taught me how to cast; how to unlock the reel on my pole and carefully lean the pole back enough to be able to flick my wrist and propel the fishing line out in front of me. That invisible line, whizzing out before me in the quiet summer air like a penny thrown in a wishing pond, lives in my memory as one of the most optimistic sounds I've ever heard. It was a leap of the imagination, a toss of the dice—flight. After we came home from fishing, Papa gutted the fluke and removed the heads on newspaper outside, then carried them in to Grandma. Grandma dipped the fish in matzo meal to prepare them for pan frying.

While she and Papa were busy with the cooking, I played on the beach, waiting for dinner. Other kids made sand castles; I made sand cakes. The wet sand was easy to pack into the shapes of my "pastries." The dry sand was powdered sugar. The pebbles and shells I collected became fancy butter cream decorations. I would contentedly watch the sea slowly eat my cakes as the day waned. Too bad it wasn't just the sea I had to bake for at LaCoupe.

By the end of February, I told Arana what I had decided.

"Arana," I said, feeling timid under her forthright gaze, "I'm going to quit."

It took a moment for my words to sink in. First she was angry—she had trained me for months and this is how I thanked her? She couldn't believe it. She let out an exasperated breath and turned her face away from me for a minute. Then she looked down for a moment more, shaking her head. I started to apologize.

"Arana, I'm so—"

But she interrupted me. "No, no," she said, "I can't blame you." There was a pause. She sighed loudly. "Do you know what I did before I came here? I was a hat designer. Yes, me, an artist, like you. I can't tell you I don't understand. This job takes over your life. If I were you, I'd do the same thing."

I took a long, relieved breath. Her face softened. Then she raised her eyebrows. I would have to tell the chef myself, she made sure I knew that. She wasn't going to do my dirty work for me. And he wasn't going to be happy about it, she could tell me that right now.

Later I told Arana I wasn't surprised that she was an artist. "The pastry is so beautiful," I told her, "all the plates look like jewels."

"Pastry is art too, you know," she replied.

I fell silent and felt my face grow hot as I imagined telling the chef my news.

"A penny for your thoughts," Arana piped.

In 1909, root gatherers were paid a penny a pound for walnut bark. The bark, green husks, and leaves were used together or separately in folk remedies to treat eczema, herpes, indolent ulcers, cracked palms and ringworm, corns, tumors, and warts, among other things. Burnt kernels taken in red wine were said to prevent falling hair. The bark alone, however, was usually boiled into a tea and served as a laxative. Considering the weight of my thoughts and the bitter tea they would make when they came to full boil, I don't think Arana realized how much she was buying for her penny.

The day in March that I gave my notice to the chef at LaCoupe was so windy, the picture windows rattled in the front of the restaurant. The chef had led me to a secluded table near the windows when I finally worked up enough nerve to tell him I needed to talk to him. A woman in an olive trench coat fighting the wind with an umbrella against a cold drizzle passed by outside as we sat down and a piece of newspaper blew onto her calf and stuck there. She struggled with the door of the restaurant and blew in with a few leaves, kicking the newspaper from her leg. When she got inside, I could see she was young. An expectant, intelligent face. Lots of dark hair completely mussed from the wet wind. Strands stuck to her face, her lips. The chef and I watched her for a moment, avoiding each other. She approached the hostess and struggled with a large envelope she was carrying.

"I'd like to drop off a résumé," she said.

I looked at my feet under the table. Someone would take my place two seconds after I left. The chef would forget me, perhaps immediately. That, combined with the impassive look on his face, made me feel like a stain on the tablecloth before him that was about to be crumpled up and thrown in the laundry cart—an insignificant annoyance that could be quickly remedied. I started to get lost in a fantasy: the chef understood, he would wish me luck, he would confess his secret dream to be a painter, I would paint his portrait, and as he sat for the photographs I would take to use as a reference, still black-and-white shots of his face and hands, like Stieglitz's O'Keeffe, he would let down his guard, his eyes would photograph dark, full of smoke . . . and then I noticed that the chef was waiting for me to say something. I cleared my throat. But I was afraid. Afraid of those eyes that held nothing in them now—no smoke, no light, nothing but concentration; single-minded, focused, fierce.

The whole thing was over in less than two minutes.

"So?" he said.

First I tried to explain. Then I interrupted myself—he made me so nervous—and just blurted out that I was giving notice. I tried to tell him that I hadn't been looking for another job, that one had just come to me. But now it was his turn to interrupt. Arana had been more hurt than angry. This, I realized, was anger.

His eyes seared through me. "I made an investment in you when I hired you. I took a chance on you—" He stopped, as if too upset even to bother to finish. But he did. "Then you just leave, just like that, and use what I've taught you to get another job—" He stopped suddenly again. He appeared almost too pissed off to speak. "You've already made up your mind, haven't you?"

"Yes," I managed to croak. I could barely look at him. He was intimidating enough when he wasn't angry.

"Then it doesn't matter what I say."

With that, he left the table, without looking back, without saying another word, without stopping. He just strode across the dining room and went down the steps, back to the kitchen. For my remaining two weeks he never looked at me or spoke to me again. My fantasy photographs dissolved in an acidic ire like oil paint in a ruthless turpentine.

Arana was unsympathetic.

"Well, what did you expect?" she asked me.

We were working on the items for the new spring menu. My

sambuca-coffee sundae and strawberry-rhubarb crisp were still on the list. I didn't say anything because I already felt I'd said enough. A delivery of produce arrived, and Arana stopped what she was doing to inspect the fruit she had ordered. I watched her bite into a pale strawberry from an open crate, then dramatically spit it into a nearby garbage pail for the benefit of the purveyor. She paused a moment before deciding whether to accept the crate or not, probably weighing out in her mind which was worse: inferior strawberries or being behind schedule on the recipe testing. With a sigh she sent the crate back; it was still too early in the season for strawberries, schedule or no schedule.

"Haste makes waste," Arana intoned as she returned to our worktable.

"Yes, but he who hesitates is lost," I countered playfully.

Arana replied without laughing at my joke, giving me a meaningful sidelong glance, "Let's hope you're right."

On my last day in the kitchen at LaCoupe, I approached the chef at the end of my shift. He barely acknowledged me.

I said, "Today is my last day. I just came to say good-bye."

No answer. He looked at me with a look that had nothing in it, with a look you look when you think you hear a sound but it's only the wind, so you look away again, unconcerned.

"I just wanted to say thank you," I persevered, "I learned so much from you."

Silence. I felt my throat tighten, so I left in a hurry, not wanting to exist in that quiet space containing only resentment, only anger.

Toward the end of the year I sent him a card I hand-printed on handmade rice paper from a linoleum block carved with a design of rhubarb and strawberries. In it I wrote a long note, trying to explain again, to justify. For this chef, presentation was everything. I wrapped the card in Chinese silk tissue paper and tied it with a satin ribbon before I mailed it to him in an envelope I had also made, with ragged edges and a gold-leaf paper lining. Working on the card, carving out the time for it late at night, was like coming home. At first I was afraid to start again—it had been so long. One of my artist friends had said, "Nan, it's like riding a bike, you never forget." And she was right. Just the feel of the paper in my hands, the ink on the roller gliding over the block, jogged my memory. From the quiet, careful folding of soft printing paper to the crinkle of tissue, I found what I thought I had lost—my art. That card was all I could manage to do, though, before my eyes nearly crossed in exhaustion and I fell on my bed, cursing a world in which the rest of my artistic visions would remain indefinitely on hold.

One day I saw him on the subway, of all places. He was polite to me, almost friendly. I asked him if he had liked the card I sent him. He said that he had, very much. But, as he walked away, I felt an ache. Now I knew how famous he was; I wondered if he remembered my name. It had been such a long time by then, nearly a year, and he had probably received a lot of cards around Christmastime. Somehow, I still felt I'd lost him. Dean and I tried to stay in touch after I left, but the city can be like that. It's as if everyone were flying around in one of those whirlwinds that takes over an intersection sometimes, blowing umbrellas inside out, and the loose posters off the mailboxes and lampposts, and if you don't reach out and take the time to tie things down, they'll just blow away out of reach. Dean and I lost touch when I got involved with my new job and he got involved with a new woman. I said, spring is windy in New York.

Fortunately, the first of the local strawberries were just starting to appear on the shelves of the city markets at around the time I left LaCoupe. On my way home after my last day there, I picked up a couple of pints and a bunch of rhubarb stalks. Cooked with plenty of sugar and berries picked at the height of their season, the harsh rhubarb will soften to a sweet and tender treat. Clearly, I had some baking to do.

There is a fish called the strawberry bass that runs in the clear waters of some northern American states. The best strawberry bass are caught just before they spawn in the spring. In Texas, Missouri, Mississippi, and Florida, fishing for the species is so frenzied that the sport is considered a symptom of spring fever. Papa Max caught mostly fluke and flounder when he went on the deep-sea fishing boats that sailed out of Forked River in New Jersey. Once he caught a swordfish while on a trip in Mexico. It might've been one of those stories about the one that got away, except when Papa discovered that the cost of stuffing the fish and bringing it home was prohibitive, he had his picture taken with it. In the photograph, a beaming, chubby Papa is dwarfed next to a six-foot-long five-hundred-pound swordfish that is hoisted up on a crane on the dock in Acapulco. There are a lot of pictures of Papa fishing, like a bald Hemingway, hugging a reel to his chest or leaning out of a flat-bottomed boat, rowing in the West Shrewsbury River with his little girls, my mother and aunt. When they went crabbing, Grandma Rae would pack them a lunch of hard-boiled eggs, kosher salami sandwiches on rye bread with mustard, and homemade lemonade sweetened with strawberry jam.

Papa's fishing pole drew a long, thin arc over the sky above my small head every time he cast his line into the ocean. I imitate him when I make art, raising my arm to draw a long arc onto a fresh piece of thick, tobacco-brown pastel paper. After I left LaCoupe, I began a drawing of Papa from a photograph I once took of him, with the beach he loved so much in the background. The drawing paper was cut in an asymmetrical shape, with panels of architectural details from the houses near the beach placed here and there around Papa's portrait. Above him, I was drawing a doll with three eyes that I had dreamed about. I looked up the meaning of the third eye at the library after I had the dream. Wisdom. Surely no better image could accompany Papa's portrait.

Time turns liquid when I'm drawing, trickling away, drowning out everything except my own breathing and the gentle rasp of pencil lead shedding onto paper. I stopped to sharpen the tip of my black Conté drawing pencil with a small, silver pocketknife and brought it to a pin-sharp point by scraping it back and forth on a piece of sandpaper. Then I held the pencil to the paper and drew the crescent moon shape of the brim of Papa's cap—one short curve coming toward me, then an angle, then another curve, this one pressed a little darker and thicker. I stood back to check that the illusion was working—a simple, flat, curved line that tricked the eye into seeing the brim of a cap receding into space.

Lines dark and light, tight and loose. Papa tugged on his fishing line and let it go slack, tugged and let go, a slight turn of the reel, a little pressure on the line. It's the same with a drawing. You can't just reel it in. You'll lose it. You have to push and pull, careful not to overwork it, careful not to get too tight. On the dark paper, the light popped when I laid it in with a soft piece of bright chalk. Artists say you have to "catch" the light. Me and Papa, we've gone fishin'.

Strawberry-Rhubarb Crisp

For the compote:
1½ pounds strawberries (approximately two very full pints)
1 pound rhubarb (weighed whole, untrimmed)
½ cup brown sugar
¼ cup orange juice
2 teaspoons lemon juice
¼ teaspoon cinnamon

For the streusel:
¾ cup all-purpose flour
Pinch salt
¼ cup chopped almonds
½ cup sugar
6 tablespoons cold unsalted butter, cut in
    small pieces

Prepare the rhubarb and strawberries: *Halve and hull about 1 pound of the strawberries (approximately 1 1/2 pints). Set aside. Hull and quarter the remaining berries, making sure that any berries that are very large are cut into bite-size pieces. Set these aside as well. Wash and trim the rhubarb and cut into 1/2-inch pieces. The thin outer skin of the rhubarb may be peeled off if desired before slicing. Add the rhubarb pieces to the halved berries.*

Prepare the syrup: *Combine sugar, juices, and cinnamon in a pot large enough to hold the halved berries and the rhubarb. Bring to a boil. Add the rhubarb and halved berries and stir to coat the fruit and rhubarb with the syrup. Bring to a simmer over medium low to medium heat and cook, uncovered, stirring occasionally, until the rhubarb is tender, about 15 to 20 minutes. Drain the fruit and rhubarb from the syrup and return the syrup to the pot. Reduce the syrup over medium heat until it is thickened and darkened in color. Add the reduced syrup back into the fruit and stir to combine. When the mixture is cooled slightly but still warm, add the reserved quartered berries and mix together well.*

Make the streusel topping: *Preheat oven to 350 degrees. Line a cookie sheet with parchment paper and set aside. Combine all the dry ingredients for the streusel in the bowl of an electric mixer fitted with a paddle, or in a large bowl to mix by hand. Add the cold pieces of butter, and with a pastry cutter or two knives, or with the machine set on low speed, blend in the butter until the mixture begins to come together and forms clumps. Do not*

overmix. Spread the clumps of dough evenly over the cookie sheet, pressing small bits of dough together in your fist if necessary to help it clump evenly. Bake the streusel for 20 to 25 minutes until it is lightly browned, turning the pan during baking to ensure even color. Cool on a rack.

To serve: *Place the warm strawberry-rhubarb compote in bowls and sprinkle with the streusel. Serve with ice cream or whipped cream if desired. Yields approximately one quart of compote and one quart of streusel topping.*

$\mathcal{Six}$ ⟶

"Walnut Creek Restaurant, Main Street,
'Meals 25 cents' "

WALNUT CREEK SENTINEL,

WALNUT CREEK, CALIFORNIA, MRS. VICKERS, ADVERTISER,

JUNE 22, 1894

 bent over a cutting board in the pastry kitchen of Prairie, the restaurant where I had my new job, carefully slicing oranges and lemons as thinly as possible for a batch of poached pears. I placed a large soup pot on the industrial hot plate behind me and poured into it eight cups of water, the sliced fruit, and a scraped vanilla bean. Then I measured out the white wine and sugar.

"C'mon, Wally," I pleaded as I double-checked the quantity of wine I had just measured, "I've got to concentrate now."

If Wally O'Sullivan asked me out once, he asked me out a dozen times. A bodybuilder as big as an ox, he towered over me. He had a round, baby face, unruly white-blond hair, and lots of freckles. He looked like the male equivalent of Heidi, wholesome and out-doorsy. Wally was handing me the measuring cups I needed from the high rack above the hot plate. When I noticed I didn't have a slotted spoon, he insisted on running to get me one. When the heavy box of pears had to be carried from the walk-in to the pastry kitchen, he carried it. And when I couldn't find a container of whole star anise on the spice shelves, he went to dry goods to requisition it for me. Meanwhile, Seth, my boss, the pastry chef, watched with amusement from the other side of the pastry kitchen, where he was spinning mint ice cream in the ice cream machine.

"Oh, I think Wally likes you," Seth sang, opening the ice cream machine door to let the fresh ice cream fall into a container. "He's practically kvelling," he said, mimicking an old Jewish man. "Go out with him already. You don't have to marry him. He's breaking my heart, the way he hangs around here all the time. Throw him a bone, throw him a latke, anything, for God sakes."

I tried to defend myself. "I have a boyfriend," I said.

"Oh, really!" Seth feigned surprise, putting his hand to his heart. "You mean that piece of rat turd you're not speaking to for the fifth time this month? Oh, *him*," he continued sarcastically while drizzling melted chocolate over the ice cream and folding it in, "I forgot." He gave me a sideways look.

It was true. I hadn't even told Seth that the rat had moved back in with his old girlfriend (strictly platonic—"her roommate walked out on her") sometime yesterday without telling me, and had called me from there in the middle of the night, waking me. But I didn't want to get into too much of my personal life with Seth. After all, he was the pastry chef.

Seth didn't look like a pastry chef. He came to work in a black denim jacket with at least twenty buttons and pins all over it. Fiercely proud of being Jewish, he knew more Yiddish than my mother. He teased me constantly. "What kind of a Jewish name is Ring? Now, Rubinowitz, that's Jewish." Once I had found a variation of my name in a book claiming to be a dictionary of Jewish names. Ringgold, Ringer. A name often given to a maker of gold wedding rings. If that was the case, I was hardly the deserving heir. To hear it from Seth, the Rubinowitzes, on the other hand, practically invented matzo ball soup, though Seth wasn't exactly the conservative picture of the devout Jew. He wore his long hair in a ponytail. It was thick, chestnut brown, and wavy, and made a beautiful curve as it hung down his back, like a shiny S-shaped cookie dipped in chocolate. Long, curly sideburns cupped each cheek. Once, he had been a performance artist, which had inadvertently led him to baking. For a friend's wedding he had placed television sets inside a wedding cake to make a statement about the "meaninglessness of modern ritual." He had enjoyed baking the cake so much, he decided baking might not be a bad way to earn a living. Unknown performance artists make about as much money as unknown painters.

Seth liked to bend the rules. He liked untraditional twists on traditional pastry. Prairie is an American restaurant, as the name implies, but they're always on the cutting edge of the creative side of cooking. That's how they got their three stars. And they kept them in a much more low-key manner than LaCoupe. Seth wasn't a slave driver. He was fair and gentle and just enough of a nut to fit in with the concept of Prairie. He put pistachios in his tortes, cornmeal in his doughs, papaya in his crème brûlée. He liked Mexican chocolate with cinnamon in it, and added maraschino to the whipped cream. Seth and I had a lot in common. I was suddenly at a stage where I wanted to change everything. He let me experiment—within reason, of course. There was a lot of work to do and he couldn't afford too many disasters. There had been complaints lately from the executive chef, mostly out of professional jealousy, that the pastry kitchen wasn't "consistent." Seth let me "crash and burn" as much as he could without raising a fuss from the chef, and in the meantime took a decided interest in my education. The other pastry cooks affectionately called the pastry kitchen "Seth Tech." I was Seth's new pupil. I still had a lot to learn. And not all of it was about pastry.

"Wally's cute," Seth volunteered after Wally had left the room. Seth poured warm water through the ice cream machine to clean it.

"Yeah, I know," I answered. I turned the hot-plate burner to high. The poaching liquid has to be boiled before the pears are added. "But he's not my type."

"That's right, I forgot," Seth countered. "You like 'em mean."

I stuck my tongue out at him. "Sounds like the pot calls the kettle black." Seth liked what he referred to as "shiksas," and not all of them so nice. But inside I felt his arrow hit its mark.

"Can I put vanilla beans and ancho chilies in the semolina bread?" I asked Seth, changing the subject.

"Weird," Seth looked doubtful, "whatever gave you that idea?"

"Eric," I said, looking in the direction of the prep kitchen.

"Oh, *Eric*." He feigned jealousy. "Well, if it's *Eric,* why not?"

Eric was one of the most good-looking guys at Prairie. Good-looking and mean. On my first day at Prairie, he had marched briskly through the pastry kitchen on his way to the upstairs kitchen, where he worked. I'm the first one to admit that love at first sight is one of those myths that blinds you to getting to know people from the inside out, but yeah, I was attracted. He seemed distant, but he lingered long enough to tell me that he was a musician—he played electric guitar in a blues band—and this was his survival job. Survival job—the magic words. Kindred spirit, I thought, feeling that voracious electrical unit in my chest I call a heart giving off sparks. He had that Italian kind of good looks, tall and dark. Thick, curly hair and deep-set blue eyes with a high-arched eyebrow over each one. The kind of chiseled face, faintly lined, that only becomes more handsome with age. Anyway, I found out pretty quickly that Eric had a girlfriend. And besides, he seemed more interested in Gemma than anyone else. It wasn't hard to figure out why. Beautiful, competent Gemma Royalton with her sexy Australian accent stood a good head above the other women in the pastry department at Prairie. And not just in height.

The first day Gemma showed up in the pastry kitchen, with her bob of tight, dark brown curls pulled neatly back in a white headband and her chin held high, I figured she was a beginner, like me. Seth had told me to show her around while he was doing inventory in the dry goods cage. Gemma asked me what there was to do. I said that there was a list, but if she knew how to roll tart shells, we needed some of those. I myself was only barely able to roll a decent tart shell. She said, sure, she knew how. I followed her to the walk-in and showed her which dough to roll, and then nervously followed her back to the metal table where we rolled dough in the pastry kitchen, thinking I'd better keep my eye on her. Seth would be annoyed if there were too many mistakes made today. The executive chef had already walked through the bakery twice, the first time to complain that the scones were too high, and the second time to complain that the new scones were too low. "Oy," Seth had said.

"Do you want me to show you how?" I asked Gemma, not sure if I should even let her do this on her first day.

"No, that's okay," she said. Then I watched, astounded, as Gemma pounded the dough into submission with a strong arm, rolled it out as fast as you can say "frangipani" with swift confident strokes of the rolling pin, transferred the dough to the pan without so much as one tear or wrinkle, and patted it snugly into the sides of the pan with another piece of dough. "That's so there's no finger marks at all," she finished.

I barely managed to whisper an awed "Wow." Gemma laughed amiably, wrinkling her turned-up nose. I looked at her with my mouth still agape. "Do you want me to teach you?" she offered. I was entranced. Then I pulled myself together. "God, I'm sorry I acted like you didn't know . . ." But she only smiled. "It's all right," she said. "You didn't know I'd been baking for ten years. I used to be a pastry chef myself, but I took a step back to assistant so I could learn more." It turned out that Gemma had more confidence, more experience, more of what it took to survive in a competitive three-star environment than any of us. "More chutzpah," Seth said, which is probably why he made her second in command only a few days after her arrival.

Trouble was, Gemma liked Rocky. Maybe because she was in the middle of a divorce from a man who was gay and had married her only to help her come to America, or maybe because she hadn't had a real boyfriend in three years, she was attracted to swaggering, macho Rocky Mendez, one of the line cooks. He reminded me of a short Ricky Ricardo with an incredible amount of energy and a sweet, affectionate smile. Rocky's honey-colored eyes made him stand out among the other Latin men, not to mention his blond hair, bleached on a dare. He kept his headphones on so loud, he couldn't hear the women giggling and commenting on his muscles and fine clothes as he danced by, shadow-boxing the fifty-pound bags of sugar and bread flour. Rocky was married, too, though separated from his wife, who would call him from Portugal periodically to remind him that his child support was overdue. Gemma lamented that Rocky was adorable but would never be accepted in her world—a world of old values and rich relatives and friends who spoke textbook French, not ghetto Spanish. So Wally liked me and I liked Eric and Eric liked Gemma and Gemma liked Rocky. It's a good thing there was so much work to do.

Well, hopeless or not, I knew Eric had once made an ancho chili soup with vanilla. Whether or not I thought it would get him to notice me, I knew I wanted some more details on that recipe before I started my bread. I headed up the stairs to find him, clutching the vanilla beans in my hand. "Eric's not in a good mood today," Seth called after me.

"Three dates!" Gemma yelled to me as I ascended the stairs.

"Three dates?" Seth asked. "What do you mean, three dates?"

Gemma and I had a bet. The first one of us who could go out on three dates with a man without sleeping with him and still have him call us back for a fourth was the winner. We shook on it, smashing our chocolate- and dough-smeared hands together like blood sisters. Pastry wenches, Gemma called us. What would we win? Just our self-respect, I guess. And maybe we would end up with a guy who was actually serious about us. Gemma had been through the same mill I had, and both of us felt as ground down as fine cornmeal. Winnie wasn't in on the bet. She lived with her boyfriend.

Winnie Hardie came from the South. Way south. Every word she said had an extra syllable and was spoken as slow as molasses. Farm girl, raised and fed on fresh cow's milk and diesel fumes. Her family should have been proud of her, making her way to the big city and using her homegrown talent (best apple buckle three times at the state fair) to get herself a good job as a pastry assistant and a future free of slop and overalls. She made the best country desserts I'd ever tasted—cobblers, crisps, pies—and she fit right in at Prairie. But Winnie was, how do you say, on the manure list with the Hardies. You see, Hardies don't live with their boyfriends. They get married.

Ten kids. Winnie was the baby. All of them with those country good looks—she showed me pictures—taut, strong bodies (Winnie's forearms were bigger than Seth's), thick, shiny bright red hair, and big, bright white smiles. Perfect skin—I guess it must have been all that fresh dairy—cherubic faces. All those kids were married, with lots of their own kids. And that was the problem. Winnie couldn't have kids. A car accident when she was a teenager killed her high school sweetheart and left her in the hospital for weeks. In the long depression that followed a horrendous series of operations, she made up her mind. She would never get married. Never. No matter how much her new boyfriend said he loved her, someday she was sure he would be sorry that she couldn't have his baby. She couldn't stand that. See, Hardies don't get divorced either. So Winnie stayed out of the game. Because as far as she was concerned, she'd already lost.

Eric gave me the ancho chili recipe, barely looking at me while he recited it from memory. He was chopping shallots so fast, his hand looked like a blur. Great knife skills, I was thinking. "You do that so well," I told him, trying to compliment him and maybe get a smile. Eric put his knife down and looked at me as if he couldn't believe his ears. "How long do you think I've been doing this?" he asked me, frowning. "I don't know, how long?" Why do I always have to blush? "Never mind," he growled, looking disgusted. I went back downstairs feeling pretty rejected.

"What is his problem?" I asked Gemma when I got back to the pastry kitchen. "Look," she said, "Eric called me last night." She was watching my face to see how I would react. It turned out that they had talked for over an hour, about nothing, according to Gemma, about life. Well, I guess that settled it. Gemma insisted Eric hadn't asked her out. But I wondered.

Just then Wally came in carrying the things we'd requisitioned from dry goods that morning. He asked me again if I wanted to go to a Tracy Chapman concert with him. I had mentioned that I liked one of her songs, "Fast Car," about a woman who feels more hopeful about her difficult life while her boyfriend has his arm around her and they're driving around too fast in his car. Wally had a car. "Say yes," Winnie whispered near my ear, and I considered it. It was awfully nice of Wally to go out of his way to bring us our dry goods. I told him I'd think about it. "Look at him," Winnie said to me as we watched Wally walk away. He turned and smiled and waved before he disappeared from view, practically tripping over a table behind him. "He's so optimistic," she marveled, "he really believes you might say yes." Her eyes were melting with sympathy for Wally. "Oh, Winnie," I said, watching that sweet look on her face. Sometimes Winnie could just break your heart.

Papa Max told us that during the Depression he worked doing odd jobs for an aunt who lived in his neighborhood. At the end of each week, she

paid him with this simple salary: a freshly baked roll and a ripe pear.
Papa's face would shine with a beatific glow when he told us this
story, his eyes would light up, his cheeks would blaze like a child's. He
would describe in detail the delicious scent and taste of these two treasures that he received as pay for his hard work and perseverance.
Never did a pear taste so sweet, never did a roll smell so aromatic as the
ones he earned himself. Forever afterward, Papa loved pears and was
known to eat one every day after lunch when they were in season. From
the moment I first heard Papa tell that story, I knew that no matter what
riches I expected to achieve, no matter what lengths I went to in order
to get them, no matter where I traveled or what I accomplished, the
greatest rewards in life would be meaningful only compared to these
things: a roll and a pear. Papa lived his life by that rule.

Pears come in hundreds of varieties. A catalog dated 1868 lists
850 different kinds. Now there are literally thousands. Their names
are like poems striving to describe their richness, their perfume,
their silky flesh. *Cuisse-dame*, lady's thigh. *Tant-bonne*, so good. Still,
none of them will ever touch the sublime character and perfection
of the pear simply known in my family as "Papa's Pear."

God works in mysterious ways his miracles to perform.

You always said that, Papa.

Being Jewish, I heard a lot about God and miracles, and I guess
if you're given to questioning either one, it makes most of those
things that Papa always said sound a lot less comforting. But it
wasn't what Papa said that comforted me, then. It was that he was
there to say it. Papa gave me an unconditional love, one that I could
never seem to find again. His generation believed in family; most of
my generation questioned it. Maybe that's why so many men my age
were reluctant to get involved. At least that's how I comforted myself when it became pretty clear that Eric wasn't going to give me
the time of day. Not that it stopped me from trying.

I kept bugging Eric all the time, just to get his attention. The

ancho chili bread came out so badly, I wasn't allowed to experiment
for a while, but I found plenty of other things to ask his opinion
about. After all, I found out, Eric had twelve years of experience as
a chef, some of it in pastry. When the sous-chef confided in me that
he knew Eric was on the rocks with his girlfriend, that was all the
encouragement I needed. Despite Gemma and Eric's friendship, he
never did ask her out, so I figured if Gemma was jealous, she wasn't
letting on. She insisted she had eyes only for Rocky, but that her
family and half of her friends would never approve, and besides, he
barely ever looked at her. I figured that was just as well since neither
of them was technically available anyway.

I banged a heavy jar of poached pears onto one of the metal tables in the prep kitchen where Eric was rolling tortillas from handmade dough. Eric avoided me. When I approached him, he moved
to the other side of the room, looking for a jar of spice he said he
needed. When I approached again, he moved to the shelves by the
walk-in, checking the avocados piled there for ripeness. "Eric," I
tried yet again. Finally, he stopped and walked right over to me. He
looked me right in the face, standing directly over me, his big blue
eyes mere inches from mine. "What?" he demanded. "What the hell
do you want?" All I had to do was reach up and put my arms around
his neck and I could hold him, he was that close. I could feel those
loose wires in my chest whapping around like crazy. I knew he
could tell he was having this effect on me and I could tell he enjoyed
it, watching me squirm. I stammered, blushing again, "I . . . I, I
just, um . . ." Oh, to hell with it, kiss me, I wanted to say. But I
didn't have the nerve. "I just wanted to know how you are today."

He shook his head, and then he almost smiled. "Lousy," he answered, breaking off his gaze. "I'm lousy, all right?" Then he went
into the walk-in refrigerator. I followed him, carrying the pears, and
placed them on a shelf. "Maybe you need a hug," I said. Boy, was I
ever taking a risk. But I figured all or nothing at this point. We were

alone. No one would see or know. "Maybe I do," he said quietly, surprising me. Then it just happened, fast. He turned to me and put his arms around me, and we hugged for a fraction of a second. I felt his body heat through our layers of chef's clothes in the cold cold walk-in, the muscles in his back under my hands. Then he went rigid again and pushed himself away. Muttering "thanks," he was out the door, leaving me standing breathless, short-circuiting in the chilly room, the vegetables and puddings and stocks staring at me like mute witnesses. Mysterious ways, I thought. Mysterious ways.

After that I was sure Eric would ask me out. But he didn't. The tension was rising like brioche dough on a hot day, and I was near the limit of my patience. When we changed in the locker rooms, the sound of Eric's voice on the other side of the wall made me breathless. I made up my mind what I would do. It wasn't 1964 anymore, and I wasn't some hopelessly naive kid traipsing around with my grandfather, waiting for miracles. I was a liberated, full-grown woman, and I was going to ask Eric out. The moment I decided, I felt tremendously empowered. Why should I have to wait for the man to make the first move? Women had the right to choose what was best for their bodies. They had the right to vote, to work, to dress and talk as they pleased. Why shouldn't they have the right to approach a man for a date?

First I would run the idea by Gemma, just to make sure she was on the level with me about her feelings for Eric. Some women may like to fight over men. My women friends mean more to me than that. After all, they were the ones who stood by me when I was fighting for my independence, fighting to prove that there is life beyond thirty without marriage, without kids. And let's face it, women have been kicked around enough in this world. We don't need to do it to each other too.

With Gemma's blessing I found Eric in the oven room, stirring a stock. I was determined to get his phone number. Gemma assured me that she was already on her way to winning the bet with someone else, and if I didn't hurry up, she'd surely beat me to the prize. A nice man, she told me, but a man she had to keep secret. "Don't worry, he's not a criminal, I just don't want to jinx it." Winnie peeked around the corner as I approached Eric, trying to hear, and I chased her away with my eyes. Seth said he still had his money on Wally, and anyway, he didn't want to hear it. "I'm too old for this nonsense," he told me. "You're making me meshuggener with all this talk about sex and boys."

When I got Eric's reluctant attention, he looked at me like I was a cockroach peeking out of the flour bin the day after extermination. How did guys do this, I wondered, feeling my feet getting cold in the cramped and steamy oven room. Two convection ovens and a ceiling-high deck oven ran furiously near the stock stove nearly sixteen hours a day. Rocky was flipping peppers around in a frying pan right next to Eric, but he couldn't hear us because of the volume of his headphones. He moon-walked to the stove, flipped the vegetables, and moon-walked back. Over the roar of the oven fans, I told Eric that I really hoped we could get to be friends, that I knew he had a girlfriend, and in fact, I had a boyfriend (a boyfriend who it was doubtful had the capacity to feel love, true, but he didn't need to know that), but didn't he want to go out with me somewhere, just the two of us, just friends, just for a laugh? You could've knocked me over with a baguette when he said yes. Yes. He said yes. Then he wrote his full name and number for me in my pastry notebook. Eric Kaplan.

"Kaplan?" I said, incredulous. I was surprised. "You're Jewish!" I exclaimed.

"Yeah, so?" From the look on Eric's face, I could tell immediately that he was thinking maybe I was bigoted. So many times I'd worn the same expression on my face that he now had on his. Unlike chivalry, anti-Semitism wasn't dead.

"Oh, no, no," I blurted out. "It's fine. Really, it's great. I'm Jewish too. I was just surprised, that's all, I mean you look . . . you look . . ." Shut up, Nan, I thought, before you blow it.

Eric's face relaxed. "Oh," he said, sounding relieved.

"Okay, so I'll call you," I said, backing out of the room and sweating profusely. "Thanks, okay? So thanks—really, thanks."

I came back into the pastry kitchen and went straight to the stove, where I was poaching more pears. I stuck a slotted spoon into the simmering fragrant broth speckled with spices and took out a pear to test it for doneness. A skewer passed effortlessly through its flesh, but it was still steaming hot. I blew on it, passing it from hand to hand. Gemma and Winnie were all over me. "What'd he say? C'mon, tell us, we can't stand the suspense." I bit my lip, enjoying every moment. Then I started grinning, and Gemma and Winnie began whooping it up. The pear, as soft and sensual as a lithe body, had cooled enough by then to hold it in one hand. It was warm, round, and smooth and fit perfectly in the cup of my palm. Maybe it was the timing, but it was funny how it reminded me exactly of a certain part of a man's anatomy—it was sexy. "Gemma," I said, carefully handing her the warm pear, "take this and feel it." "What?" she said, uncertain, taking the pear. "What does it feel like?" I asked her, watching her face as she cradled the pear in her own hand. She paused, unsure of my motive for giving it to her. "Oh, Nance, you've got a dirty mind." "Give it to me," said Winnie, and after a moment began smiling like a Cheshire cat.

"Promise you'll tell me what it's like with him," said Gemma quietly, admiring the pear glistening in Winnie's palm. "Now, Gemma," I admonished her. "Remember, we've got a bet." "Screw the bet," said Winnie, "get in his pants." I was about to answer her, when Seth came in the room, carrying two empty pear jars. "Fill these jars when the pears are done, Nancy," he said, and looked up at us quizzically. "What are you girls doing with that pear?" he accused us. Then he answered himself, "Never mind, don't tell me. If it has anything at all to do with sex, just don't tell me." We laughed. But we didn't have the last laugh.

When I called Eric that night to set up the date, he changed his mind and turned me down. My heart felt as empty as a pear prepped for poaching, its core gouged out. He said he loved his girlfriend and didn't want to go out with anyone else, not even just as friends. He sensed that friendship wasn't all I wanted. I gave him ten points for being faithful to his girlfriend. Still, I returned to work the next day determined to forget all about him. I would immerse myself in my work, I decided.

Maybe what I needed was to give this pastry career a chance. Working long days wasn't doing my artwork any good anyway. I still didn't have the time or energy to go home to my studio and paint when I had to be at Prairie dressed in my uniform and baking bread by six-thirty in the morning. I was just about to pitch my palette for good, when an opportunity presented itself that might prevent that.

In addition to his job at Prairie, Seth also worked as a consultant setting up and staffing new pastry departments at other restaurants. He began talking to me about moving up, about grooming me for a job he had in mind for me when I was ready. This job, he promised, would require a mere eight hours a day. He convinced me it might be better all around to get a promotion—more pay, more creative freedom, and maybe, I thought, more hours left in the week for my art. I began to believe that if I persisted a little longer, I would eventually have time to paint with artists' as well as pastry brushes.

A walnut tree can take four and up to ten or twelve years to bear its beautiful nuts. This does not make it unattractive, however, to the gardener. In the meantime, it spreads its wide branches of open, lacy foliage and grows into a tall and graceful garden ornament, casting a cool and restful shade. Even a walnut tree has both its art and its work to consider. The artist in Papa Max thrived at his construction sites, where he worked with architects and even learned to make renderings and blueprints. He seemed to live his life happily enough between his business and his fishing pole. Maybe I could do the same. Besides, I had a hunger for the taste of Papa's Pear, and the pastry chef position looked ripe and sweet to me, hanging from a branch close enough to reach if I just climbed up a little higher. As it turned out, it would take more than a mere stretch to reach that fruit. It would take work. Hard, hard work.

I had some bad days, like the time I tried to do too many projects at once—Seth and Gemma were trying to teach me how to juggle things so I could use my time more efficiently—and left four dozen corn and pepper muffins in the deck oven for six hours, ruining the muffins as well as the pans. There was also the time I poured pounds and pounds of warm chocolate into dozens of ice-cold eggs (don't rush your recipes, Gemma kept telling me, think ahead, get that chocolate on *early* and let it cool) and all the chocolate seized into rock-hard bits of cement. I was good at all the basic things by then, so I could help Seth and Gemma get the production done on the crème brûlées and ice cream bases and cookie doughs. Gemma, seeing that I was trying so hard, took me under her wing and taught me all her tricks, like spraying the breads with water while they baked so they would have a nice crisp crust, or freezing the tart shells before we baked them so they would hold their shape better. Still, so many times when they taught me something new or complicated, I ended up screwing up, fighting back tears, and starting over. Wiping the sweat from my forehead with a wet, chocolate-smeared sleeve, I would apologize and start over. Start over, and start over, and start over.

After weeks of trial and error and practice, the day came when I was glazing some mousse cakes with a warm dark chocolate ganache. The ganache was just the right temperature and thickness. I had stirred it patiently and slowly so it had no bubbles or streaks of cream left in it. I raised the bowl of ganache and let it pour onto the top of the cake in a velvet stream. It spread evenly and flowed down the sides of the mousse with one perfect swipe of my spatula. Not one extra drip marred its smooth, glossy surface.

"Very nice, Nancy," said Seth, "very beautifully done."

A roll and a pear, I thought. And even though I kept reminding everyone that this was still just my survival job, there was another part of me that was hooked. Because when I finally got hold of one of the pears in the pastry tree, I saw one above it that looked bigger and juicier and would surely be an even better meal for a starving woman like me—starving for recognition and validation and security. Sure enough, after I reached that pear, I spotted yet another higher above, even larger and more tempting, and climbed up after that one too. Looking back, I still flinch when I see myself climbing up and up and up, dangling from the highest branches, perilously swaying on a creaking twig, a fool out on a limb. Still, when Seth offered me the pastry chef position at a Vietnamese restaurant called Toy downtown, I accepted.

If everybody in the world got together and put their troubles up for sale on the table, you'd grab your troubles back and run away.

You're right, Papa. And that's what I kept repeating in an effort to comfort myself during the summer before I left Prairie.

After a long dry spell without enough business to keep a pickup truck in spark plugs, my father was forced to liquidate the fabled New Jersey branch of Ring Bros. and sell the house we mostly grew up in. Along with the cardboard boxes of dishes and old photographs, I felt I packed a whole era of my life away that I would never be able to retrieve again.

Around the same time as my last, sad weekend visits to my family home, my cat died of leukemia—the same orange-and-white cat with one white toe on his right front paw who had played with the torn ends of my street-inspired sculptures; a cat who although barely celebrated on a daily basis was deeply loved. His life was short and his death tragic, especially during a time of so much loss and loneliness in general. It was also during this summer that my beloved Papa Max took to his bed for the last time and never rose again. In addition—as if this soup weren't salty enough with my tears—Seth had been fired.

The executive chef had decided that Seth was getting a little too independent—he had stopped even bothering to try to placate her temper tantrums. He didn't seem surprised, had seen it coming, in fact. Meanwhile, I was having second thoughts about leaving, feeling vulnerable and afraid I would lose touch with Seth, Gemma, Winnie, and, yes, even Wally—and, of course, even Eric. Maybe I wouldn't like working in an all-Vietnamese kitchen, I worried, where I would be the only American. Without Seth, though, I got a bad feeling about the future of the pastry kitchen at Prairie. That's why I was crying and Winnie was whining while Seth was packing his things—his rolling pin, his knife kit. Then suddenly Gemma rushed into the pastry kitchen, her apron smeared with blood. She looked as white as fondant icing.

"It's Rocky," she cried, "he dropped a sheet pan of focaccia and he had his chef's knife in his hand under the pan and he fell and—" She stopped, unable to speak, her eyes flooded with tears. She took a breath. "He refuses to go to the hospital, because he's not legal." Gemma said these last two words with a bitterness I had never heard before in her voice. Then she put her face in her hands, sobbing violently.

"It's all right," Seth said, reaching to put his arm around her. "His friends will take care of him. You know those Spanish guys, they all stick together. They're macho, mamacita," he tried to cheer her, winking at me and Winnie. This was so typical of Seth, comforting someone else when he himself had troubles.

"No, no," Gemma wept, wiping her eyes with the bottom of her apron. "It's not like that. I *have* to worry about him."

"Gemma, what are you talking about?" I asked her. "He's not your responsibility."

She looked embarrassed. "I won the bet, Nance," she said, exasperated.

With Eric, I thought, not understanding her train of thought and feeling a pang of jealousy. Then I realized she wasn't changing the subject. "You mean with Rocky?" I asked, replaying all those times she had sworn he could never fit in her life.

"Yes, but I won it a while ago, that's the trouble." She was shaking now. "I feel faint," she said, and leaned against the counter.

"So." I began to figure it out. "So you slept with him. Are you in love with him?" I still couldn't fathom it. Gemma actually going out with Rocky. She was just telling me last week how her family and friends would disown her if she even looked at a poor Portuguese man from Hoboken, New Jersey. A poor, *married* Portuguese man from Hoboken.

"Our divorces came through, one after the other," said Gemma, as if reading my thoughts on my face. "We were married last week at City Hall. I'm sorry I didn't tell any of you, but I couldn't."

"Married!" I blurted out. My mind struggled to accept this new information. How could Gemma, whom I had grown so close to and had thought of as my kitchen confidante, keep such a big secret from me?

"Gemma, isn't this a little sudden?" Seth asked. He must have been thinking exactly what I was—that Gemma had never, to our knowledge, been the impulsive type.

"She's pregnant," a voice from behind us said with the conviction of someone who knew a lot about her subject.

We turned our heads to stare at Winnie, who looked close to tears herself, and then back at Gemma, who nodded sadly, another tear coursing its way down her wet cheek.

"I'm so scared. What am I going to do?"

There was no answer. There we stood: Gemma, pregnant and crying, her lover's blood on her apron. Winnie, ever the stoic, in the background. Seth, unemployed, his empty hand generously stretched out to Gemma. And me, helplessly watching, a witness gathering experience, gathering stories. We looked like a Caravaggio painting. *Gemma Tells The Pastry Cooks She Is With Child.* Too bad the fluorescent lights in the bakery had none of the drama and romantic feeling of Caravaggio's chiaroscuro. In that glaring, relentless light, it was all too obvious that this was no rendering.

It was real.

"Gemma," I said quietly, "are you and Rocky ready to have a baby?"

"I don't know, Nance." She wiped her cheeks on the back of her sleeve and lifted her eyes as if someone or something might be listening from above. "I don't know," she repeated miserably to the ceiling, to one of the fluorescent light fixtures, buzzing and blinking intermittently, the way they do just before they burn out.

Holding Papa Max's hand by his bedside as he lay dying, I spoke to him, unsure if he could hear me, unsure if he even knew who I was anymore. His hand felt small and fragile, as if it were made of crepe paper and pipe cleaners. I made small talk. But inside I was pleading with him, begging him for answers he could no longer give me.

"Papa, you taught me so many things," I asked him in my mind, "why didn't you ever teach me how to say good-bye? I don't know how to do this," I yelled silently at the tubes attached to him. "I can't do this!"

"Max?" Grandma practically hollered in his ear. "Look who's here."

I could tell she was testing to see if he recognized me. We all stood frozen in his moment of hesitation.

Widening his eyelids with effort, he answered, "Nancy."

Oh, thank God.

Then he closed his eyes and lay breathing uneasily, lost again. I told Papa I loved him. That I missed him. He squeezed my hand, but I wasn't sure whether he was being reassuring or only twitching in his fitful sleep. Maybe it didn't matter. Papa's whole life had been reassuring.

Even though a walnut tree takes nearly a generation to become fruitful, once it produces, it can yield nuts for as many as fifty years. As I prepared to leave Prairie, I put my faith in this harvest of the future—nets swelling with fish, trees heavy with nuts, fragrant pears, each one as sweet as Papa's, hanging low on weighted branches within easy reach just waiting to be plucked.

Poached Pears

4 large pears (about 2 pounds), ripe but still firm
Juice of ½ lemon
1 vanilla bean, split and scraped
1 cinnamon stick
2 cups sugar
8 cups water
1½ cups white wine
1 thinly sliced lemon
1 thinly sliced orange
1 piece staranise, whole
2 pieces cloves, whole

Use a corer or small spoon to remove cores from the bottom of pears, leaving them whole. (A baby's spoon or espresso spoon works well; however, a melon baller is too large and is not recommended.) Slice bottoms of pears so that they will stand. Peel pears, trying to leave the stems intact, and place them in a bowl of water that has the juice of half a lemon squeezed in it to prevent the pears from turning brown.

Place all ingredients except pears in soup pot and bring to boil. Add pears to liquid. Reduce heat to simmer. Cover pears with a piece of parchment paper cut to fit inside the pot, with a hole cut in the center to allow steam to escape. Cook until a paring knife or skewer can be inserted into the pears easily, about 15 minutes. Remove pears as they are done. When all are done, measure 5 cups of the poaching liquid, unstrained, into a separate container and set aside to cool. Reduce the remaining liquid, also unstrained, to ³/₄ cup for light syrup, approximately 20 minutes. Strain. Store syrup and the pears in the cooled poaching liquid separately in the refrigerator. To serve, spoon some of the syrup onto a serving dish and place a pear in it. Serve warm or cold. Yields 4 poached *pears and ³/₄ cup light syrup.*

Chef

Seven ⟶

"To dream of Walnuts portends difficulties and misfortunes in life: in love affairs, such a vision implies infidelity and disappointment."

PLANT LORE, LEGENDS AND LYRICS,

RICHARD FOLKARD, JR.,

1884

emma didn't tell any of us where she was going that muggy day in June. It must have been a Tuesday or Wednesday, because those were my days off at the time, and I was home when the phone rang. Of course there was nothing out of the ordinary about that except that when I said hello, all I heard at the other end of the line was hysterical sobbing.

"Gemma?" I said. I knew the sound of her crying—lately I had heard it often.

More violent sobs, and then she managed to get out one word and one word only before she started howling again, and that word was:

"Twins."

It turned out that Gemma had actually gone to an abortion clinic, convinced that a baby she couldn't afford and wouldn't have time or energy to take care of properly was worse than an aborted baby. But after her examination, she was told that she was carrying twins.

"It was hard enough, Nancy," she wept, "to kill one baby. But two!"

I worried about Gemma's decision. If she didn't have the time or money for one baby, how was she going to handle two? That she had gone to the clinic at all made me believe that she herself was ambivalent about the decision. But the fact remains that she did leave, and with both babies alive. From that day on, she never looked back. Slowly, she figured out what it all meant, she told me. She knew she must try to be the calm, nurturing center of what she had come to know as a chaotic world, not only for herself but for two new lives as well. This was something she didn't fear, but welcomed. She wanted to be a mother. The only thing was, she would have to do it alone, because Rocky wouldn't be there.

Rocky had refused to go to the hospital with such vehemence that his friends were powerless to convince him otherwise. Rocky said he knew he would be deported and he couldn't go back to the poverty of his life in Portugal—he would rather die. Unfortunately, like so many of his friends at other restaurants who either were paid their small salaries in cash, or, like Rocky, had procured false identification to obtain work legitimately, he feared discovery. Illegal aliens being paid off the books do not qualify for employee benefits like health insurance, and the ones who are given insurance under false names, as Rocky was, are afraid to use it.

Rocky's leg became infected. His fever rose to a burning white heat. And on a still summer morning, lying on the drenched sheets in his tiny bedroom, his breath left him in a pained flutter like the sound of the pigeons lifting from the fire escape outside his window. He was twenty-one years old. Gemma was lost on the subway, trying to find her way to the Queens apartment he shared with six others, without hot water, without a phone, that his pride had never let her visit. When she finally got there, he was already gone.

The news of Rocky's death, when it reached Prairie, was greeted with a stunned, immovable silence that fixed itself onto everything—the stained white cement walls and floors, the scratched face of the gray time clock, the flour-dusty surfaces of the metal tables—and stayed there, muting and dimming everything it covered with a dull, palpable outrage.

They say life comes from death. When Papa Max died, the family speculated about which of the young women was pregnant or would become pregnant soon. If it's true, Rocky's death must have been especially powerful in its ability to make new life. Because in addition to Gemma's twins, we also were amazed by another miracle.

Doctors have told many people that they will never walk again after bad accidents, and they walk. They tell people they will die, and despite the odds, they live. Which is why none of us doubted it when Winnie told us she was pregnant. Winnie's doctors had been so sure that she would never bear a child after her accident that long ago Winnie had stopped bothering to use birth control. Quietly and secretly, her body had healed over the years, just as grass and wildflowers poke through the cracked, crooked pavements in the city.

Winnie's boyfriend proposed, and not long after Seth was fired, she happily moved away to the suburbs to raise her kid. That left me and Gemma, who was grieving for Rocky and struggling with her morning sickness, to stick it out at Prairie. At least until I left for my new job at Toy and Gemma decided what she would do. The owners of Prairie made Gemma "interim" pastry chef, expecting her to do all the work that Seth had done, but without a raise or promise of being given the job permanently. We suspected that they didn't want anyone loyal to Seth to have the position. Nobody left at the restaurant besides me knew Gemma was pregnant.

It was a difficult time—the workload was staggering and we had to train someone to take Winnie's place. Against the advice of her doctor, Gemma was putting in fourteen-hour days, and she didn't take a day off for weeks. One morning when we arrived, we discovered that no one on the overworked night crew had noticed that the trays filled with glasses of chocolate pudding had been left out of the refrigerator overnight. It was deep summer by then; the kitchen was hot, and the pudding had spoiled. In addition, the bread flour that Gemma had ordered had never shown up because the bill wasn't paid, so Gemma had to send a porter out in a cab with a check to get it from the warehouse downtown. That set back bread production nearly two hours. To make matters worse, when I went into the walk-in to retrieve the chocolate cakes, I discovered that someone had pushed a container of eggplant back on the cake shelf and the eggplants had spilled out onto the fragile cakes, smashing their glazed tops.

I could see Gemma's already pale face turn a shade paler as she quickly put me to work making a new batch of pudding as well as redecorating the cakes. Then she took over the baking I usually did, which included decorating and setting up the pastries for lunch service, besides seeing to her own responsibility of inventory and overseeing bread production—one hundred onion rolls, eight loaves of sandwich bread, four brioche loaves, and six dozen corn muffins.

When the flour finally arrived, there was barely enough time to make the dough, let alone proof and bake it. Because it was such a muggy, humid summer, the flour had more moisture than usual and when the new assistant added the amount of water to the dough prescribed by the recipe, the dough became too wet. To compensate, he started adding flour back into it—too much flour. Then, of course, he had to add water again. As a result, the breads never proofed properly. But Gemma and I didn't know that. The new assistant was so afraid of admitting his mistake that he baked the clay-like, leaden rolls and breads and delivered them to the lunch kitchen for service. With only ten minutes to go until lunch began, Gemma flew through the pastry kitchen spewing orders, carrying a tray of cookies, crème brûlées, whipped cream, and fresh fruit on one shoulder, and her clipboard under her other arm. Suddenly, she slipped on a patch of oil that the hurried prep cooks had spilled and not bothered to clean up, and the tray went down, spilling the fruit and pastry all over the floor.

As Gemma stood cursing at the mess, the new assistant marched up to her and whined that the other cooks had used up all the roasted peppers he had prepped for the corn muffins and now there were no muffins for lunch. The cooks said they couldn't wait any longer and would have to take them off the menu for the day. In exasperation, Gemma waved away the new assistant, who offered to clean up the floor, and sent him off to roast more peppers. I saw everything but was unable to leave my spot near the stove without risking scorching the pudding. I opened my mouth to offer to pull the pudding off the stove and help Gemma, but she interrupted me.

"Just tell me the pudding is fine," she said in desperation.

I looked at the pudding just in time to turn down the burner before it boiled over.

"The pudding is fine."

Just then Wally appeared out of nowhere with a mop, and as Gemma numbly took it from him and started mopping the floor, the executive chef ran up to and shoved what looked like a deflated baseball under her nose.

"Gemma!" the chef yelled. "Did you know that the rolls and breads are all ruined? We need them in ten minutes for lunch! What is all this mess? And why are we eighty-six on corn muffins? I'm going back to my kitchen and I expect to see some kind of bread up there in half an hour!" With that, she stomped up the stairs to the main kitchen.

Then it happened. I watched Gemma crumple; her hand slid down the mop handle as she slumped down and sat right on the floor. She started to cry, then sob. I pulled the pudding off the stove and ran over to her.

"Gemma, none of this is your fault," I tried to comfort her. Gemma was the strongest, most organized cook I had ever met— if she couldn't make things work that day, then no one could. But these tears weren't for spilled fruit and cookies or missing peppers or spoiled puddings or smashed cakes or lumpy onion rolls or even menus without muffins. These tears were for Rocky, for the babies that kicked her every time she lifted a pot or hoisted a sheet pan, for the hours and hours of overtime she put in without one extra dime in return.

I helped Gemma to her feet and after the new assistant confessed his mistake with the bread, we convinced Gemma to explain things to the chef, ask if she could buy some bread from another bakery, just this once (Gemma usually had the kitchen running like clockwork, surely the chef would understand?) and pick up the bread herself so she could get some air. Wally gently took the mop from her and finished cleaning up the floor, then volunteered to replace the fruit and cookies Gemma had spilled with new ones while I finished the pudding. Gratefully, I accepted his offer. As soon as the pudding was safe and sound, cooling in parfait glasses in the refrigerator, I ran upstairs and informed the waiters that we were out of chocolate cakes until further notice, then rushed back downstairs. When I arrived, out of breath from taking the stairs up two at a time and sprinting back down, I found Wally still in the pastry kitchen, helping the new assistant whip up a new batch of muffins.

"Thank you, Wally," I said earnestly, then fell in beside him to begin buttering the muffin tins that would receive the batter. A feeling of calm soon returned.

Over and over, Wally helped us without asking for anything in return. But it was hard for me to reconcile this saintly persona of his with the Wally I knew outside of work. I had finally relented and accepted one of his invitations, then spent the next few weeks making up excuses why I couldn't see him again. Finally, he gave up. I still shook my head in disbelief when I thought of that crazy date. He took me to a seedy neighborhood bar and while he drank enough vodka to fill a fish tank, he confessed to me that his whole life was one big drug-dealing, gambling, dangerous mess. It turned out the only kitchen he'd ever cooked in before he came to Prairie was in prison and everything on his résumé that he had used to get his job was a lie. Wally turned his cherubic face toward me and smiled while he mopped. I smiled politely back at Wally and looked away. I was lonely, but not lonely enough to get involved with him. When Eric walked through the pastry kitchen, I gazed after him sadly, but there was no use in pursuing that any longer. Besides, I was starting to believe that romance and ambition just didn't go together.

Esther Hanna begged Papa Max to bring home a girl for her to talk to, someone who would bake with her and gossip with her and walk with her to the markets. Bring me home a sweet girl. What are you waiting for? What's the problem, eh? A nice Jewish girl. A daughter-in-law.

Max was the last of Esther's children to remain single and living at home. Esther nagged and nagged and nagged Max to bring home a wife to make little grandchildren for her, but Max was in no hurry to get married. In an attempt to humor her, since he had no intention of looking for a bride, he bought her an extravagant gift—a hinged wooden wind-up Victrola and a stack of records. All the music she loved: Jewish folk songs, opera, the famous Caruso. On an impulse, Max had it delivered to Esther one day while he was at work.

The card read: "Here's your new daughter-in-law. She'll sing to you all day."

Of course, all of that changed when Max met Rae.

Rae was beautiful. She stood out from the crowd, Papa Max said later about the night he met her on the Knights of Pythias boat ride. The boat ride had been advertised for months as the biggest party happening anywhere south of Grand Street, and everyone had their escorts picked weeks in advance. Grandma Rae and Papa Max each had dates, but not with each other. That didn't stop Max from hovering around Rachel all night, trying to get her attention.

"Every time I turned around, there was this boy," Grandma Rae told us later, nearly blushing. I say nearly because Grandma Rae wasn't one to blush. She was always in control, always dignified, always the lady. She never left the house without being completely "dressed," which to Grandma Rae meant a neat coif, manicured nails, stockings, girdle, full slip, and brassiere underneath an unrevealing dress with matching purse and shoes. We would often laugh when we heard this story, amused to think of our prim and proper grandmother flirting with men. Grandma Rae mistook our gaiety for mockery.

"Well," she said defensively, "I didn't always look like the old lady I am now, you know!"

Grandma Rae, with her dyed black hair teased up high on her head, and her lips drawn on with bright red lipstick—Grandma's lips were thin so she drew on her face!—was quite a character. It was hard to imagine her without the subtle contours of her age—her soulful eyes dimmed by the years with a large bag under each, like an oyster shell drooping from her lower lid; the slight hook of her long nose; the set of her mouth with the wrinkled corners drawn down, ever so slightly; the slope of her shoulders, just so; the freckled skin creased over her knuckles; her thick ankles, leaning in toward each other just a little as she stood in her solid, low-heeled pumps. But the Rachel that Max saw on the boat wasn't that old woman we loved so well. It was the Rachel in her wedding photograph—the soft features of her smooth oval face framed with dark curls and lace, a long strand of pearls resting on her high, firm bosom.

Three months after the boat ride, Max surprised Rae and her two sisters in the living room of their apartment one day with a diamond ring and a proposal for Rae. Rae loved Max. She had known that ever since the day they met. Even so, she knew that marrying Max, who worked in the city, might mean never getting out of the Lower East Side, away from the smelly pickle barrels, and the greasy locksmith who parked his cart in the street right in front of her building. Away from the thick, deformed legs of the old women who had scrubbed too many floors walking too slowly in front of her, blocking her way—these women, like her mother, Bella, who lived and died in tenement apartments with bathtubs in the kitchens and toilets down the dark hallways. Away from her volatile father, Nathan, who shouted at her mother in a drunken rage over the sound of the heating pipes that clanged and clanged and woke you, cramped and perspiring, in a room you shared, in a bed you shared.

It was understood in those days that when a woman married a man, she lost her autonomy. Where they would live was not a joint decision. If Max's work kept him in the city, it would keep Rae in the city too. Torn between her love for him and her desperate need to get away from her squalid surroundings, she told him she needed to think about it. Max sat on the landing outside Rae's apartment the rest of the day and into the night, refusing to leave until Rae gave him an answer.

Grandma Rae began working as a teenager, scrubbing floors, cleaning, and baby-sitting for an aunt, who paid her a quarter. Later, after she and her sisters all passed the civil service exam, she worked on Governors Island, where they were shipping arms to Europe during the First World War, and after that she was a court stenographer during Prohibition. I remember her telling me with her round brown eyes opened wide that she took down the minutes at the trials of pharmacists accused of forging prescriptions to obtain alcohol illegally for bootleggers. She might have even kept on living as a single workingwoman—if only Max hadn't proposed to her.

Grandma Rae, with her girdles snapped up tight and her breasts restrained in an unforgiving corsetlike bra, repressed her ambitions as well as her flesh. That's what women did in the twenties when a man proposed. For marriage, you would gladly give up everything, never dream of being selfish, never put your own needs first, ahead of your family's. Rae believed it was her birthright to be a mother and a wife, to bless a husband with children. How could she refuse Max's hand?

In the morning Rae told Max that she would accept his proposal, but only if he promised to get a job outside the city. Max called his brother, Izzy, who had a construction business in Newark. Izzy gave Max a job, and on November 16, 1924, Grandma Rae and Papa Max were married. Rachel Wiener became Rachel Kasoff, moved to New Jersey with her new husband, and never held a job again.

And poor Great-Grandma Esther Hanna was still lonely until

Sundays, when Rae came back to visit, first alone, and then with Esther's new grandchildren: my mother and her sister.

Grandma Rae would ride the Hoboken ferry with my aunt and mother, two pink-cheeked children of ten and six. The girls dreamed of the potato knishes they would buy at Yonah Schimmel's on the Lower East Side near Grandma Esther's apartment, and dreaded their visit to Great-Grandma Bella, as fragile as parchment paper in her wheelchair at the Beth Abraham Home for Incurables. I can imagine them all standing in the wind on the ferry deck: my grandmother, tall not just in height but with the tall of surviving and believing, in a short jacket and straight wool skirt with braid at the collar and cuffs (Oh! How I wish she had saved those clothes!) and square-heeled pumps, and her daughters, in velvet dresses with lace collars that Great-Aunt Bea had made, and long wool coats buttoned up to the neck. In those days Grandma Rae had a head of thick, curly black hair that must have ruffled gently in the softer breeze as the boat slowed, pulling into the dock of New York City.

In early September, a few short months after Seth was fired, Prairie hired another pastry chef and demoted a resentful Gemma back to assistant. The new pastry chef was a heavy-handed woman with the sunken-eyed appearance of a nocturnal creature. She was a personal friend of the executive chef's, and upon her arrival she coolly announced that she had been given permission to fire all of us if she was greeted with any resistance.

Gemma was the leader of that resistance. After all her hard work, she was loath to hand over her position to a woman with half her experience and all the style of a regulation army bunk bed. Gemma didn't wait to get fired, however. Instead, she quit and took another job as the pastry chef of a prestigious restaurant downtown, where she stayed until she started to swell alarmingly with the burgeoning weight of the twins. The twins were in an odd position—the birth would be difficult if not dangerous—and Gemma was exhausted and ashen with the strain of carrying them. Just about the time I left Prairie, Gemma's doctor recommended that she stop working. Her employer put her on full disability. She was bedridden.

Seth continued working as a consultant until he could get a new full-time job. In fact, I saw a lot of Seth at that point because he was still the consultant for Toy, and he was training me into my new job.

It might seem odd that a Vietnamese restaurant would want an American pastry chef. But the owner of the restaurant, Mai, was a very good businesswoman. She treated her staff like family, feeding us well and taking an interest in our personal lives. A plump character with long, silken black hair, she favored black tent dresses, cowboy boots tooled with flowers, and a signature ten-gallon hat decorated with a coral-colored silk rose she was hardly ever seen without. She had an ageless, shy smile with perfect, even white teeth, like a delicate glowing crescent moon, which gave her a deceptively benign look while all the time the gears in her head were turning with the aggressive precision of sharpened knives. She was smart. She knew that New Yorkers, no matter how sophisticated their palates were, would not assimilate easily to traditional Vietnamese desserts such as red bean paste cake and caramelized rice noodles. So she hired Seth as a consultant to make her a menu of American favorites combined with eastern flavors. We made coconut lime meringue pie, tropical fruit crème brûlée, and ginger ice cream sundaes. Combining East and West may have been a fairly new idea in the kitchen, but it was old beret in the art studio. I had already seen it so many times—the French impressionists borrowing compositional devices from Japanese art or Franz Kline painting his calligraphic black brush strokes. I picked it up like a brush soaking up ink. Seth trained me in two weeks flat and then I was on my own. Mai put my name on the dessert menus, giving me full credit. It was an exceptional opportunity and had been handed to me on a silver platter, but there were a few drawbacks.

A lot of kitchens are in basements and a lot of those basements, being in New York City, are rather primitive. Toy was unheated—as the winter deepened, I took to working in cutoff gloves and a hat, with a wool jacket over my chef's coat. I was so excited at first to be a pastry chef and receive credit and compensation for my work that I put up with the conditions for longer than I should have. It wasn't just the cold, mind you. I think it was my third or fourth day at work when I turned around after I entered the kitchen early in the morning (the baker is always the first to arrive) because I heard a rustling near the door and saw not one, not two, but *five* slinky, large rats jump nonchalantly off the dry goods shelves near the kitchen door and prance lightly across the floor. Their long, skinny, greasy tails dragged behind them, not a yard away from me, to a spot under the ice machine on the far wall.

I always wondered what I would do if I were caught off guard in a frightening or emergency situation. Would I freeze? Would I act quickly and calmly? Would I run away? Now I know. I screamed like a banshee. Then I went directly to Mai.

"Mai! I will quit! I will walk right out of here if those rats aren't eliminated immediately!"

"Chill a pill, Nancy," the chef said in his broken English slang, taking me by the arm and walking with me away from Mai. He gestured to Mai as if to say he would handle it while speaking to her in fast Vietnamese. He smiled at me through clenched teeth. "I see you met our little friends."

"Little friends! Are you kidding? Can't you get an exterminator? And that's 'take a chill pill,' all right?"

"We have exterminated. Many times. We'll follow up on it, I promise."

But they didn't. I imagine it had something to do with the equal parts of expense and futility that extermination probably entails in an aging New York City building, but I was never really given a reasonable excuse. It's true, the rats didn't often get into anything because all the dry goods were sealed in impenetrable bottles or cans or hard plastic bins with lids. It didn't stop the ambitious rats from trying though, and when someone was careless and left a lid ajar or an opened bag of coconut outside of its container, the rats had a veritable picnic. I complained bitterly to Seth, who impressed upon me how important this job was for my career and that I would be stupid to leave it—jobs were scarce and pastry chefs were a dime a dozen. He tried to arm me with reason.

"Rats don't attack unless they're cornered," he said with an air of authority, as if he were a researcher studying rodent behavior. "They're more scared of you than you are of them, believe me."

"Don't even try it, Seth," I said, "I'll bet that's what Goliath's mother told him right before David came to town too."

Seth didn't laugh. No sympathy there. Who knew if what Seth said was true? Who cared? The rats scared and disgusted me in a primal, gut-wrenching way. My niece had silky, cute rats as pets in California. Once she got uppity with me about my animal prejudice.

"There are good and bad rats, just like good and bad people," I told her. "Yours are suburban, law-abiding rats, wearing baseball caps and little high-top sneakers and barbecuing leftovers from your garbage on your patio grill at night while you're asleep. These are city gangster rats. They've got little guns and pointy shoes. They eat people, I swear. It's different."

I couldn't call the health department because if they closed down Toy, I would lose my job and Seth's friendship too. Hey, where the circumstances are irrational, you can be sure there's rationalizing. And while walnut leaves were reported to chase off houseflies or treat the bite of a mad dog (or mad human, for that matter) that didn't mean they would help me a bit with the rats. So I invented what I called my "ritual" and put up with the situation for as long as I could.

This is what I would do: Each morning when I entered the restaurant from upstairs through the dining room, I would grab an empty bus tub (the heavy plastic tubs that the busboys use during service for the empty glasses and plates they collect while working the floor). Bus tub in hand, I would go to the top of the steep stairway that led to the basement kitchen and flick on the light—the kitchen was pitch dark in the early mornings, as there were no windows. At the top of the stairs, my ritual began. First I would shout with as much bravado as I could muster, "Okay, you rats, I'm coming down!" hoping to scare them with the sound of my voice. Then I would throw the bus tub down the stairs with all my might and it would bounce down the steps, making a frightening racket. I would descend the stairs with my heart pounding, pick up the bus tub again, and throw it at the locked kitchen door, hoping to scare them with the sound once more. Then with one terrified motion I would unlock the door, fling it open, and quickly reach inside to click on the light. With my eyes squeezed tightly closed and holding my breath, I would then throw the bus tub one more time as hard as I could into the kitchen. At that point I would always hear the rats scurrying from the dry goods to their home under the ice machine. Immediately, I would beat a panicked retreat to the bathroom outside the kitchen door to change my clothes, panting and shivering in repulsion. Once changed, I would wait an extra minute or two, giving the rats a little time to disappear completely. Then and only then would I venture warily into the kitchen on tiptoe. Every so often a dawdling rat would streak under my feet to the ice machine, knocking me off balance and causing me to cry out with a piercing wail, but for the most part the ritual worked. This I did every single morning, five and sometimes six days a week, for the better part of a year.

Once my day was started and I lit the burners on the stove for warmth, it was fine. I would return the bus tub to the dining room upstairs and the rats would stay put until the next morning. I often wondered if the anxiety produced by my ritual outweighed the good aspects of my job, but I always ended up resigned to it. Mai let me experiment as much as I wanted. Where else would I get this kind of creative freedom? I had worried when I left Prairie in the autumn that I wouldn't know how to handle the responsibility of running an entire pastry department, but when Seth lowered me into the bowl of the small kitchen at Toy with an inventory sheet and a daily schedule, I baked. I juggled menu changes and special requests, organized my department, and got into a routine. Soon I was baking with all the strength and confidence of a pro.

Gradually, I discovered that I had a talent for making up and developing my own unique recipes. Until I was ready to replace Seth's menu with one entirely of my own creations, however, I dug through my recipe file and used tried-and-true recipes that seemed to fit the flavors preferred at Toy. I was expected to fill a cookie plate each day with an assortment of cookies that could be arranged artistically on an oversized shiny black platter that was displayed prominently in the dining room. So I made mint chocolate chip cookies, pistachio shortbread, caramel peanut slices, passion fruit tuiles, and Rachel's Cakes. Rachel's Cakes was Grandma Rae's cookie recipe, which yielded a sweet dough rolled up like a jelly roll with apricot puree and flaked coconut inside, coconut being a favorite ingredient in Vietnamese cuisine. The cookie was beautiful as well as delicious with its pretty orange-colored pinwheel of filling curled inside a golden dough. Mai and her staff loved them. They ate them warm from the oven before I even had a chance to get them onto the platter, so I began baking extra Rachel's Cakes each day, just for the staff.

Despite my love life, which closely resembled a depleted cookie platter after a busy night, life seemed to take a decided turn for the better at Toy. Warm weather lingered into October, and on a sultry Indian summer weekend I went out to the beach with a Care package of Rachel's Cakes to visit my old friend, Karen, whom I had gone to art school with in the seventies. We settled down into our familiar niche, fitting together like worn bleached bones from the same prehistoric animal, and talked about our three favorite subjects: food, love, and art. I still lamented the small amount of time I had to make art, as did she, but we came to the conclusion, as we always did, that life was for learning. We passed the weekend doing what most women friends do together—untangling ourselves from the constricting tentacles of the world and finding solace and strength in each other. At some time during the weekend I checked my phone messages, still nervous about my new job and fearing a disaster in my absence. There was one message, but it wasn't from work. It was from Eric.

Eric Kaplan's reappearance in my life was tentative. On our first date he shook my hand when we said good night. On our second date he kissed me on the cheek. This might have concerned me at other times in my life, but at this juncture it was just the kind of caution that I could appreciate. Gemma may have already won our bet, but that didn't mean I had given up trying to even the score.

If Wally was a bitter cookie that looked deceptively sweet, Eric was the opposite. It's true; Eric protected himself by keeping people at arm's length. This distance could easily be mistaken for meanness. And the clothes he favored at the time—his black leather jacket, black wool beret, and pointy-toed boots—only contributed to his already aloof demeanor, especially when he was onstage with his band, playing a blistering electric guitar for some raunchy, mean-spirited, down-home blues. Love for me up until then had been a difficult recipe, one that always seemed to require a lot of care and attention to detail. I was always screwing up, so I wasn't very confident. Eric listened to me, took the time to get to know me, even asked permission before he finally kissed me full on the lips. Amazingly, the batters didn't separate, the cakes didn't fall.

When we had gotten close enough for me to invite Eric into my bed, it was well past midnight, but typical of new lovers, we weren't tired. I decided to bake a batch of Rachel's Cakes while we talked—it seemed such a romantic thing to do, so spur-of-the-moment. I had a kitchen the size of a broom closet at the time, so baking in it was no small feat. Finally, at nearly two o'clock in the morning, I put the cookie logs in the oven and set a timer.

"Well, what should we do for thirty or forty minutes?" I asked, trying to look innocent. The answer was obvious.

On walnut trees in the early spring, male and female flowers occur on the same tree. Staminate flowers are borne on the catkins, usually four to six inches long, which emerge from buds on wood grown the previous year. As many as two million pollen grains can be released by a single catkin, and a mature tree might have several hundred catkins. The pistillate flowers are borne on the new season's growth, and contain an ovary and a short style, and look like a little nut. Most shoots consist of two flowers, but some have three or even clusters of up to nine or ten flowers. When the stigmas, which grow out of the ends of nutlets, are soft, moist, and velvety, they are ready to receive a dusting of wind-borne pollen from a catkin.

I fell into a sweet, light sleep.

My bed was near a wall of paned French windows, and the

moonlight fell across the blankets in rectangles like confectioners' sugar through a stencil. The timer went off, waking us—it was now near three in the morning. I got up and stumbled into the kitchen, concerned about the cookies—I hadn't even turned the tray they were on to make sure they baked evenly. I hastily put a full-length apron over my naked body and a pair of thick mitts on my hands, then gently lifted the cookie sheet from the oven. On it were perfectly golden-brown cookie logs, maybe a little more done on one side than the other, that smelled like heaven. I heard Eric follow me into the kitchen, but when I turned around proudly with the sheet pan in my hands, I was stunned to see that he was dressed. In a state of apparent panic, he told me he was sure he shouldn't be there with me at all. I tried to get him to talk to me, but he refused. In the following nightmarish seconds, he grabbed his motorcycle jacket, bid me a hasty, unfeeling good-bye, and left. The hot pan slipped from my hands and crashed to the floor.

In the morning I decided it was over. However much Eric had led me to believe that our relationship was built on mutual respect, obviously all he had really wanted was to get me in bed. As soon as he won his prize, he lost interest in the game. Irate, I found his watch next to the bed, where he had forgotten it. I had found possessions of my other boyfriends before in my apartment after a problem or argument. They had always used these things as an excuse to call when they wanted to see me again. Invariably they would come to retrieve their glove or book or bowling ball, and lure me into another unhappy sail with them that usually ended with me alone, baby-sitting one of their castoffs which washed up on the shore as the hateful waves receded. Not this time. I dressed for work, left the house, and headed for Prairie, where Eric still worked. I would give him back his watch and I would give myself back my life.

I found Eric in the upstairs kitchen, preparing for lunch service. He was already in his chef's whites, with a bandanna tied around his forehead instead of the requisite cap. He looked even more like a pirate than I supposed him to be in this cavalier head-gear. He was surprised to see me. He started to say something, but I interrupted him, throwing his watch at him, which he caught just before it hit him in the chest. "Here's your watch," I fumed, "so you don't have to come back and get it." I had re-hearsed this speech on the way over and it came out perfectly now, on the crest of a wave of adrenaline. "I thought you were dif-ferent, but you're not. You're just like every other guy who's afraid to be close. You think you can just walk out and not have to look at me again like I'm something you can toss away, like an old kitchen rag!" Then I started crying, something I promised myself I wouldn't do. The rest of my speech eluded me. "Fuck you," I yelled through my tears, shocking myself as well as Eric, and ran out the door without looking back.

On most walnut trees, the male flowers release their pollen too early or too late to dust the female flowers on the same tree, so that the tree pollinates itself poorly if at all.

On the train downtown to Toy, the shell-shocked predawn subway denizens stared rudely at my tears in dull fascination, like I was on television and couldn't see them. This made me cry even harder. Not only was I heartbroken, but my pathetic reaction was on dis-play. Mortified, I cried all the way to Toy.

As the train neared my stop, a vision of Grandma Rae and Grandma Selma appeared on each side of me. Short and plump, Grandma Selma's legs barely reached the floor of the train.

He's a son of a sea cook!

I looked in her imaginary direction.

Son of a sea cook! Doncha know that's the biggest insult there is?
Grandma Rae interrupted her from my other side.

Oh, stop it, Selma! Can't you see the poor girl is beside herself?

Then she whispered to me, loud enough for Selma to hear, *Take it from whence it comes and charge it to ignorance.*

My grandmothers disappeared. In reality, neither of them would venture into the subway anyway. Grandma Rae didn't even like it when anyone else took the subway. She thought it was dangerous. When she was my age living in Hillside, New Jersey, with two small children in tow, the proper thing to do was to take the bus or a taxi, which she couldn't afford during the Depression anyway. Grandma Rae was always too nervous to drive herself. It even made her nervous when Papa Max would drive into the city to pick up Esther Hanna. So if there wasn't a bus, they walked—to the corner butcher, or the corner newsstand, or the corner greengrocer. When Grandma Rae needed sliced salami from the kosher deli, she would put little Norma in the stroller, and dress up my mother, Dorothy, big enough to walk next to the stroller now. Short, round-faced Great-Aunt Bea would come along, as would vivacious Cousin Mimi. Then they'd make the five-mile round trip to the Kosher Market on Bergen Street in Newark. But Grandma wasn't my age anymore and I didn't have any children. Cousin Mimi moved to Philadelphia, so I didn't have anyone to walk with that day. And besides, I had to get to Toy, over one hundred blocks away, and that meant taking the subway whether Grandma would like it or not.

"Good morning, ladies and gentlemans," she said, curtsying deeply in the middle of the crowded subway train aisle. "Today I will like to dance for you."

She's one of the beggars I always see on the subway—the ones you get to know by their speech and routine—their "shtick," as

Grandma Rae would say. This one is a young Asian woman, her hair bleached blond, in shabby pink tights and leg warmers. She put down her knapsack and began to dance, a little stiffly but obviously once formally trained, like the tutu'd ceramic ballerina inside a music box I had as a kid. She never stopped smiling.

Once, when I saw her with a friend of mine, he said, "Look at that face. That's the face of happiness, of truth."

Momentarily, I felt envious of her. She was probably living more fully the artist's life than I ever had. But it was only momentary. I looked at her backpack again, where she most likely had all her possessions, and the stains on her clothes, from sleeping in whatever could be salvaged for a blanket on the subway platforms, or, worse, in the street. I emptied all the change in my pocket into her tattered paper cup. Part of me feared her—if not for my detested survival jobs, I would be in the same predicament as she, a predicament I had been taught to avoid at any cost despite my burning desire to be a full-time artist.

You don't know what it means to be poor, to be afraid. You're spoiled.

I remember Grandma Rae telling us the stories she knew about the Holocaust, about the Depression, her eyes shining with held-back tears. She would lean her chin into her hand, her elbow propped on the kitchen table before her, *tsk, sigh,* and shake her head slowly. Only my Grandma Rae could put more feeling into this pose, into the sound of this *tsk!* and this *sigh* than any other person alive. It would speak volumes. It was the final statement, the ultimate appraisal of years and years of oppression, murder, outrage, financial ruin, and personal tragedy. What couldn't be expressed in words, what was too difficult to explain, could always be summed up by my grandmother's sad face resting wearily in her palm, her heartfelt *tsk!* and her soul-stirring *sigh.* If she were sitting impossibly on the subway with me, I'm sure this would have been her response to the little dancing beggar in pink, the subway, and my love life.

How could I have been so wrong about Eric? I asked myself as the train wore on through midtown and the Village, SoHo, and finally into TriBeCa. I was thoroughly depressed. I wouldn't worry about love anymore, I decided. Being in love was ruining my image anyway. How could I perpetuate my stance as the intense, misunderstood, and lonely artist if I were walking around, God forbid, happy? Everyone knows an artist must suffer, I lied to myself. I had a reputation to uphold, after all. Enough with this love stuff. I was through. Besides, I was certain I would never hear from Eric again.

Walnut pollen can be carried for many miles on a strong wind. The farther the pollen blows from its source, the more widely it spreads, and the less likely it becomes that it will ever fall on a receptive female.

Bang bang bang! Crash! Clonk!

When I arrived at Toy, I performed my ritual with more vengeance than usual. After I confronted Eric with his watch, throwing the bus tub down the stairs was especially pleasurable.

"Okay, you rats! Get out of my way! I'm coming down!" I yelled at the top of my lungs. I ran down the stairs into the basement, my heart racing. Then I picked up the bus tub and threw it at the kitchen door. Crack! I unlocked the door, flipped on the light, and threw the bus tub one more time, hard, into the kitchen, clenching my eyes shut tight when I heard the rats scampering. Then I retreated into the bathroom to change into my uniform, as usual. This time, though, when I came into the kitchen, I was so disgusted about Eric, about my ritual, about everything, I just left the tub where it lay, upside down, on the basement floor.

Let somebody else pick it up and carry it back upstairs, I thought unhappily.

I began to lay out sheet pans for Rachel's Cakes, banging each one on the metal table harder than usual while muttering to myself about Eric. I could hardly concentrate on the recipe. I climbed up into the dry goods area to get a big bag of coconut out of its plastic bin in order to refill the nearly empty coconut bucket I kept in my station. Unfortunately, rats like coconut as much as Grandma and I do. The plastic coconut bin in dry goods had been pried open, and on the edge of the thick brown paper bag were the unmistakable marks of busy rat teeth. Tears burned my eyes again. Angrily, I threw the gnawed bag of coconut back in the box.

"Oh, hell," I said to no one in frustration. "I can't leave my work undone. I'll just have to open a new bag of coconut." Just then the phone rang. I grabbed a new, sealed bag of coconut and climbed down, cursing. The bus tub still lay upside down on the floor, inches from my feet, making it impossible for me to walk in a straight line to any of my destinations. Still, I didn't move it, just skirted around it. Let it lie there, I thought bitterly. On the way to the phone, I grabbed from my station the scissors I would need to open the heavy coconut bag and lugged it with me. Then I grabbed the kitchen phone and wedged the receiver between my ear and shoulder while I started cutting into the new bag.

"Kitchen," I said, expecting the voice of a purveyor looking for the chef. It was Eric. Before I could say anything, he responded to every word of my botched speech. "You're not an old kitchen rag, I can be close," he pleaded, "you're right, I got scared. Give me another chance, please, I want to be with you."

I tried to lift the heavy bag of coconut onto the counter in front of me with the phone on my shoulder and almost dropped the bag on my foot.

"Can you hold on?" I said. I took a deep breath and set the phone down, then reached for the coconut bag. What was I going to say? I hadn't expected Eric to call—and certainly not so quickly. At that moment the dishwasher, a large-bellied Dominican man named Ramon, arrived. I saw him brush past the bus tub, about a yard away from me, knocking it lightly with his foot. It moved—twice. We both stared at it and at each other in shock. There was something under there, and it was alive.

Forgetting all about the coconut and the phone, I streaked to the end of the room, and while peeking out from behind the kitchen door, watched horrified as Ramon lifted the bus tub, revealing a rat two feet in length from nose to tail. I couldn't believe I had been nonchalantly prancing around this rat all morning. Ramon beat the rat senseless with a rolled-up newspaper, then swept it into a dustpan and dumped it, bloated and limp, in the garbage pail near my station. Trembling, I insisted he take it outside.

My hands were shaking so much, I didn't know if I could work, but I tried, returning to my pastry table to set up the electric mixer for my cookie dough. I was still thinking I could forget all about it, when I pulled the top off the coconut bucket to pour the contents of the new coconut bag inside and saw what I was certain was the end of a long, skinny tail peeking out of the coconut that was left in the bottom of the bucket.

"Ramon!" I screamed, jumping away from the bucket and cowering in the corner. "Ramon, look in the bucket, get it out, get it out, please!" I was hysterical, sobbing.

Ramon gingerly touched the end of the tail with a long-handled spoon while I shrieked from nearby. It didn't move. "Oh, God, there's a dead rat in the coconut," I moaned. Visions of beaten, swollen rats burned behind my closed lids like waves of heat coming off a grill. Then I peeked and watched astounded as Ramon reached into the coconut with his pudgy fingers and slowly lifted out the long, slender hull of a vanilla bean, which I must have dropped in the coconut myself by mistake.

We both laughed. Suddenly I remembered Eric, and ran over to pick up the phone. He was still there.

"What the hell is going on there?" he said. "Are you okay?"

I tucked the phone under my chin again. While I emptied the old coconut into a bowl so that I could wash and refill the bucket, I explained to Eric why he had been hearing such a racket. Then I accepted his apology.

Eric and I learned to harmonize our differences just like my cookie dough for Rachel's Cakes rolled up around its filling of coconut and apricots, making one delicious dessert out of distinct, separate ingredients. By winter we agreed to take the next logical step and move in together. This wasn't as easy as it sounds. I felt as fragile as a walnut seedling about to be transplanted, hoping that the farmer would wrap me well in burlap to protect me from the sun and tie me securely to a stake so I wouldn't get stepped on. So what if I had never considered my old apartment permanent, never bought a proper bed, never hung curtains, never had the cracked tile in the kitchen fixed—even a walnut dropped by accident into a patio pot or flower bed grows into a tenacious young tree, difficult to pull out. The stems of a new seedling may not look like they're growing, but all the time the little taproot is descending to a formidable depth. What if I couldn't dig myself out after all those years alone? What if my roots were too crowded at Eric's, what if my shadow threw a pall over his garden? I was terrified.

Walnut borer, walnut moth, walnut scale, walnut weevil. Worm and blight and spider. So much could go wrong. Persian walnuts bud early and are vulnerable to spring frosts. But Eric was a confident farmer; if there was a sudden cold snap, I knew I wouldn't suffer too much damage. And I was no mission walnut, small and weak. Eric may have practically had to pack my bags for me and drag me out the door, but I survived the grafting.

One Sunday when Toy was closed, I gathered up all my photography equipment and had Eric drive me down to the restaurant in his car. Mai had said I could come in on Sundays if I wanted to photograph my work in the dining room. Finally, I had replaced all of Seth's recipes with my original ones. For the first time since I had started baking professionally, just over a year ago, I had my own menu. When I arrived at Toy, I went into the kitchen and located the garnishes, sauces, and pastries I would need to plate one of each dessert, then carried everything up into the quiet dining room.

Proudly, I arranged the slices of cake and platters of pastries for their photographs, taking into consideration the elements of visual design: the color and texture of sauces and garnishes balanced with the height and forms of the desserts, which were sometimes fashioned into new, nontraditional shapes. My work wasn't just pastry anymore. It was sculpture and painting, joining a tradition of pastry chefs back through history, the same tradition that had prompted the famous chef, Carême, to state, "the fine arts are five in number—painting, sculpture, poetry, music, architecture—whose main branch is confectionery."

I set up my floodlights on stands and my thirty-five millimeter camera on a tripod. Using a handheld light meter and a professional gray card, I took a reading and determined an exposure. Then I focused on my subject: a perfectly arranged cookie platter. This camera at one time had been my father's. His first darkroom shared the tub with my older sister's bathinette in the Stuyvesant Village apartment he and my mother rented in Union, New Jersey. Photography was his refuge from the pressures of a businessman's life, but he never took a break from supporting my mother and the four of us kids to pursue it full time. I have fond memories of picture-taking expeditions in the snow that we used to take together on his days off when I lived at home briefly after college. Ironically, it was the hard work that kept him away from his photography that ended up making it possible for me to attend art school.

He photographed my artwork, then taught me to do it myself. When I first moved to the city, I used to borrow equipment. Over and over I tried to save the money to buy what I needed, but an unexpected bill would always set me back. I'll never forget the day my father suddenly gave me his camera and all the equipment I needed to photograph my art. It wasn't my birthday or any particular holiday. He just knew I needed it, and he was buying another, smaller camera for himself. It was an extravagant, thoughtful, and generous gift, and so like my father to give it.

In addition to the cookie plate, I set up a chocolate peanut butter mousse cake, balanced pointed nose up against a triangle of chocolate peanut bark under which ran a river of caramel sauce; and a pear and sun-dried cherry spring roll (an Oriental name that Mai preferred but which was actually a strudel gently rolled into the shape of a firecracker) dusted with powdered sugar, spanning a tiny lake of pear sauce accented with a lightning rod of cherry sauce and garnished with a round, clean scoop of Tahitian vanilla ice cream. I had already photographed my pistachio-and-raspberry ice cream sundae sitting as tall and regal as the Chrysler Building with a crown of free-form tempered white and dark chocolate, and my cashew pie in a circle of bitter chocolate sauce studded with large polka dots of cashew anglaise. I piped a perfect curl of peaked whipped cream onto the plate next to the strudel, and tucked a full, bright green mint leaf under the cream, then stood back to assess the effect. Outside, the rain fell in a steady, drumming stream.

Maybe my pastries weren't paintings exactly, but I treated them as if they were. I taped the photographs neatly onto squares of black paper and clipped them into a red loose-leaf notebook with plastic page protectors, which I then took to calling my portfolio. What Mai didn't know was that I was already using my portfolio to look for another job, and it wasn't just because of the rats. Aside from the cold, which was a major concern now that it was nearly February, I was frustrated and impatient with the tiny, crowded kitchen. Furthermore, for all of my hours of overtime, I still was going to get only one week of vacation for the whole year, unpaid, in the summer, and a raise, when Toy's unpaid bills were frequently posted on the bookkeeper's bulletin board, was still out of the question. Even though I knew the same was true for nearly every other cook in the city, I took no comfort in having company for my misery. On top of that, I still didn't have time for my artwork.

The drawing of Papa with the three-eyed doll that I had begun the previous spring was finished by then, but that was the last full-scale drawing I would have time to do for a long time to come. Every day after work I returned home and worked on a series of small pastel drawings. They were all abstract, mostly fields of color that dissipated at their edges. Passive and nebulous, the little drawings hung on my drawing board like a chain of ladder rungs going nowhere. I knew I wouldn't be happy until I could give them the attention they deserved, but now I was thoroughly involved in my pastry career. Should I keep baking, or throw in my kitchen towel?

Once when we were visiting Grandma Rae's apartment, Eric found her sharpening steel in a drawer in her kitchen when he reached in to get a can opener. The large, professional steel, with its carved, worn wooden handle and long, heavy top, surprised Eric. "What's your grandmother doing with a big steel like this?" he asked me.

"Sharpening her knives." I smiled at him, enjoying the surprise on his face.

Grandma Rae was a cook's cook who never came to visit without a foil-wrapped dish containing one of her creations. The quality of her ingredients and cooking tools mattered to her as much as they matter to professional chefs. She would make daily trips to the butcher, to the greengrocer, and the fish market to pick out the things she needed with a discerning, practiced eye.

There's a family chestnut about Grandma Rae that comes to mind whenever the family tells stories about her. They say that if you rang Rae's doorbell, in the short time it would take her to walk to the door and answer it, the table would be laden with food. Her stuffed cabbage, baking in a fogged glass dish in her oven, produced a smell so bewitching that we had to wonder if she was trying to put a spell on us. After all, she was born on Halloween, as she would often tease us with a smile, "with the rest of the witches."

But didn't people need art as much as they needed food? Does a full belly keep our spirit from starving as well? Grandma Rae would say no. She loved art. My paintings hung all over her apartment, and she read incessantly. She would be happy to discuss politics with you, even religion, or current events.

But first you should eat.

It wasn't just Grandma Rae's opinion that helped me make up my mind what to do next. While I was snapping pictures, there was a knock on the window. Through the rain-streaked glass I thought I saw a familiar face. I walked over and rubbed a circle clear on the fogged pane.

"Arana!"

I opened the door for her and she stepped inside, shaking water from the leather jacket and baseball cap she wore backward on her thick, shaggy mane. She talked to me about the desserts I was making and seemed proud of me—it was good to see her. She told me that she had eventually gotten her name on the dessert menu at LaCoupe, but decided she missed her native Wisconsin and was going back home to sing in her brother's rock band, Blender Heads. We laughed and talked about old times, and then, just before she left, she handed me a rolled-up magazine. "I thought you'd like to see this," she said. I unrolled it as she disappeared out the door and down the block.

It was a recent issue of *Dessert Masters* magazine, a bible for pastry chefs and a showcase for exceptional ideas. The cover promoted a feature article about LaCoupe, so I opened it up and found a full-page glossy photograph of a tall, glistening ice cream sundae. The caption next to the sundae said "Coffee-Lover's Parfait." The sundae had been my idea, but Arana had been left with the hard work of making up and testing the recipes for its components—sambuca white chocolate sauce, espresso sorbet, and cinnamon ice cream—after I left. I didn't know if she had ever completed it and doubted I would get any credit for it if she had. But the credit at the bottom of the page was large and clear: "Pastry Chef Arana Power, Assistant Pastry Chef Nancy Ring." I was thrilled. I felt the recognition course down my back in a cool, exquisite shot of energy. "Thanks, Arana," I said to her out loud, even though by then she was gone. I cited the article on my small but growing résumé and put the pages from the magazine in the red notebook along with the photographs of my desserts. This would help me move on. The only question now was, where?

As I was taking the last photographs, I heard the horn of Eric's car blaring outside. He was early, but he was leaning on the horn in such an urgent way that I ran outside in the freezing rain to tell him I needed more time. He spoke before I did.

"Nan, hurry up! Gemma's in labor!"

One of Gemma's twins had moved into an even more awkward position than before just as she was ready to give birth. In order to try to save the ill-positioned baby's life, her doctor had to perform an emergency cesarean. This was something for which Gemma was not prepared. Despite her difficult pregnancy, she had been assured that the birth would be natural. She panicked and screamed when they began the operation.

"I swear, I could feel them cut me. I wasn't ready!" she cried when we visited her, then lowered her voice, gesturing toward the crib, fresh tears beginning again. "Every time I look over there, I wince. I know I have to forget, but it's so hard."

Eric sat uncomfortably next to me on the bench near Gemma's bed, holding the flowers we had brought. I walked over to the crib and looked in.

"Well, we all made it," Gemma said with obvious relief.

One girl was much smaller than the other, but they were both healthy and pink, as translucent as tissue paper. The smaller one looked exactly like a female Rocky, with a thin brush stroke of glossy, dark hair. The other was the spitting image of the girls in Gemma's family—big-boned and with a head of wispy curls. Roxanne, one hospital wrist tag read. I peeked at the other one— Rachel. I leaned over the crib and smiled at Gemma.

"I named them for Rocky," Gemma said quietly.

The pregnancy, the birth—none of it compared to the real test that Gemma had coming, and all of us knew it. Although, the next time I visited Gemma at home, true to her incredible ability to get organized and survive, she was sitting with a baby in a basket on each side of her and a bottle in each hand, feeding them simultaneously as if she had done it a hundred times before. Looking at her that day, I almost believed it's true that life never gives you more than you can handle. Still, I feared for her. It's one thing to be valiant. It's another to be valiant and alone. Shortly after the babies were born, she packed up everything and moved south to a Baltimore suburb, where the same money that paid for her tiny apartment would pay for half of a house with a yard and garage, and the streets were lined with trees for the girls to climb instead of parking meters and overflowing garbage pails. I missed her, but we stayed in touch, exchanging recipes over the phone and catching each other up on our lives. Gemma understood why I wanted to leave Toy. It wasn't just the expense that turned her away from New York. It was also the rat race—no pun intended—in New York's fiercely competitive professional kitchens.

Rachel's Cakes

<u>For the pastry:</u>
2 ½ cups flour
Pinch salt
2 teaspoons baking powder
¼ pound unsalted butter, softened
1 teaspoon grated orange zest (optional)
½ cup sugar
2 eggs
1 teaspoon vanilla extract

<u>For the filling:</u>
6 ounces dried apricots
Water
3 tablespoons strawberry
      preserves
¾ cup flaked coconut

Preheat oven to 350 degrees. Line a cookie sheet with parchment paper, or grease it and set aside.

Prepare the filling: Place apricots in a medium saucepan and fill with just enough water to cover them. Bring to a boil, reduce heat, and simmer until apricots are tender and can be pierced easily with a sharp knife. Add more water during cooking if necessary to keep apricots covered. Drain apricots and puree them in a food mill or food processor fitted with a metal blade, or mash the fruit with a fork as finely as possible. Add strawberry preserves and mix well. Cool mixture completely and set aside. Place coconut in a small container and set aside.

Prepare the pastry: Mix together flour, salt, and baking powder and set aside. Beat butter with zest, if using it, in the bowl of a mixer fitted with a paddle, or with a wooden spoon until light. Add sugar and beat until thoroughly incorporated. Beat eggs, add vanilla extract. Add egg mixture, a little at a time, to butter, beating on high speed or vigorously with a wooden spoon. Do not add more egg until the first addition is thoroughly incorporated. Add dry ingredients all at once, with mixer on lowest speed, or gently mix with wooden spoon until just incorporated. Do not overmix. Divide dough into three pieces approximately 7 ounces each.

Assemble the cakes: Working with one piece at a time, roll each piece of dough out on a floured pastry board into a rectangle $1/4$ inch thick. Spread generously with apricot puree and sprinkle with

3 to 4 tablespoons of coconut. Roll dough up jelly roll fashion, being careful not to break the dough. Wrap each log in plastic wrap and let it rest in the refrigerator for two hours.

Bake the cakes: Place the chilled logs on the baking sheet. Make shallow cuts in the top of each log $3/4$ inch apart with a paring knife, where the logs will be sliced after baking. Bake for approximately 30 to 40 minutes, until the logs are light golden brown, turning the trays during baking to ensure that they bake evenly. Cool on a rack for at least 15 minutes before cutting each log into thick slices. Store in airtight container. Yields approximately 28 cookies.

Eight

"If a woman is suspected of being a witch,
a walnut dropped into her lap will
prevent her from rising."

BIZARRE PLANTS,

WILLIAM EMBODEN,

1974

eople think being a chef is so glamorous. They romanticize a pristinely white-coated and poufy-hatted cook tasting a simmering broth with a silver spoon and adding a pinch of something or other with a supremely confident air. The steam wafts up into his cherubic face like a flowery, clement sauna. Actually, it's more like being a construction worker. Thickly muscled, grunting kitchen workers hoist enormous boulders of doughs, meats, and plucked birds onto cold metal tables and carve them with sharp, forbidding knives. They suffer back injuries and knee operations and surgery for hernias from lifting or carrying or shouldering some enormous and unwieldy

food. Like most chefs, I always managed to forget my bodily pain and hunger, inspired and mad with devotion. I would lose myself in the incredible flow of time, time that slips by like a fast river in a dream, with the kind of concentrated rush of feeling that occurs only when you are doing something you love.

Finally, I gave notice at Toy. I would soon discover, however, that most restaurant kitchens in New York City are pretty much alike. There weren't resident rodents in all of them, but the conditions were hardly exemplary. For the next two years I slowly climbed the pastry ladder, gaining a little more knowledge here, a little more experience there. The climb was steep. I worked hard, long hours, in ill-equipped kitchens with limited space and old machinery and ovens. I worked in kitchens where the temperature rose to over a hundred degrees in the summer with no ventilation or fans, and it wasn't just for myself that I despaired, but for my melting butter cream rosettes and wilting chocolate curls falling hopelessly out of temper.

I didn't quit baking though. My love for baking is such that it would take more than a few hellish kitchens to quell it. I believed despite everything, despite the fourteen-hour workdays and the cursing, sometimes abusive chefs, that I would soon discover the perfect job. Finally, after a long search, I thought I'd found it.

He wanted a frozen dessert, a hot dessert, a room-temperature dessert, and a dessert that combined hot with cold, a custard, a cake, three flavors of ice cream as well as sorbet, with a preference for figs, crème fraîche, bittersweet chocolate, and berry flavors. He also had a list of dislikes. No pomegranates, no food coloring, no marzipan, no soufflés, and nothing trendy, too fussy, or smothered in whipped cream. He had experience in pastry himself, but he didn't have time to run the pastry department as well as oversee the rest of the

kitchen, so he needed me, he said, to get the pastry department organized for him. And one more thing. The executive chef of Acroama
added that he loved oranges. I left my second interview with a handshake, a notebook full of sketches and lists, and the job.

The chef boasted openly, "Acroama is gonna be *the* place to go,
you wait and see. It'll be the hottest new restaurant in town, and I
don't mean just New York, but any town, the entire East Coast—
why not? Maybe even the whole country. You watch, we'll be the
center of attention in the restaurant industry." When I looked at him
uncertainly, he added, "I've got some major press and critics interested in us already. We're gonna knock this business on its ear, set
some standards around here." The owners, beaming like twin fat,
contented walruses, clapped him on the back and chortled happily.

"Why do you think we named it Acroama?" one of them asked
me.

"What does it mean?" I asked.

"Greek word," the chef said, "found it in *Larousse*. It means," he
paused for emphasis—"that to which one pays attention."

Normally I would be skeptical of such big claims, such flagrant
bragging. But the chef of Acroama was an understated young man
who wore tortoiseshell-rimmed glasses. His boasts were spoken
softly and shyly, almost as if someone else had put them in his
mouth. There didn't seem to be a shred of ego in this man's shy,
genuine smile and warm handshake. My smile mirrored his invol-
untarily as he shook my hand and my head bobbed up and down,
yes, yes, like one of those toy dogs in the rear window of a speed-
ing car. While the chef shook my hand, he told me that the staff
would have to accept moderate salaries to stay under budget (yes,
yes) and work extra hours at first to make the deadline of opening
day (bobbing, smiling) but he promised we would receive full
credit for our work in all those rave reviews we'd be getting (yes,
yes) as well as raises and more normal hours. I felt high on the ela-

tion of getting the job over a lot of other applicants (their unfortunate résumés lay on his desk in a pile as thick as a telephone book). Although still wary of the restaurant business in general, given my recent experiences, I believed him. I should have paid more attention to his shoes though. I've always felt you can tell everything about people from their shoes. I didn't think much of it at the time, but the chef was wearing a pair of black, thick-soled, lace-up army boots. With steel tips.

They say hindsight is clear sight. I kept telling myself that I should have seen something wasn't kosher at Acroama. I should have read the signs. I should have known. But even Great-Grandma Reba would have told me that no one can stop hard times when they're hell-bent on coming. Fate is like bread dough, rising in a warm spot. Even if you punch it down, it rises again.

When Great-Grandpa Frank Dondershine sailed to America in 1902, hot on the lace-up heels of Reba Lohmachinsky, his sweetheart from Romania who had come to America the year before, he didn't hold out much hope of finding her. Reba had fled her unhappy childhood home in a hurry, and she had deliberately made her footsteps difficult to trace to elude the father who beat her. Remarkably, through diligent sleuthing in the small world of immigrants, Frank found her working and living with relatives in New Jersey. Shortly afterward, they were married in New York City, without the prerequisite dowry and exchange of expensive gifts that would have been required in the Orthodox temples of Romania. The couple didn't own much aside from the wealth in their hearts. But by the time they had eighteen-month-old Selma and her three-month-old brother, Nathan, to feed, they had saved enough to buy a small grocery store on Prince Street in Newark, three steps up from the bustling street and with an apartment in the back. Soon Harry was born, then the twin girls, Gussie and Rose. Five kids, three rooms. Still, that didn't stop the family from believing that if they worked hard enough, they could make a success out of the store.

Selma delivered bagels to the neighbors as soon as she was old enough to remember the route, and the boys helped Great-Grandma Reba stock the shelves and take care of customers. And despite his chest that whined like an old oven door, Great-Grandpa Frank delivered milk by horse and wagon. When the children became alarmed at their father's wheezing and gasping, they asked what was wrong. Great-Grandma Reba hesitated before answering, glancing at Frank, who shook his head, indicating that he feared the children wouldn't be able to handle the truth. Reba told them that their father had asthma. In truth, he suffered from a serious lung disease.

The family still wasn't rich, but there was enough money coming in for Frank to keep the store stocked with goods, and for Great-Grandma Reba to bake the pastry and breads the children loved, filling the small store with the aromas of yeast cakes and challah. You couldn't say the hours were long, because the hours never ended. Work and life were as intertwined as schmaltz, fried onions, and chopped liver.

They say hard work never hurt anybody. I'll bet you a baker's dozen that Great-Grandma Reba would say they're wrong. But I wasn't thinking of what Reba would say, or how she would stand out in the kitchen of Acroama, in her long, full skirt and ruffled apron, when I took my new job. Besides, I knew Reba could take the pressure. At Acroama I was promised health insurance, three full-time assistants, and a brand-new kitchen that I could equip just the way I wanted from scratch. Even though I had promised myself no more fourteen-hour days, no more working without benefits and adequate pay, I figured, for all this, I could work a few hours of overtime and receive a few nickels less. Ambition drove me to take this job, this job that threatened to take over my life once and for all. It was more pressure, more responsibility, more pastry than I had ever agreed to before. I did it because I was ready, because I wanted the challenge, because I was sick of walking the fence, of constantly being torn between my art and my need to survive. I did it because Eric had gotten his first executive chef position, and that inspired me to look for a promotion as well. I did it because I was crazy from the heat.

Summer. Not just any summer, but New York City summer. Forget Martha and the Vandellas singing "Dancin' in the Street." Summer in the city is as hot and heavy as overworked bread dough, too thick to rise and too tight to roll. No one is dancing. But they are working. Just because the tar is melting in the street like fudge over a double boiler doesn't mean that anybody's getting the day off. To make it worse, the kitchen of Acroama wasn't designed properly. Even in the 1700s people knew enough to plant a black walnut tree over the farm dairy since the tree provided enough shade to cool not only the stone milk house but also the spring running beneath it, where they could keep the jars of milk chilled. No shady walnut kept the heat from the cook's grills and ovens at Acroama from spiraling like a swarm of bees toward the pastry corner and hovering there, harsh and inhuman.

"This menu is printed wrong," Bernie said to me.

I was the pastry chef and Bernie was impossible. If Bernie could qualify as an assistant, then I was the Queen of England. And I don't mean her skills weren't excellent. They were. It was her heart. She was reckless. She was moody. She was glib. Only this time she was right.

I squinted at the menu Bernie was holding, trying to read it while I grated orange peel at the same time. *Ch-ch-ch-ch.* Pause. *Ch-*

ch-ch-ch. The smell of orange, sharp and invigorating, was punctuated by blasts of fishy smoke from the smoker that sat like a small oven next to the pastry station. Every time the cooks opened the door to check the thick slabs of salmon inside, an asphyxiating cloud came pouring into our space. All my requests to move the smoker had been answered with excuses. Bernie coughed loudly and glared at the cooks. Wiping my watering eyes with the edge of my apron, I peered at the menu again.

"See," Bernie said, "it says *burnt* orange ice cream instead of *bitter* orange ice cream, like you said. I'll go get the manager and tell him for you."

Whatever, I muttered to myself. It took all my energy just to keep going let alone worry about details like typos on the rough draft of a menu. We had been working these crushing twelve- and fourteen-hour days without breaks, and today was no exception. A to-do list of things we had to get done before we could go home spun inside my head: train the night assistants to make the new cookies for the sorbet plates, pipe jam into the cardamom petit fours, fill out an order sheet for— Suddenly I thought about what Bernie had said. I ran after her and caught her before she got out the kitchen door.

"Wait, Bernie, forget changing the menu. I like the sound of that burnt orange ice cream. I want to try to make it."

I had been thinking about an orange ice cream to go with a chocolate walnut tart that the chef wanted dressed up. He had already approved my chocolate orange pâte sucrée for a crust and the addition of ice cream for a garnish. I knew that plenty of rind would make the sweet flavor of orange ice cream pleasantly bitter. *Bitter* orange ice cream seemed properly elegant, just the right combination of the restraint of an adult and the sweet tooth of a child. But *burnt* orange ice cream conjured up ideas that I hadn't even thought of yet: deep, dark caramel and fresh juices reduced almost too far until they were syrupy, thick, and intense. Forget restraint. Here was the possibility for rapture, for passion. Also, I'd never seen that flavor before. It was a first. It was an Invention, capital I. It was a tour de force. This was the hot, hot summer of 1992, and as far as I knew, there wasn't a burnt orange ice cream on any other menu in the city.

I had gambled when I took this job. I gave up making art completely. I gave up every other interest I had in my life except for Eric, and at the beginning even gave up seeing my friends. The job became everything for me: my identity, my baby, my religion. It was a hard job, a shroud of details and endless hours of labor that hung heavily over my head, threatening to suffocate me at times. But I clung to it not because I wanted the fame and glory that the chef promised was at the end of this hard, steep climb, but because I was curious. What would happen if I put all my energy into pastry, every bit of it, not just my time in exchange for money, but all my creativity, all the persistence and ambition that I had saved up for painting and trying to get recognition for my art?

Pliny the Elder wrote in the first century A.D., "The shadow of the walnut tree is poison to all plants within its compass." Pliny didn't know it yet, but it wasn't the shadow of the beautiful tree that was so deadly. The roots of the walnut tree secrete the chemical juglone: 5 hydroxy-1, 4 naphthoquinone. The symptoms of juglone poisoning are usually dwarfing, wilting, or yellowing of leaves, but if the plant is especially intolerant, death. I thought I had found the job of my dreams at Acroama, a job like a spreading, tall, and lovely walnut tree, sheltering, shady, from all appearances perfect.

"Shit, the flash didn't go off!" Bernie complained, peering around the edge of the Polaroid camera and checking the flashbulb.

We took pictures of all the new desserts to help teach the night assistants how to plate them for service. Bernie had borrowed the camera, and it wasn't working. "Give it to me," I said, and she returned, grumbling, to the dough she had been rolling before we started taking pictures. I glanced over at her as she worked, as lean and tall as the thin French rolling pin she used with its smooth, tapered edges. Her long fingers pushed the pin quickly and expertly over the dough.

Bernie had enough experience to be the pastry chef herself. When I first met her after she was hired by the chef, she had confessed her reluctance to take on the pressure and responsibility of being a pastry chef. I was puzzled because when I had seen her résumé in the chef's office earlier, it had included numerous pastry positions and a stint studying in Italy. I asked her right away why she wanted to be my assistant instead of being chef. She matter-of-factly told me that she wasn't particularly creative, not that she was putting herself down for it. She just knew that about herself, the same way she knew the size of her shoes. Her answer convinced me. Now that we were actually working together, though, I could sense her frustration with being second in command.

"Bernie, could you let that dough rest in the refrigerator before you reroll it? I don't want it to get overworked," I said to her.

"Don't worry about it. After it's rerolled, it rests in the fridge." Her dark eyes dared me to contradict her. "It's the same difference, you know."

I put the camera on the shelf above me, making a mental note to have someone fix the flash later, and began cracking eggs for a recipe. Impatiently, Bernie pushed my bowl of eggs two inches closer to my side of the table.

"This station is way too small when we're both here at the same time," she whined, stopping to take out her hair clip and redo it for the fourth time that morning. She stuffed the clip in her pocket and shoved her straight black hair behind her ears with annoyance. "The kitchen where I worked before spoiled me. It was twice this size and I had it to myself." She rolled her eyes and groaned, "I hate this rolling pin! It's so cheap."

Bernie's talents were speed and production. And complaining. She didn't like the name of the restaurant. She didn't like the restaurant's decor, the chef, or the chef's clothes. She didn't even like the desserts we were making. On some counts I had to agree with her. The chef did dress like a suburban science teacher from the fifties. But what Bernie lacked in congeniality, she made up for in skill. For every cookie the other assistants rolled, she rolled four. For every recipe they mastered, she mastered two or three. She pointed to the metal shelves called the "speed rack," where we placed all the finished desserts to rest before we wrapped and stored them. The rack was full, brimming with tart shells and cookies and pies we had been making all day.

"See," she said, explaining herself, "your happiness is a beautiful dessert displayed on a plate like a piece of art, and mine is a full speed rack." For a brief moment I thought I understood her. We were two sides of the same coin. Between us, we had the creativity and speed of a pastry giant. The only trouble was, we still had to take our chances when the chef flipped that coin. When I won the toss and needed Bernie to follow my directions, she rebelled. If I instructed her to do something one way, she invariably had a reason to do it another way. Everything was an argument.

Juglone is also produced in the leaves of the walnut tree. Rain dripping from the leaves carries it to the ground. I reached up to put my bowl of eggs on the shelf next to the camera and thought I felt a drop.

I sought Eric's advice on the matter, but he seemed to think the main problem was that I hadn't been allowed to hire my own assistant. The executive chef had hired Bernie and me in separate interviews and then introduced us to each other afterward. Chefs usually hire in pairs. Our chef was no exception. He had hired two night assistants for me (both of them young, inexperienced, and starry-eyed since this was their first job ever), and two sous-chefs. Two of each cook—grill, sauté, pasta, and garde-manger—one for night and one for day. It was like Noah's Ark, and unfortunately, just as feral.

The sous-chefs were as different from each other as frozen pizza from French cassoulet. Tough, solidly built Maria Madrid, the nighttime sous-chef, was a pushy, obnoxious woman with a sporty cap of short, dark hair crowning her cherubic, almost pretty face. If you put a bonnet on Maria, she could pass for Isabella Beeton, the famous cookbook author and model wife of nineteenth-century England. Unfortunately for that face, however, nearly every other word out of Maria's sneering mouth was an oath. Every chef has their bulldog—that tireless animal that does all the dirty work so that the chef can be left in peace to create—and Maria was it. She was the one who screamed at the cooks when they were late and got on the phone to yell ultimatums at purveyors when they didn't deliver. She was also the one who stayed in the restaurant until three in the morning defrosting the broken ice cream freezer with a hair dryer when the repairmen didn't show. And she was the one who figured out we could order wide plastic tubing from a hardware store to cut into cake molds instead of buying hundreds of dollars' worth of specialty cake rings. We needed her, but she drove me crazy. She was constantly visiting the pastry station, breaking off bits of everything we made to "test it for the chef," and she was always coming up with "suggestions" that invariably meant more work for me.

The daytime sous-chef, Arthur, on the other hand, was quiet, with a hangdog face that looked permanently exhausted. He always had large rings under his eyes and a low-key, sleepy demeanor to match. If Maria was a bulldog, then Arthur was a basset hound. One particular day, at about two o'clock, Maria had just come in to work. She had stopped in the pastry station, as she always did on her

way in, and was stealing petit fours off the speed rack while she be-
rated one of the cooks who wanted to go home early because he
didn't feel well.

"Hell, one time I worked *two* fuckin' doubles in a row," she said
to him loudly enough so the whole kitchen could hear, "went out,
drank a fifth of vodka and ate half a pizza, came back to work without *ever* goin' home, threw up in a fuckin' garbage pail, and worked
all the next day with a hangover that would make your cold feel like
a fuckin' party. I *never* go home sick. Goin' home sick is for wusses.
Ya hear me? Huh? I'm tawkin' to you."

The rest of the cooks laughed mercilessly. No one could get
over Maria, with her sweet Mrs. Beeton face and her Billingsgate-
fish-market mouth. She was just the type of woman, though, that
the burly cooks would let boss them around. They were always having these verbal contests to see who was the most macho—or
macha, in Maria's case. All the contests started with "One time I
worked . . ." and each statement got ridiculously longer until cooks
were swearing they had worked thirteen doubles in a row, with
104-degree fevers in kitchens the temperature of hell and under
slave-driving chefs who made the army's basic training look like
nursery school. This time, though, like most of the time, no one
could compete with Maria. The sick cook went back to his station
with his ears burning bright red.

It was all propaganda, as far as I was concerned, designed to
whip the cooks into a workaholic frenzy that would ultimately benefit the restaurant. Not everyone can be convinced to sacrifice their
lives for the greater glory of a restaurant, however. It takes a
predilection for this type of behavior, this fever. I couldn't help myself from laughing at Maria's outrageous delivery. Underneath,
though, I hated it. It hit too close to home.

"You know, Maria," I couldn't resist teasing her, "there's a life
out there, and believe it or not, it's got your name on it."

"Yeah, tell it to my husband," she said as she walked away. "You and him got the same fuckin' ideas."

It was hard to imagine Maria's husband. Who would marry that mouth? Maria continually bragged about him, saying he was coming in for opening night. None of us could wait to see him. I measured a quart each of cream and milk into a pot with the orange zest I had grated and set it on the stove next to the caramel to scald. My legs ached as much or more than when I was a waitress and my head throbbed with exhaustion. My sweaty chef's coat stuck to my back. Maria's barking filled the kitchen with a frantic tension and Bernie scowled nearby. But I didn't care. I was inspired. And I had the fever.

After a while, Great-Grandpa Frank could hardly lift the heavy aluminum milk cans that he had to pick up at the railroad station each morning. Selma, by now five, and Nathan, by now four, went along. Frank hoisted the cans as best he could while Selma and Nathan quickly placed the glass milk jars underneath to catch the fresh milk as he poured. When all the jars were filled and loaded on the wagon, Great-Grandpa Frank slowly climbed in, coughing and sweating with the exertion, picked up the reins of his horse, and cracked them gently on the animal's back.

"Bye, Papa, bye!" the children cried after the wagon as it tottered down the cobblestoned streets. Great-Grandpa Frank turned and waved with difficulty, his mouth held in a pained "O" around the sound of the good-bye that he was unable to shout back at them through his wheezing. Frank was only thirty-six years old, but his breath was already as short as puffs of steam from a dry kettle. Despite that, he had taken on more and more accounts. He never said no, not even when the deliveries kept him out well past suppertime. He wasn't greedy; it's just that he was trying to save a little, so the children could go to school, so there would be new shoes for Chanukah.

Selma and Nathan ran back into the grocery store after their father drove away, raided the candy jars, and scooted, giggling, under the tables heavy with sacks of flour and grains, around and around the spinning stand that held packages of nuts and spices, playing hide-and-seek behind the icebox and the pickle barrels. A bag of flour overturned and broke open, erupting in a white cloud of powder, while the younger children crawled around on the wooden floor, opening packages of sweet cakes and rolls.

"You're eating up all the profits!" Great-Grandma Reba yelled at the children, catching Nathan and Selma by the wrists before they whirled into a tall display of scouring soap. A pile of tobacco cans crashed to the floor when they were knocked over by the twins, Rose and Gussie. Reba let go of Nathan and grabbed the candy from him and his sister. "You know you can't eat that! That's not kosher!"

The first customer of the day banged in the door, jiggling the little bells attached to it.

"Get in the kitchen and sit down at the table!" Reba admonished the children in a hoarse whisper, wiping her perspiring face with her forearm. "All of you! Now!" Reba tried to smooth her dark hair, tried to smile so her haggard cheeks would plump, making her pretty face look less tired.

"May I help you?"

"I need a long-handled wooden spoon," I said to Bernie while I watched my caramel for burnt orange ice cream quickly darken. Bernie grabbed the spoon from the shelf near her and handed it to me. Developing a recipe is mostly error and trial—first you err, usually several times, and then you try again. A new night assistant, Vikki, worked alongside me.

Clara, the other one, had arrived late, her blond ponytail flying behind her, and was downstairs changing into her uniform. Clara was impossibly slow; being late would set her back even more. The night assistants came cheap because they were so inexperienced, which made the chef happy, but it also meant that it was a lot of extra work for me to train them. Three hopeless assistants before Vikki had been fired by the chef at my request. You get what you pay for.

"Write down everything I do, so we can repeat it," I told Bernie, then turned to Vikki. "Can you please get me a vanilla bean from the fridge?" I asked her.

"What's a vanilla bean?" Vikki asked.

Bernie and I looked at each other. Not again. But then I gave Vikki the benefit of the doubt. Vanilla beans weren't something that you found in every kitchen.

"Excuse me," I said, stretching my arm around Vikki to retrieve the vanilla beans from the refrigerator on her other side. In my other hand I held a measuring cup of reduced orange juice that I was just about to pour into the cream and orange zest that was scalding on the stove. "Bernie, quick, whisk this into the cream for me," I said, handing the measuring cup off to her while eyeing the caramel pot on the stove behind me. I was pushing the caramel beyond where I would normally stop it. After I had dug the vanilla beans out of the fridge, I turned around just in time to pull the smoking caramel from the flame.

"Damn!" I yelled. "Vikki, can you please scrape and split these beans, now."

I grabbed the pot of zest-infused cream and milk and poured some into the caramel, to temper it. It bubbled up violently, threatening to boil over the top of the pot. A rush of steam burned my hand where I held the wooden spoon that I was using to stir. "Ouch!" I yelled. Bernie quickly handed me a kitchen rag, which I wrapped around my burning hand.

Out of the corner of my eye I saw that Vikki didn't know how to hold a knife properly. "Bernie, please show Vikki how to scrape the vanilla beans," I said, starting to really sweat. Too many cooks, I swore under my breath. I could see Bernie struggling to teach Vikki how to scrape the slippery, small beans. "Bernie, you do the vanilla bean, get Vikki to separate some eggs," I said in frustration. She must be able to do something to help us, I thought. We just had to find out what it was. When the caramel settled down to a golden hot soup, I poured all of it back into the cream. Then I returned the pot of cream to the stove to scald once more, and threw in the vanilla beans that Bernie had scraped for me.

I checked that Bernie was whisking the vanilla extract into a bowl of sugar, then ran to the ice machine with a bucket. We needed an ice bath to cool off the ice cream base the minute it came off the flame and prevent it from overcooking. This was something that should have been set up beforehand but in the confusion was overlooked. Vikki came back upstairs with the eggs, stopped near me at the ice machine, and asked how to separate them.

Exasperated, I put down the bucket of ice I was carrying. It was time for some questions.

"Vikki, I thought you told the chef you worked in a bakery."

"I did," she answered me timidly. The silver barrettes she used to hold back her long brown hair glinted at me, reminding me how young she was. Thin bangs hung in her eyes.

"Well, how could you not know how to separate eggs, then?" I asked as gently as I could.

"We only baked bread," she said, looking as anxious to please as a puppy.

"Oh, my God," I said, noticing the cream I had put on the stove starting to boil over. "Get that cream," I started to say to Vikki, who was standing between me and the stove, but when she looked around behind her, uncomprehending, I just thrust the bucket at her and pushed her aside, barely making it to the stove in another cloud of fishy smoke. Just then Maria interceded and grabbed the pot of overflowing cream, pulling it off the burner.

"Keep your wits about ya, *pastry chef,*" she snarled at me, waving the smoke from her face and emphasizing the title as if I had better prove I deserved it.

I stopped coughing and took a deep breath. So much for my three full-time assistants. One was Bernie, and the other two were useless. I sent Vikki on an equipment hunt—with drawings—for a chinois, a ladle, and a spatula. Then I turned back to the burnt or-ange ice cream.

Bernie worked next to me without saying a word. Her jaw was held in a tight line. My attempts to make conversation with her by joking about the night assistants were greeted with a smug silence. Finally, while I whisked the yolks to temper them with the scalded cream, I asked, "Are you all right?" She didn't answer me, so I let it drop.

When the ice cream base was finished and set on the ice to cool, I tasted a little of it. It was wrong. "The flavor isn't intense enough," I sighed to Bernie, "we'll have to do it again. I can tell already. It's not your fault. You helped a lot, it's just that the recipe isn't—" That's when I turned around and caught Bernie in the middle of making a sour face at me that she thought I wouldn't see. I didn't need this right now. "Bernie," I said, pushing my damp hair from my forehead, "it's four o'clock already. Why don't you just quit for the day and go home." I just wanted to get her away from me for a few hours, and besides, Bernie and I had been working doubles to meet our deadline of the restaurant's opening. We'd worked fifteen days straight without a day off, and I knew the chef wouldn't notice if she took off early. "The night assistants are already here," I told her, "they'll clean up and take over." Suddenly I preferred the night assistants' cheerful incom-petence over Bernie's bad attitude.

"No," Bernie said shortly. She banged the dirty pots one inside the other loudly.

Caught off guard, I suddenly realized that this was it—the battle of wills that had been brewing since we met. But I was in no condition to fight. "Bernie, I don't think you understand," I told her wearily but firmly, "I'm telling you to go. Now go. I'll see you tomorrow." I just needed some respite from her, from her moods, her tantrums. The night assistants made me dizzy enough without Bernie buzzing around me like a bloodthirsty mosquito.

She raised her voice. "No, I won't!"

Shocked, I turned to face her. In the heat, her hair had frizzed out in a dark halo around her head. Striped shadows fell across her face from the venetian blinds in the picture window behind me. "You don't have a choice, okay?" I said, trying to keep my voice even and not escalate this into a major scene. My head pounded. Sweat trickled down my back, my sides. Bernie glared at me as one of the stripes of light burned in her eye, making it flash at me, electric gold. The cooks at the other end of the kitchen were starting to look in our direction. But Bernie didn't care what they heard. Like a temperamental child, she lost control. She shouted, "I refuse!" Every head in the kitchen turned. Vikki, who had just returned with an armful of equipment, stopped in her tracks and turned white.

"Come outside," I said quietly to Bernie, "right now." With the ovens and smoker running all day, and the grill blasting on high, the kitchen was well over one hundred degrees. Though hard to believe, outside in the eighty-degree heat with a small breeze was refreshingly cooler. And more private. As I led Bernie out, I tried to take into consideration how tired we both were. Tempers were bound to get short. My eyes ached deep behind their lids. When this is over, I thought, I'm staying in bed for a week.

"How do you think it looks to the night assistants when you talk back to me like that?" I reprimanded her. "Never mind them. How do you think it feels to me?"

"You patronize me!" she yelled.

"I patronize you?"

"Yeah, you're always telling me that I did a good job, that I helped you so much!"

"This is my crime?" I was flabbergasted. "This is a first." I couldn't help laughing. All my other assistants, now and in the past, had appreciated my ability to let them know that they were doing well. Bernie opened her mouth to say something else, but then her face reddened and her eyes filled with tears. My laughter turned to concern.

"My life is so out of control," she sobbed. She told me about a boyfriend who needed her too much and a lover who didn't need her enough. A father who never stopped criticizing her, thus her inability to tolerate compliments. She was broke and in debt and not being paid enough. She said the chef had lied to her about her salary. I listened in surprise to her unexpected monologue and then promised to talk to the chef the next day about getting her a raise. She was doing a good job despite the problems I had with her. Still, something about the whole situation stuck in my side like one of the teeth on the docking tool we used to prick holes in tart shells.

At home, I tried to talk to Eric about Bernie, but Eric had his own troubles. The owner of the restaurant he worked in was a high-strung, nervous woman who drove him crazy about her budget. She was making him weigh and measure every single ingredient on his menu so they could cost it out and find out where the nickels and dimes were going. Eric felt so tormented that he could barely concentrate on his work. He was also worried about his music career.

"I've been thinking that I might not want to cook anymore," he said. Seeing the surprised look on my face, he tried to explain. "I mean, I'm making a little money with my band now and I have some savings. If I didn't cook, I'd have more time to get gigs."

I silently mulled it over. Before he had finally relented and accepted his last job, Eric had turned down several promotions. He wanted to make sure he'd have time for his music. This was difficult to explain, especially to the chefs who had liked Eric and wanted to help him get ahead in the kitchen. I understood. However, I could hardly pick up the slack financially if Eric quit his lucrative chef's position. Eric and I lived together now. When he was working, he had paid most of the bills, not because I expected him to, but because he made more money. Pastry chefs are routinely paid less than food chefs; Eric's salary was higher when he had been a line cook, third in command, than mine when I was a chef, in charge of a whole department.

Worrying late that night in bed, I finally fell asleep going over the burnt orange ice cream in my head, imagining the flavor I wanted and trying to pinpoint how to achieve it. One of the ingredients was wrong, or being added in the wrong proportion. It should be sweet and bitter at the same time, I thought drowsily. And intense. Sweet, bitter, and intense.

"I think I'll name my first child Burnt Orange," I said sleepily to Eric. "What?" he muttered. "Nan, you're delirious," he whispered. "Go to sleep." I felt his warm side next to mine, the cat purring loudly near my ear, her claws kneading the pillow under my neck, tangling my hair. I was too tired to stop her. Then blackness, sleep so heavy it made my aching body feel like it was all broken bones in a cast. I dreamed I awoke in the dry goods storage room at Acroama, believing that I had fallen asleep there during work from sheer exhaustion. When I came hurrying out, the restaurant was filled with circus performers—jugglers, acrobats, clowns, dwarves, and freaks—and none of the desserts was ready. The next thing I knew, my heart was pounding me out of a dead sleep just before dawn and the radio alarm was blaring the blues station that Eric had set to wake us up. I managed a tired laugh when I recognized the song. Willy Nix was belting out "Bake Shop Boogie."

When I went to the chef that afternoon to ask for Bernie's raise, I was surprised to find out that Bernie had already been there. But not to ask for her raise. She had gone to the chef to complain about me behind my back. I was shocked, and then angry when I was put on the spot to defend myself. The chef told me that Bernie thought I was trying to control her too much, that she thought it was unfair to be expected to do things my way when she had so much experience herself.

"I was only trying to keep the pastry department consistent," I said, hating myself for sounding so defensive. "Isn't that what you wanted?" I had come to the chef to fight for Bernie's raise, but now that I knew Bernie had spoken against me, coupled with her aggravating behavior ever since she was hired, I decided to ask for something else instead.

Before the chef could answer me, I said, "Look, forget that. The truth is, even though she's a great worker, I don't think she's an asset to your kitchen or to me anymore." I paused to build up my nerve, then continued with as much self-assurance as I could muster. "What I really want is permission to let her go."

The chef didn't seem to know what to say. He hemmed and hawed and refused to take sides either way. I tested his commitment to me further. I requested that if he wouldn't let me fire Bernie, would he please mediate for me in a discussion with her. The chef refused. He stressed how disappointed he was that the two of us couldn't get along better. All I was thinking at that point was how Bernie probably couldn't get along with Miss Congeniality from the goddamned Miss Universe pageant. But I didn't say it. Before the chef threw me back into the fray, I barely remembered to ask why we didn't have our health insurance yet, which all of my assistants had questioned. The chef assured me our benefits were coming. They were just "delayed."

"Oh, and by the way," he said as I was leaving, "if Bernie needs money, we'll pay her extra for working a seventh day each week until we open. But no way is she getting a raise. Money is becoming a problem for the restaurant, but don't repeat that. The owners have never owned a restaurant before, and they're panicking over the amount of money it costs. Bernie was never promised that she would make more than she is making. She is mistaken," he said curtly, turning his back to me, "you tell her."

I left the chef's office with my teeth clenched so tightly I could have ground coffee beans with them. "Great," I muttered, "I go to bat for her and meantime she's throwing me a curve. And now what am I supposed to say? Oh, gee, I'm sorry, Bernie, the owners never had a restaurant before and they're fresh out of the green stuff, but don't worry, there's always plenty of money for *traitors!*" I returned to the pastry department in a huff and decided to keep my mouth shut until I could talk this over with Seth. Seth had a great new job as pastry chef of a stylish, popular restaurant. Unfortunately, he had just undergone a hernia operation from lifting too many huge bowls of dough, and was recovering at home. I would visit him later and get some advice.

Back in the kitchen, I stood at the stove, once more making my burnt orange ice cream, trying to calm down by concentrating on my work. I placed a copper pot filled with sugar for caramel on one burner, and on a second burner, a pot of orange juice, Cointreau, and zest-infused cream. One of the cooks, Janet, worked beside me. Janet was the beauty of the kitchen with her blond curls and her characteristic lipstick the color of bright red peppers—a welcome contrast to the blur of stainless steel and white chef's coats. She was grilling vegetables. Like women usually do while they are cooking together, we started to chat, about recipes, where we lived, what we did. I mentioned that I was an artist and that baking was my survival job.

"I'm an artist too," Janet said, surprised.

"You are?" We turned to look at each other, her with a forkful of zucchini poised in the air, and me with my wooden spoon stopping abruptly mid-stir.

"I'm a painter," she said.

"I'm a painter too," I replied.

We laughed when we each looked around to see if anyone else was listening. It was more like saying to each other "Okay, you can take off that mask now" than just discussing our hobbies. Art, like Judaism, is not just a religion; it's a way of life. Artists continually hide their real feelings about their survival jobs from other people they work with for fear of jeopardizing their relationships with those people. Most employers and co-workers assume that artists are not serious, stable workers. Hence, our disguises. Bernie came up behind me to see how the ice cream was going and I put my mask firmly back in place.

"Okay, here we go," I said to Bernie. I pulled the copper pot bubbling with a dark caramel from the stove. I had been through several incarnations of the burnt orange ice cream recipe by then and knew that I nearly had it down. All it needed was a little fine-tuning.

"Write down to bring the caramel to a point slightly darker than an Irish setter. Write down to temper it with the reduced orange juice and cream mixture. Change the vanilla in the recipe to Cointreau extract."

Bernie wrote while I whisked the caramel with the orange cream until it incorporated and turned a rich sienna brown. We both tasted.

"Wow." Bernie's eyes opened wide.

"We got it," I said happily. A rush of bittersweet satisfaction.

Nobody else had anything like it yet. We had done it. But at what price? Our health? Our sanity?

"Get this on the stove to scald," I said to Bernie, "and temper in the sugar and yolks. Then chill it down right away so we can freeze it for the chef later on." I checked my clipboard where I had the lists of the recipes and inventory we needed for tomorrow's opening. Everything was ready. The night assistants were at least trained to send out the desserts properly, even if they didn't know exactly what all of them were. That would come later. In all, I had developed and produced over twenty original recipes for Acroama, each of which included the desserts themselves as well as sauces, garnishes, ice creams, sorbets, and plate presentations. Janet took her pot off the stove and she and Bernie peered over my shoulder at the clipboard for a minute. Janet gave me the high sign.

The chef walked by and interrupted us sarcastically. "Can I get you girls a cup of coffee, maybe, or a doughnut?" We scattered like water droplets bouncing off hot oil.

It wasn't until I collapsed on Seth's couch later that night that I realized again how tired I was. I had called him from the street to ask if he needed anything. And what did the pastry chef want? "Sticky buns," he said, "from Village Bakery. They have the best ones."

Seth took the bag of pastry from me when I got to his door and padded into the kitchen to make us tea. He was wearing baggy plaid cotton pajamas, the kind my father wore when we were kids. His long hair was loose and a little flyaway with static electricity. "Great pajamas," I said. His collection of sixties paraphernalia, Day-Glo posters, and pop-art paintings covered every inch of wall space in his apartment and vibrated in the eerie glow of black light. Every time I went to Seth's apartment, I wanted to walk out and come in again, just for the bizarre effect it had of entering another era.

"You look tired," Seth said tactfully. He could have said worse, considering my condition. I may have been doing a good job, but my life was completely out of balance. I barely had time for my friends or Eric, and I never took the time to exercise or eat right. But this lifestyle wasn't even considered extreme by restaurant owners and most chefs. Quite the opposite. It was expected. Seth listened patiently to my troubles concerning Bernie.

"Listen," Seth said wisely, "every assistant gets a little restless when they're ready to become a chef themselves. That's why I moved you to Toy's. I knew you needed more responsibility. I knew you were bored. In your nice way, you drove me nuts too." I gave him an indignant look. "Okay," he conceded quickly, "you were never as mean-spirited as Bernie. I'm just saying, get her out of your face."

He was right. I knew that Bernie was champing at the bit. That didn't excuse her behavior, though, any more than the various reasons for beating a walnut tree to increase production of nuts could excuse that old, horrendous rhyme "A woman, a dog and a walnut tree, the more you beat 'em the better they be." But the strange thing was, I told Seth, Bernie insisted she didn't want to be chef. Bernie wouldn't listen to me and she wouldn't leave.

"She'd rather stay at Acroama and torture you," Seth joked before he continued. "Look, she sounds like a real pain in the *tuchas*. Your job is to keep your department consistent and teach assistants to do things your way to ensure that. Bernie has too much experience to take instruction from you. You've got to confront her one-on-one. It's the only way." Seth and I spent the rest of our visit munching our sticky buns and laughing over the album of his bar mitzvah pictures. "This one got fat and married an eye doctor," Seth said, pointing to pictures of his friends, little girls and boys in ill-fitting suits and sixties department-store dresses, "and this one committed suicide while on acid, and this one became a madam for an escort service." All the little faces were so innocent and hopeful in the photographs. It's all about choices, I reminded myself.

So Bernie and I had it out. The next morning I dragged her into the dining room, where exhausted construction workers were putting the final touches on the bar area for the opening that night. The sound of electric saws and hammering clanged and buzzed on and off behind us. There was the pungent smell of sawdust mixed with freshly cut flowers and paint. Large reproductions of Greek statues leaned against the stark white walls, waiting to be placed on their pedestals. Bernie let out a rush of accusations, most of them concerning my refusal to stop directing her while she baked. "I know how to whisk!" she yelled at me while a saw shrieked behind her.

"And that's the trouble!" I shouted back at her over the clamor. "You should be a pastry chef *now*, Bernie." My words bounced too loudly off the walls, startling us, in a suddenly quiet moment. I lowered my voice. "You *are* a pastry chef."

Bernie was silenced by this statement. She unfolded her arms, which had been tightly crossed over her chest.

"Bernie, look, you're not doing either of us any good by hanging around here when you know you should be a pastry chef by now. If you want to find another job right away, I'll give you a great reference. But in the meantime, let's try to get along, since we're stuck here together. I'll even let you do things your way"—at this she looked doubtful, but I continued in a voice that let her know I meant it, even though it wasn't easy for me—"as long as the desserts are consistent with mine." This last statement seemed to placate her. Then I sent her back into the kitchen and went downstairs to the chef's office for our morning meeting.

It was hotter than usual the day that Great-Grandpa Frank rounded the corner on Prince Street, about to make his last stops. The sun burned his felt cap into a fiery circle around his scalp, his feet turned leaden in his lace-up boots. Reba was in the store, three blocks away, arguing with an old man about the price of coffee beans.

"Such a *schnorrer*," she whispered behind the man's back. Something about this old man, this haggler, made her angry, asking for his pennies off on a bag of coffee. Pennies, pennies, pennies; all the pennies she counted and double-counted, never having enough, and every old man who wanted one or two. For every three she placed in the register, four flew out the door—for the children's shoes, for potatoes, for the striped peppermint sticks the babies pilfered from the glass jars when she wasn't looking. And so she took the pennies off the price of the beans, like watching the russet-skinned onions she wanted for tonight's dinner disappear from her plate, but she did it anyway, adding up the stack of groceries the old man piled on the counter, taking the man's dollars, and pressing the register keys, one dollar and . . .

Three blocks away, Frank's lungs convulsed inside him. He balled his fists and pulled the horse's neck around too fast. The horse swerved into the busy road, nearly colliding with another wagon, causing her to rear up . . .

. . . seventy-five cents . . .

. . . and crash into the silk tie pushcart, knocking over a barrel of tomatoes. Shouting, then the horse's scream cracking the sky. Frank, gasping, was thrown from the cart . . .

. . . Reba slowly placed the crumpled dollar and warm, heavy coins in the drawer before closing it with a clank.

. . . and felt something cold rushing toward him as he lay, unable to move on the sidewalk—something unbidden, something rattling a tin cup and voraciously hungry.

Reba turned, bumping into the large, open bag of coffee beans which toppled, spilling all the beans like dark paint rushing over the floor.

Great-Grandma Reba would tell you the spilled beans were an omen. *Tsuras*, she'd call it. Heartache, trouble.

We finished setting up for opening night ahead of schedule and actually ended up with a few hours to spare in the afternoon. I took advantage of the unexpected windfall and rushed home to take a walk in the park and a shower. I hardly had time to go to my beloved park anymore, and as I walked there in the bright sunshine under a postcard blue sky, I felt light, happy. When I entered the park, though, I was surprised to see Eric coming toward me on his bicycle from the other end of the sun-dappled cement path that wound through tall oak trees in the full leaf of deep summer. It was the middle of the day. He should have been at work. He slowed to a stop in front of me, and leaned on the bike, smiling, but sadly. "No," I said, already sensing something was wrong. "Yes," said Eric, "the owner resolved her budget problems with my salary. I was laid off." Then he added in a bittersweet voice, "I guess I'll have all the time I want to play my guitar now."

I returned to Acroama late that afternoon. At five o'clock, just as my assistants and I were getting ready for opening night service, Maria ran into our station, breathless. She told me that we had just received a phone call from a very important pastry chef who worked at another restaurant. He was coming in for dinner at Acroama with his girlfriend in order to propose to her. They would be here in three hours, at eight o'clock. This pastry chef, who was known for his wild chocolate sculptures, wanted a dessert that could conceal a diamond ring. Maria had volunteered me for the project, and bragged to the famous chef that I was an artist.

Bernie and I had worked three weeks without a day off, most of them doubles, to get ready for this night. Except for the few hours we had stolen that afternoon, we had never taken a break during any of those days. To say we were exhausted was the understatement of the year. I listened wearily to Maria's enthusiastic suggestions, one of which was for me to design an elaborate chocolate cage with a chocolate bird and an abundance of fruit and mint around it. It sounded like a great idea, but there were a few problems with it.

First, the kitchen at Acroama was hot enough to wilt Maria's new permanent. How were we going to temper chocolate in that heat? Second, and more important, it wasn't my style. All my desserts were modern and the designs were abstract, closer to Mondrian than to the Old Masters. And last but not least, I didn't know one lick about chocolate sculpture and didn't have time to learn. "Why doesn't Mr. Famous Pastry Chef make his own cage?" Bernie whispered to me. When I said no, that the customer hadn't given me enough notice, Maria went to the chef to ask him to make me do it. She had promised the dessert already, and now it wasn't about me anymore. It was about her swollen pride. She was relentless. She convinced the chef to tell me I had to make the cage.

If only I had said no just one more time and made it clear that I would not agree to every impossible whim. But saying no would have been admitting that I was human. I can't blame Maria or the chef for forcing me to concede when I shouldn't have. It was my own fault. I saw Maria's cage as the fruit on the tree of perfection. It tempted me, and I bit it.

Neither the chef nor Maria had ever made such an elaborate chocolate sculpture themselves, but they insisted that they would show me how to do it. For the next two hours I worked in frustration as the chef, Maria, and Arthur, the daytime sous-chef, gave me unreliable instructions in the art of sculpting chocolate that all ended up in melted, out-of-temper disasters. Bernie and I consulted books and called our friends, but chocolate sculpture was something that was mostly practiced at hotels and in larger, more conservative restaurants. There was no way I was going to master such a complicated technique so quickly, no matter what my artistic abilities were in other mediums. In desperation, I constructed a chocolate dome by squeezing melted chocolate through a paper cone in crisscrossing stripes over the outside of a bowl that had been covered in plastic wrap. Then I placed it in the coldest walk-in refrigerator to set.

As I left the walk-in, I felt sad, but I couldn't pinpoint why. Then it came to me. I suddenly realized that the reason the chocolate cage bothered me so much was not because Maria was such a bully and not because I was expected to do the impossible on such short notice for opening night, but because I was making a surprise for another woman who was about to be engaged. Making the cage had opened up a Pandora's box of mixed emotions.

How can I describe the equal parts of despair and longing I felt when I gazed at my grandmother's sepia-toned wedding photograph? What does a wedding dress look like to an artist with more paint on her hands than time, more dough in her kitchen than in her pockets, and who deliberately picks her men, even wonderful Eric, for their matchless inability to make a commitment? A good studio rag, maybe, if cut into manageable pieces. Every bar of the impossible chocolate cage seemed to imprison me in my own ambivalence.

At seven-fifteen I pulled the chocolate dome carefully out of the walk-in and wobbled with it up the stairs to the kitchen. The stairwell was hotter than the kitchen itself. By the time I made it to the top of the steps, where Maria and the chef were waiting for me, my poor chocolate dome was as crumpled and damp as wet tissue paper. The prospect of it making its way to the dining room was about as dim as my ever being on the receiving end of that diamond ring. When the chef set his eyes on the dome, or what was left of it, I saw his smiling face change to reflect the anguished face in Edvard

Munch's painting *The Scream*. My heart sank fast into my stomach, like the soft, heavy center of a falling soufflé.

Luckily, I have always worked well under pressure. I ran into the upstairs walk-in, quickly dug out my tuile cookie dough, and threw a nonstick sheet pan in the freezer. A tuile is a cookie that is very light and thin and can be formed while it's warm into any number of shapes: curled, round, wavy, spiraled. I warmed the dough on top of the oven while I helped my assistants begin sending out desserts to the opening-night crowd. When the tuile dough was softened enough to use, I spread it into a large round circle and a long rectangle on the frozen pan. I mixed a portion of the dough with my raspberry sauce, and squirted it through the fine tip of a squeeze bottle to make fluid red abstract designs on the pale circle and rectangle. When the cookies were lightly browned in the oven, I pulled the rectangle off the sheet pan, and while blowing on my burning fingers, as I held the hot cookie, formed it into a standing ring, like a cake pan without a bottom. The other cookie, the circle, I placed on top when it cooled. This was what I had wanted to make to begin with—a cookie box— and not only did it take just ten minutes, but it was starkly modern, unusual, and very simple. "Elegant," my assistants complimented me. The chef and Maria had to accept it because it was all there was, but they each admitted it was beautiful. About five minutes after I fashioned it, the famous pastry chef and his girlfriend arrived and the diamond ring was carried into the kitchen. I placed it carefully in the box and gave it to my assistants to serve.

Opening night, despite my apprehension, was thoroughly successful. The chef presented me and the sous-chefs with French chef's jackets embroidered with our names in gold letters and encouraged us to get out in the dining room and play celebrity. Even Arthur's gray pallor seemed to shine in his toggle-buttoned and impeccably tailored white jacket. The cooks were impressed with how organized my department was and how sublime the desserts were.

"You got your shit together." Maria beamed at me.

"Um, thank you, Maria." I smiled at her. I knew this was Maria's highest praise. I didn't even complain when she intercepted my cookie box to overzealously festoon the plate with a plethora of mismatched fruit and scavenged sauces from my dessert fridge. Maria's style and mine would never agree. Maria's husband, on the other hand, was a vision of refined taste in a copper-green linen suit. "Opposites attract," Bernie whispered to me. Maria seemed to glow on his arm while she introduced him to everyone, as if she were a tacky lamp that suddenly transformed into something gorgeous when plugged in. My name at the bottom of each dessert menu shone in triumph. Eric came for dinner with his sister, and Gemma, out for the first time since the twins' birth, shuffled in on Seth's arm. And the famous pastry chef popped the question amid a smattering of applause, some for my cookie box and some for his tearful, grateful girlfriend, smiling and waving at everyone like a prom queen on a float in the town parade.

The restaurant was packed with invited guests until well after midnight. That's why it was such a shock when business fell off in the month that followed. The famous pastry chef's dessert proposal got a mention in an article about weddings in the Style section of the Sunday *Times,* but Acroama wasn't mentioned anywhere. The restaurant was new. We all comforted each other that it would take a little time for it to attract a following. Unfortunately, the famous critics and important press the chef had promised us never materialized, much to the chef's embarrassment.

It was pretty slow. But that didn't mean we had nothing to do. The chef wanted desserts so complicated that it took us the better part of a day just to keep up with production. Pastry is considered a luxury by most restaurants, and a pastry chef is the first one asked to make sacrifices when money is tight. Instinctively, I began preparing myself for the inevitable questions about which assistants I could let go and which expensive ingredients we didn't really need.

The chef grew increasingly irritable and critical. "Take the chocolate praline mousse cake off the menu," he demanded one morning as he hurried by. "Why?" I asked, hurt. The mousse cake had been a favorite of his until that very moment. "Because it sucks!" he barked back over his shoulder. I heard the owners were harassing him about money beyond his endurance, so I tried to understand his outburst. Chocolate and nuts are expensive. Rumors circulated in the kitchen that he might walk out. Each day I saw him speaking in a low whisper to his sous-chefs while they stood in a private huddle at the end of the kitchen.

Up until then I was always welcome in the chef's office and even greeted with smiles when I arrived there to use the phone or a book or to talk to him. In the following weeks, though, I was shooed away when I tried to enter, and the office door was unceremoniously shut in my face. I could see that the chef was inside with the owners and his sous-chefs. Something was up. I felt our relationship change with the same instinct that told me when something was burning in the oven. Finally, the chef called me down to his office for a meeting.

In the windowless, dank basement underneath the main kitchen was the purgatorial prep kitchen that one of the cooks fondly called "the dungeon," an appropriate name for a place where we often suffered the tortures of the damned. The prep kitchen was on the way to the chef's office. Janet was down there peeling a bag of carrots. For cooks, hell is an airless place where one peels a bag of carrots that never empties, with an old, dull peeler, while a devil in a red chef's suit yells at you in a thick, incomprehensible accent. Janet looked anxiously over her shoulder at me when I entered the room, probably expecting the chef and fearing a scolding for not working fast enough. She relaxed visibly when she saw it was only me. Then we both shook our heads in disbelief at the level of tension. The air was so thick with it, you could cut it with the proverbial knife.

The chef's office was small and cluttered with books and papers and too many desks. We sat in swivel chairs, facing each other, too close. I could see the blood vessels in the sleepless whites of his eyes, and I had to turn my chair so that our knees wouldn't touch.

Unfortunately, the chef didn't ask me to fire assistants or curb my spending. He fired me.

My head swam. I was speechless as thoughts raced through my mind. Yesterday I had come to work and discovered the manager with a stack of new dessert menus that didn't have my name on them. He had covered himself by saying they'd been reprinted to correct a typo and my name had been left off by mistake. "The manager," I blurted out. "You had my name taken off the menus yesterday!" I couldn't believe what I was just now understanding. "You couldn't wait until I left?"

"Look," he answered, "I know you think this has something to do with what happened between you and Bernie, but it doesn't."

"Oh, yeah?" I countered. "Then how come you're not asking me if I'd take a cut in pay or if I could reduce my staff or my budget?" The chef looked away uneasily. "Oh, I see, you picked me. You decided I was the one who was dispensable. I set up the whole department and developed all those recipes for you, and this is the thanks I get."

The chef tried to defend himself. "I was told to eliminate a certain amount of money from the payroll. Your salary—" But I interrupted him. "Sure, I guess now that you have a trained pastry staff and a menu, you don't need me anymore. How can you do this?" Without waiting for an answer, I turned to leave the room.

"You shouldn't burn your bridges like this," he threatened my back. I turned around. Now the snake shakes his rattle, I thought, burning with outrage.

"*Me* burn *my* bridges?" I let the words sink in. "Don't forget, *you* are firing *me*." I stared him down. "*You* are the one who is burning bridges."

With that, I left the room. I rushed past Janet so that she wouldn't see the tears burning my eyes, and climbed the steps to the kitchen with my thoughts slamming against the inside of my brain like a giant steel stockpot crashing down a flight of stairs.

Reba was stunned when they carried Frank through the front door of the store, barely alive. When her shock dissipated, she saw all too clearly that Frank grew worse instead of better. Over the next few sweltering weeks, he lay in his bed, struggling for breaths, each one like the slow, gasping bubbles in thick, boiling sugar syrup. He was soaked right through his nightshirt with fever. *Pneumonia* was a big word to tell frightened children. Finally, one evening, he died. In that moment, Reba became a widow with five children to support by herself.

Life changed suddenly, drastically. Her mind couldn't contain it. How would she support her children, keep the store going, pay the bills? Great-Grandpa Frank left the sweating, churning, voracious world of Prince Street as if he were a bit of something wonderful bought far too cheaply, bagged up for a greedy customer and carried away forever. Reba felt robbed.

Reba blamed the wagon, the grocery store, Frank, herself— even God. If only they hadn't had such a rickety old wagon, the wheels so thin and unbalanced they could throw a person right out of his seat if the horse bucked just once. If only there had been a few less deliveries that day, Frank wouldn't have gotten so hot, so worn out. If only she had taken the money they used to repair the broken screen on the front door of the store and used it for a doctor before

Frank got so sick. How could God punish them like this after all their hard labor?

Reba and the children worked in the store together to try to keep it open. Somehow, there was never a profit. Finally, the boys figured out that the wholesalers were cheating their mother out of hundreds of dollars a year. Even after they began to buy elsewhere, though, they could barely make ends meet.

Reba was forced to sell everything she owned—most of the furniture and dishes, all her silver, what little jewelry she had, and her linens. Selma tells me all they had to eat was potatoes, potatoes, and more potatoes, except for sometimes when there were onions as well as potatoes. When Reba called the children to dinner, she spread the table with newspapers instead of a cloth. The children fought. If one of them got a scrap more food than the others, they would practically kill each other over it.

Some say that learning about oneself is like peeling an onion, slowly revealing layers and layers of thin, translucent skins. To me, it's more like taking the shell from a black walnut. The black walnut's shell is hard and thick, and stories of its obstinate seal are legendary. One farmer recommends placing the nuts on a hard surface and rolling them under a heavy-booted foot. Another asserts that backing a truck over them is the only solution. Several authorities seem convinced that the most expeditious way is to use a vise. Whatever the method, the black walnut is sure to take some effort to crack and will leave its mark on whoever is dogged enough to keep trying—the shells dye the fingers with a dark, brown stain. The nut rewards those who persevere, however. Richly flavored and intense, it does its origin in the gold-bearing gravel beds of the Sierras proud.

Bakers especially prize the black walnut for its exceptional flavor. Maybe that's why I kept trying to crack those shells, however difficult it proved to be.

As I made my way back to the pastry station, I searched and searched my mind for a reason I should be the one picked to take the fall. Did Bernie purposely steal my job from me behind my back? Did the owners plan from the very beginning to let me go as soon as my staff was trained? Did they ever have any intention of giving us our raises and benefits, or was that just a ploy to get us to work for them when they were already nearly bankrupt? Did the chef use me for as long as he could afford to and then selfishly take credit for my work, or was he just as much in the dark as he claimed to be?

Tears coursed down my cheeks despite my efforts to not cry in front of Bernie. "You should quit too," I said to her as I packed my books and tools for the last time, knowing she wouldn't. "But not for me. For women. For pastry chefs. For all the women pastry chefs who are underpaid and overworked and anonymous. None of us should work this way again until things change." I paused at the door, wishing she would say something. Then Bernie took me off guard by asking if she could hug me. She looked genuinely stricken, whether by guilt or by pity, I'll never know. Without waiting for my answer, she put her long arms around me. Conflicting feelings washed over me. "And don't give them my burnt orange ice cream, Bernie," I said ruefully as she let me go. "You're the only one who has the recipe, and you know they don't deserve it." With that, I fled out the door.

On the way home, I realized the full impact of what had just happened. Eric and I were both unemployed. When I walked through the door of our apartment, Eric had his guitar slung over his shoulder. "Listen," he said before I could get a word out, "I've been practicing this one for you all day." Then he started singing "I'm Your Ice-Cream Man" by John Brim. But he trailed off when he saw the look on my face. "No," he said. "Yes," I answered.

When the smoke cleared, Eric and I sat down to decide on a plan. "I'll get another job," Eric offered right away. He still hadn't made up his mind whether or not to end his chef career. "Don't worry."

"Eric, stop," I said. "How can I tell you that I don't want you to be a musician if that's your first love?" I pointed at myself. "She who worked as a waitress for eight years and went into debt so she could paint." We both laughed, then stopped abruptly, realizing the risk we might be taking.

"If we're gonna live like starving artists now, that's fine with me," I reassured him. "Do what you need to do."

"What about you?" Eric asked.

"I'll be a miserable pastry chef." I pouted.

Eric put his hands on his hips, letting his guitar dangle from its strap around his neck. "Nan, you know the only reason you have such a hard time putting in all those hours when you're working as a pastry chef is because you really want to paint. Tell me you don't lose track of the time when you're in your art studio. You'll work for twelve, fourteen, hell, you'd sit there twenty-four hours a day if I let you. So who are you to say that chefs aren't happy? If that's all they want to do with their lives, they just work at it, like anybody else with a vision. Look at that crazy Maria! She's happy! Now, I'm not saying you should go back to waitressing so that you have more time to paint, but—" This was where I interrupted.

"No way am I ever going back to—" But this was also where I stopped. What was I going to do?

Fortunately, I hadn't left Acroama empty-handed. Janet and I stayed in touch and became close friends. And I had all my new recipes, which would help me get another job. All except one, as I was soon to find out.

My burnt orange ice cream was endlessly reproduced on menus everywhere and finally languished in mediocrity. It became a symbol for everything bittersweet about being a pastry chef for me. Eventually, I would come to understand from this experience that a recipe really belongs to no one, and I wouldn't hesitate to give one away now, and with extreme pleasure. After all, where would I be if my grandmothers had kept all their baking secrets to themselves? Still, I obsessed over the fate of this particular recipe a long time before my lesson was learned.

It could always be worse.

How could I argue with Great-Grandma Reba, a woman who raised five children in three rooms and ran a store by herself? My problem should have seemed so little, so easy to solve compared to hers. But it didn't.

Eventually, Reba's children grew old enough to go to work, and help the family survive. The boys became so successful as businessmen, and Selma married so well that later Selma's husband, Eddy, and Reba's sons treated their mother to summers at a fancy hotel on the shore. To Reba, the beach was paradise, but the boys worried that the food at the hotel wasn't good enough for her. After all her years of hunger and denial, though, Reba had realized something that the pressure in most restaurant kitchens belies. There's more to life than food. "Don't worry, boys," she told her sons in her thick, Romanian-tinged English,

I don't come for the hits (eats), *I come for the hocean* (ocean).

Burnt Orange Ice Cream

2 tablespoons sugar (for yolks)
1 tablespoon orange extract (optional)
1 cup heavy cream
1 cup whole milk
2 tablespoons grated orange zest
2 cups fresh orange juice
1/4 cup plus 1 tablespoon Cointreau
1/4 cup plus 2 tablespoons sugar (for caramel)
3/4 cup egg yolks

Place 2 tablespoons of the sugar in a large mixing bowl. Add orange extract, if using it, and whisk to combine. Set aside. In a medium saucepan, scald cream and milk with zest. Steep 30 minutes or more off the heat. Meanwhile, simmer orange juice and Cointreau until reduced to 1 cup. Whisk reduced orange juice/Cointreau into cream mixture and strain. Return the orange cream to the pot and set on low heat just to keep it warm. Have a pair of oven mitts or a kitchen towel nearby for the next part of the recipe. In another pot, caramelize $^1/_4$ cup plus 2 tablespoons of sugar to very dark (just past the color of an Irish setter). Do not stir the sugar vigorously at any time while it caramelizes. Instead, swirl the sugar gently in the pan by tilting the pan if necessary to ensure even color. Remove the caramel from the heat. Using the mitt or kitchen towel to protect the hand you stir with, immediately temper the caramel by adding a small bit of the warm orange cream to the caramel while stirring vigorously. The steam that occurs will be very hot. Keep adding cream slowly until the caramel stops bubbling violently. Whisk all of the tempered caramel back into the remaining cream, and place it on the stove over medium heat to scald once more.

Add yolks to the sugar in the mixing bowl and whisk together when the cream scalds and not before. Temper the yolks with the scalded orange cream by pouring a small stream of the hot cream into the yolks while whisking continuously. Pour the yolk/cream mixture back into the pot, and return to the stove over medium heat. Stir continuously with a spatula until mixture thickens enough to coat the spatula and a line can be drawn through it with your finger. Cook the base only until it is just thickened or it will curdle. Immediately strain the finished ice cream base and stir it to release the excess heat. Place plastic wrap directly on the surface of the base to prevent a skin from forming. When cool, chill the base in the refrigerator. Freeze in an ice cream machine according to the manufacturer's directions.

Nine ———

*"The dark chocolate tones of this wood, and the ease with
which it could be worked made it ideal for furniture. . . .
From cradle to coffin, walnut served."*

"Down Come the Walnuts,"

George Laycock,

<u>Audubon</u>,

May 1980

his time I didn't lie. I told the personnel director at
the Easton Hotel that I was an artist and that baking
was my survival job. This was something I had
learned not to do in the past. It labeled you. You
artist, you. You lazy, antisocial, radical, unreliable you. None of
those yous was me, but I waited for the inevitable questions, prepared to defend myself.

"Tell me what you think is your worst attribute."

I tried not to smirk. This interviewer was my age, my demo-
graphic. We both knew what we were doing—playing roles—but

neither of us made a move to fall out of character. All her questions really said, "Show me you're willing to play the game," and all my answers said, "I'm playing." Everything she said I translated before I answered. When she said, "Tell me your worst attribute," I knew she meant, "Show me that you're smart enough to recognize this trick question." My worst attribute? I could reveal something truly bad about myself, like the uninitiated, or I could turn a negative into a positive.

I looked at my interviewer's short strand of pearls, her black cashmere sweater, the A-line skirt. She impatiently tapped my résumé with a thin gold pen. Was she as conservative as she looked, or only posing in order to fit in at this old-world hotel, where pinkies lifted on coffee cup handles, and bellmen extended a white-gloved hand to help guests out of their limousines. Ladies first.

"I'm a perfectionist," I said, nearly grimacing at my own brown-nosing, "I drive myself crazy until everything is perfect." Translation: I'll be your slave, I'll give you exactly what you want. I looked down at my lap, trying not to explode. Not with laughter, though, with rage. Inside I was furious. Inside I was barely able to control the urge to leap out of my seat and shout at this woman who sat so demurely, asking me questions like "Where do you see yourself in five years?" and "Use three words to describe yourself."

"Insane, perverse, and bizarre," I wanted to lie with a smile, just to see her eyes widen and her mouth drop open, just so I could laugh and laugh and laugh, instead of controlling every normal human impulse in my body. I wanted to lean my elbows on her desk. I wanted to say "shit." I wanted to yell at the top of my lungs and race up the stairs away from the office and slam a door, hearing it reverberate throughout the hotel. I wanted to say that I didn't want a survival job, that I didn't want to bake seventy hours a week and then make art with the tiny scrap of energy I had left, if I had any energy left. Yes, I wanted to bake, goddammit, but not at the expense of the rest of my life.

I wanted to rebel. Instead, I took a deep breath and finished the interview quietly, reasonably. It wasn't in me to be so childish. Because if I had acted out like a spoiled infant, I wouldn't turn around to see behind me the luxurious, grand, carpeted hallways of the hotel, dappled by the light of crystal chandeliers. I would see Great-Grandma Bella, glaring at me from the dank, dilapidated hallway of a Lower East Side tenement.

Great-Grandma Bella carried her round metal teapot to the communal faucet in the hallway of her building. At least this was an improvement from the pump in the yard behind the buildings that had meant climbing four flights of stairs every time she needed water. Still, the faucet was old and rusted, the wall around it cracked, the stained sink mildewed where the pipes leaked. Bella held the teapot under the trickle of water, careful not to let the filthy wall or sink touch her clean dress. The hallway was nearly completely dark. Only the light from her door at the end of the hall allowed her to see, and that light was dim—there were only two windows in her apartment and a few oil lamps. One window was over a fire escape, looking out on the alley striped with crisscrossing laundry lines above rows of garbage pails. The other one faced a brick wall. These tenements were reputed to be better than the older ones on the other side of Orchard Street, because they had air shafts between the closely spaced buildings, supposedly to let in air and light. Bella kept that window closed—the only thing coming in besides the murky light was tuberculosis.

Bella carried the teapot past the tiny rooms off the hallway, where the toilets were, and went inside her apartment to put it on the stove, carefully sidestepping the wrought-iron crib in the middle of the room. Then she leaned on the crib, wrapping her hands around the iron curlicues, and peered in. She remembered when her youngest daughter, Goldie, used to sleep there so soundly. Soon she grew too big for the crib and had to sleep in the bedroom with her sisters, seven-year-old Rae and five-year-old Dotty, in the one small bed they shared. Dream, Goldie, dream, Bella used to muse silently over the child. Dream of a wide featherbed all your own and rooms full of sunlight, poor little thing, because you won't see them when you wake. And I will dream of having time to dream.

Time passed so quickly. Now Goldie was herself grown, married, and pregnant, and she and Nathan were saving the crib for their grand-child. Bella sighed. Rae and Dotty were also married and out of the house, and only Goldie lived at home until she and her husband could find a place of their own. Bella put her hands on her hips and squinted in the dim light of the apartment, looking around and mentally check-ing off her chores. The washing was finished, hanging from the line out-side, the breads were baked, the shopping was done for supper, and Goldie napped blissfully, worn out from helping her mother. The sewing could wait until tonight. Nathan wouldn't be home for an hour or so. When the water in her kettle boiled, Bella poured herself a cup of tea. This was a good time to work on her crocheting.

Bella hung her shawl on a nail in the crowded closet. She won-dered if Nathan had asked around for a door for that closet yet. She had begged him to do it so many times, but it was hard to tell if he heard her through all that whiskey in his ears. Bella frowned, push-ing her thin lips out, wrinkling her long nose in disgust. That man was headed for trouble, there was no doubt about it. Maybe if he worried more about his own behavior instead of always criticizing her and the girls, he could avoid disaster. No, disaster smelled good to Nathan, like prune and farfel tzimmes roasting in the oven. She'd watched him sniffing for it, poking his nose into everything volatile, everything unstable. Thank God he was also as vain as he was reck-less, or he would never put on his handsome suit and go to the gar-ment district to work. Bella thought of Nathan, admiring his own large, heavily lidded brown eyes and high cheekbones as he adjusted his felt fedora in the carved mirror by the door. She shook her head. Her short, thin frame wouldn't allow her to reach the high shelf in the closet, so she carried over one of the high-back chairs and climbed up on it. From the crowded shelf above her shawl she pulled down her crochet hook and the fine white cotton thread she used to crochet lace.

The pockmarked, bowed shelves behind the glass doors above the stove looked better with the embroidered napkins she had made to line them. Now that dark window on the air shaft cried out for a fine piece of lace to obscure its view of the brick wall. No matter that the building was nearly falling down, with every inch of wall spotted or peeling, the floors uneven, the ceilings cracked. Bella would scrub and decorate and make it a home. Anyway, there had been nowhere else to go when they arrived in America over thirty years ago in 1895. Nathan was a merchant, not a farmer, so they had to stay in the city, and besides, a lot of other immigrants from Austria lived there, on the Lower East Side of Manhattan. It was good to stay together. The important thing was that they were alive and had a chance to start over, however bleak it seemed. She pulled the chair up to the bathtub in the kitchen, let down the pine board that covered it so it could be used for a table, and placed her ball of thread on it. As she sat, she smoothed the hem of her dress under her.

Bella wound a loop in the thread and slipped her crochet hook into it with her right hand. She held the thread taut with her left pinky and looped it around her left forefinger, leaving it slack enough to give when she needed more thread to crochet with. Holding the knot on the hook steady, she pushed the hook forward letting the thread loop over it, and twisted it neatly until it formed another stitch pattern, then pulled it taut once more. This she could do with her eyes closed. Loop, twist, pull, loop, twist, pull. As her hands worked, she let her eyes wander back in her memory, back to

Austria, to her mother, Great-Great-Grandma Gootah, patiently teaching her how to crochet in the sunny window seat at the front of their house in Vienna. But Bella also remembered hearing sounds outside that window, sounds more animal than human, bleating and barking, heavy black boots pounding the streets, whistles as sharp as hunting knives, and the crack of wood hitting bone, the bone of people named Wiener, just like Bella's family, or Schwartz or Weissman, for no other reason than because they were Jewish. Bella's mind quickly turned back to the future and firmly closed the blood-spattered window behind her eyes. No, it was better to be here, even in the darkness, even in the dank, airless cocoon of a stinking, dilapidated tenement. Loop, twist, pull, loop, twist, pull.

Loop, twist, pull, loop, twist, pull. I pushed a long piece of twine through the back of a circular piece of worn, flat metal and pulled it through the front again, beginning to form a knot between the metal and a piece of rubber hose. I was repairing one of my street sculptures made from found objects, the one I called *Pregnant Woman*. Eric came in the room, leaned against the door frame, and watched me for a moment. Then he told me that someone had offered to hook his guitar up to a computer for him and make it sound like a harmonica. We both laughed at the thought of Eric, the blues man, ever wanting to make his guitar sound like anything but a guitar. "Sounds more like something you would do, huh?" he teased me, nodding in the direction of my sculpture.

My education in realism was very similar to Eric's in the blues: We were both purists. But where Eric balked at the idea of seeing how many weird sounds he could get out of his guitar, I was the opposite. However much I loved my realist roots, I still felt the need to test the limits of my boundaries sometimes, even if I did end up coming back to realism over and over. Interestingly, my pastry work was visually very modern, while a lot of my artwork wasn't.

As I was working, I heard the mail hit our apartment door, thrown there by one of the workers in our building—a sound I had become attuned to since I was home more often. Most of the time, I was waiting for letters from galleries or show juries where I had sent slides of my artwork. Everyone knew the rejection letters were sent out last and that artists who had won a grant or gotten into a show received their letters weeks ahead. It was early for me to hear from some of the shows I had applied for—I still had a chance to open that door and find good news. The thump of the mail made me feel immediately hopeful. I opened the door and gathered up the envelopes, spotting the return address of the Easton Hotel on one of them. There was nothing else for me. Sitting down at the kitchen table, I tore my letter open and read it quickly. My hope dissolved before I could finish it.

"Don't look so sad, Nan," Eric comforted me, thinking I was having my heart broken by a rejection letter from some gallery.

"No, no, Eric, it's not about my artwork, it's this," I said, holding the paper out to him. The letter said that the hotel had decided not to hire a pastry chef after all, and instead they had hired a sous-chef with pastry experience. They added that they would let me know if the situation changed.

"Oh, sure," I sniffed, "two for the price of one. I don't envy the sous-chef. You know that job will come with some heavy overtime."

Eric patted me gently on the back and handed me the classified section of the *Times,* which he had been perusing. I gave it a disgruntled scan. There were several ads for pastry chefs, as usual. I never lacked for interviews, just for reasonable jobs at the end of them. The Easton would have been an exception, with its unionized staff receiving overtime and full benefits. Most of the jobs were advertised by tyrants who promised the moon but were sure to deliver nothing, like Acroama. I could recognize all the clues by now. Chefs who couldn't give a straight answer about benefits, didn't offer contracts for things they promised, and were vague about what was expected were suspect.

The phone rang and I absently picked it up.

A professional-sounding voice at the other end asked for Nancy Ring.

I cleared my throat and tried to sound more alert.

"Speaking."

"Nancy, this is Chef Weyland from the restaurant Quince. I was wondering if you could come in for a second interview."

I turned around and gave Eric the high sign. I had seen the ad that Quince had run in the *Times* looking for a pastry chef the week before and submitted a résumé along with sending about twenty other résumés to an assortment of restaurants. The first interviews are always like cattle calls. It's getting called back that counts. Quince, named for a tart, perfumed fruit, was a restaurant that Eric and I admired. It was large but homey, like eating in somebody's living room. The chef was our age and had a similar style of cooking to Eric's—rustic and grounded in the classics, but not without innovation. Part of the pastry chef's job was shopping at the farmer's market each morning for fresh seasonal ingredients. And Quince was fair. The pastry chef had weekends off and worked no more than eight or nine hours a day.

Quince's philosophy and mine couldn't have been better matched. If I had wanted any of those jobs that I had applied for, it was this one. The chef asked me to bake a sample pastry for him, anything I liked, and bring it with me to my interview a few days later. In his 1656 treatise, "Art of Simpling," William Coles wrote that if a vegetable or plant looked like part of the human body, then that was its "signature" and it could cure or diagnose that part of the body. A walnut, because it looked like a head, was long thought to cure or cause headaches. If only I could have known which Quince was to be for me—cause of headaches, or cure?

When I hung up the phone, I knew immediately what I would bake. My peach and honey upside-down cake. I had combined Great-Grandma Bella's honey cake with another recipe for upside-down cake. The last peaches of September, tender and sweet, were a favorite among chefs. I threw on my jacket and ran out to the market to buy the choicest fruit and other ingredients I needed for baking, despite our depleted budget. What I didn't know was that someone else was also called for a second interview at Quince. Someone I knew.

I had scheduled an afternoon interview for the following day with Quince, knowing that if I awoke early and set right to work baking, the cake would be as fresh as possible. The next morning I drew the kitchen curtain back and turned to my worktable, where I had piled the ingredients for my peach and honey cake. Wanting a job too much, like the way I felt about Quince, made me nervous. What if I screwed up the recipe? An anxious baker isn't a good thing, I reminded myself, and tried to relax. Fortunately, the sight of the smooth, curved peaches leaning into each other gently in the diffused kitchen light helped to soothe me. An artist's eye is calming. See how beautiful this world is, the peaches seemed to say, and how perfectly imperfect.

I stood on a stepladder and reached into the highest shelf in our cupboard for my round cake pan, the one that used to be my mother's. It shone darkly, dull with use. It was probably my grandmother's pan as well. When my mother moved to Florida, she had given it to me, along with a bunch of other baking equipment—glass measuring cups and metal bowls and wooden spoons. It continually surprised me that I would sooner part with most of my possessions than with the sifter my mother used to teach me how to bake when I was a child. All of those old tools were aged by a process that rivaled the provenance of the finest antiques. They were aged by bakers, but not just any bakers. For the bakers who darkened the grain of my wooden spoon, who dulled the round edge of my sharpening steel, were family: my mother, my grandmother, my great-grandmother. At times I thought about throwing the whole collection away and buying new, modern things, things without history, without stories that I wasn't sure I could listen to anymore. But something stopped me.

As I cranked the handle on my sifter, I saw them before me, like one of Rembrandt's group portraits. But instead of staid old men in black robes and starched white collars, I saw aprons, ringed fingers holding spatulas and whisks and brooms. I saw teased hair and red lipstick and support hose. Great-Grandma Bella and Great-Grandma Esther, strong, with her plow; Grandma Selma, stubborn, hands on hips; and Grandma Rae, vigilant, her head leaning on her hand in her characteristic pose, about to *sigh* and *tsk!* These were the heads of state in our world, the matriarchs, the queens.

The hurdy-gurdy man outside the candy store down the street from where Bella lived cranked the handle on his instrument. Inside the store, the Austrian Jews Social Club was meeting, and the faint strains of tinny music drifted in and out of the conversation like the aroma of a baking cake wafting through a kitchen.

"Here's my recipe for honey cake, like I promised you last week," Bella said to her friend, Soreh. "If you have any trouble with it, ask Rachel, she makes it the best." Bella put her arm around her daughter Rachel's waist. Rachel, who lived in New Jersey and had brought Bella's grandchildren with her, and her sister, Dotty, were visiting Bella and Goldie for the day. Bella loved to bring them to the socials to show them off.

"Such beautiful girls you have, so grown-up now," said Soreh, clasping her hands under her large bosom and beaming at Bella. "My Sonia is here. Did you see her? She's tall now, like her *father*." Bella heard the emphasis that Soreh put on the last word and knew what was coming next. Soreh, with her bright-eyed, pink-cheeked face, was always digging for gossip as energetically as a rabbit digging for carrots. Bella said nothing. She had no intention of encouraging Soreh by giving her what she wanted, drops of poison about Nathan to feed her neighbors. But Bella couldn't avoid Soreh either. She enjoyed these meetings too much, where all the families who had lived in Vienna gathered to tell stories of home and give each other news and advice. Soreh wasn't so bad, really. "Where's Nathan?" Soreh finally asked directly, then chattered on. "The last time I saw him was at shul, on Rosh Hashanah. That was quite a hat you wore that day, Bella. I loved the feathers in the brim." Oh, so she thinks she can catch me off guard by complimenting me, Bella thought, still revealing nothing. Soreh was unruffled by Bella's silence. She craned her short neck around the room. "Is Nathan here?" she demanded loudly.

Rachel's face lost its smile at the mention of her father's name, as if she had just heard a sour note being played. She excused herself quickly before her mother answered. "Mother, I really want to see *The Polish Jew* when it plays in the basement of the school," she said. "I'll just go check the poster for the time."

"Soreh, do you see Nathan?" Bella asked Soreh rhetorically, looking straight in her friend's eyes. Soreh frowned, and shook her head. "Then Nathan's not here," Bella said, ending the conversation. She looked again toward the front door of the candy store, when the screen door banged, letting someone in. No, it wasn't Nathan, as she'd hoped. "He's coming," she said with the conviction she practiced in front of her daughters when her husband was late, and then changed the subject.

"Soreh, tell me, did you get any letters from Austria this week? Did your half brother write to you? How is he? Any news from Vienna?"

Before Soreh could answer, Rachel came back to her mother's side with her sisters, Dotty and Goldie, and interrupted. "Mother, there's a picnic next week for all the families in our social club. Are we going? I would love to bring the girls back in for that." Bella's granddaughters raced up behind Rachel, and four-year-old Dorothy began asking permission for things, a penny to give the hurdy-gurdy man playing in the street, a piece of cloth for a new dress to wear to the picnic. Bella started to speak, then before she could scold or wag a finger, Nathan arrived and threw his arms around the crowd of his family. Bella flushed with pride to be in the circle of his strong arms, feeling reassured by his presence. She smiled broadly at Soreh. Of course Nathan was coming, here he was! And that was all that mattered, to be here with her family, all of them together. This was happiness—the glint of the penny Nathan pressed into Dorothy's palm, the scent of fresh, cold night air on Nathan's good, long wool coat as the sleeve brushed her cheek; being surrounded by her tall, handsome family—little Bella, held in their embrace as if they were a good string of pearls, strung tight and fastened with the secure, strong clasp of Nathan.

What Bella refused to see was that the necklace was not strung so well, that the clasp was loose. Soon she would turn her head to look away one time too many, and foolishly test the strength of that unreliable clasp.

It cost me ten dollars to buy the things I needed to make my peach and honey cake, including the sauce ingredients. I traced the round edge of the cake pan onto a fresh piece of parchment paper with a sharp pencil. This had better work out, I thought as I cut the piece of parchment paper to fit in the round pan.

"She never eats," Eric said, trying to get our new cat, Sammy, to lick butter from his finger, "and she's too skinny."

"You sound like my grandmothers, Eric," I teased him while I brushed my round pan with butter. "How were your interviews?"

"Broomstick," Eric called to Sammy in the same voice he would use to call her name. He was always trying to prove that cats don't really know their names, but just respond to a tone of voice. Much to her credit, Sammy ignored him. "Lukewarm," he answered me, and then turned back to the cat. "Doris," he called her, "Radio." Sammy sat and gazed at her water bowl, unperturbed. Eric left the room.

I measured sugar into a pot to make caramel. "I need this job," I said to the sugar in the pan, to the kitchen around me, to the spirit of my great-grandmother watching over my shoulder, watching my caramel and my heart turning darker and darker.

"Clammy," I called softly to the cat, and Sammy looked up at me, gold eyes shining, expectant. I laughed.

"What's so funny?" Eric called from the other room.

"Nothing," I replied, smiling at the cat, who opened her mouth and as far as I'm concerned, smiled back. Encouraged, she jumped up onto the windowsill next to me and watched me, stretching her neck to sniff the delicious aromas I was producing.

"Stay," I warned her, lightly touching the gold fur diamond in the middle of her dark face. Her whiskers brushed the flat of my palm. "This is hot."

Along with the butter, I whisked my hope into the caramel— hope that the chef at Quince would like my cake, hope that he would hire me. Before I gave up completely on my pastry career, I wanted to know that I had tried as hard as I could to find a position that was right for me. I poured the thick, glossy caramel over the peaches that I had peeled, quartered, and placed in overlapping spirals in the buttered pan. Then I placed the pan in the oven to bake the caramel and the peaches together until they bubbled and darkened. While they baked, I measured out the rest of the ingredients for the batter, and then poured a cup of the coffee Eric had made that morning into a saucepan with a jar of honey. I turned the flame on under the pot, and gently stirred the coffee and honey, watching it slowly melt together. Honey and coffee, I thought. Once again, bitter and sweet. This was a family recipe.

In the early evening, while Bella was setting plates down on the clean newspapers she had laid over the board on the kitchen tub, she heard a knock on her door. Who would knock right before the Sabbath meal? Everyone was busy preparing dinner, hurrying to find the candles and lay out the good dishes before sundown. Maybe it was Nathan, but why would Nathan knock on the door of his own home? Bella's daughters were in the bedroom waking the grandchildren from their naps—traveling from New Jersey made the children so sleepy—and dressing them for dinner. The women came to the bedroom door and peered into the dim kitchen at the sound of the knocking. They all exchanged shrugs, no one could guess who could be there. Bella moved to the door and opened it.

The sight of the young woman before her made her forget her manners. Who was this blond woman, with her hair such a mess and her bruised face streaked with tears? And what kind of woman threw her clothes on in such a hurry, buttons undone at the neck, no gloves, no hat? A hesitant voice said hello to Bella, with a thick brogue. Irish! thought Bella. What is she doing in this neighborhood? How does she know my name? Several doors in the hall opened and Bella saw her nosy neighbors, among them Soreh, poke their heads out to see who was standing in the hallway outside Bella's apartment. Bella ushered the woman inside and quickly shut the door behind her, glaring most accusingly at Soreh.

"My name is Patty Murray," the rumpled woman said, drawing up

her tiny shoulders as if she had spent hours in front of a mirror bol-
stering herself up for this meeting. She glanced at Bella's daughters
uneasily before bringing her blue eyes back to lock with Bella's. What
was it in this woman's demeanor, this total stranger, the nearly whispered, urgent words she spoke, that made Bella grab her shawl and
follow her down the narrow alleys and streets without question, past
the pushcarts closing up for the evening, vendors calling out to them
to get a good end-of-the-day bargain before the Sabbath began, the
kind of bargain Bella would never walk away from if she weren't following someone she had never met to a place she had never been,
like a sleepwalker in a bad dream. At the end of the walk was a neighborhood just like Bella's, but where the pushcarts were not closing
up so early for Sabbath, and where the cries of the vendors were in a
language Bella didn't understand, but knew the sound of, like this
woman's. And that's how Bella found herself climbing the steep steps,
not unlike the ones in her own building, that led up to Patty Murray's
apartment in the Irish section of the Lower East Side.

Bella followed the woman through a narrow kitchen, a mirror
image of her own, dark and crowded, filled with unsmiling people,
people like her own family; children, so many in so few rooms,
crowded in like animals. None of them spoke a word, though Bella
saw the look that passed between Patty Murray and one of the men,
and she knew at once the source of the bruises Patty Murray had on
her face. Then Bella stopped walking, having been led to her destination. There, on the bed in front of her, was Nathan.

Nathan was lying faceup, his arms and legs resting heavily on
the blankets, sunk into the bed. "Nathan!" Bella cried out in shock,
but he didn't move. She drew closer to him and called his name
again. "He's drunk, isn't he?" she cried. "What's he doing here?"
Then she noticed that Nathan wasn't dressed properly, his clothes
were on in a very haphazard way, more haphazard than this Patty
Murray's, as if someone else had dressed him as carelessly as a rag

doll, as if he— Bella's mind finally took in the extent of Nathan's betrayal. She looked at Patty Murray, then back at Nathan, then at Patty Murray, and suddenly the pearls on that weak necklace clattered to the floor with a frightening racket. She swung back her arm and slapped Patty Murray with all the force that her tiny arm could contain, screaming in Yiddish all the names for a shiksa like Patty Murray. Bella's ears filled with shouting, so many voices, her own, not her own, all yelling at once. One of those voices was Patty Murray's and now Bella could hear her, drowning out the other voices and filling Bella's throat so she couldn't utter another sound but only listen to the impossible thing this other woman was saying with a voice like a scalding, bitter soup. "You ignorant woman! He's not drunk! He's dead! He's dead! And he died here, in my arms!"

Bella froze the Murrays behind her eyes, distancing herself from them. "My people will come for him" was all she said before she pushed her way out of that choking kitchen and walked slowly back to the scattered pearls of her family. Her stoic pride wouldn't permit her even one tear as she walked to her apartment through the darkening streets. Not one tear at the funeral either. Even though the necklace of family that had held her tight had been strung unreliably, she managed to pull it back together. Bella didn't lose one pearl. Nathan was nothing more than a cheap bit of metal, ill-chosen for a clasp. She broke it off, and took its place herself.

Rustlers with chain saws have heartlessly felled many a beloved walnut tree, some that have been part of a family's history for generations. The ambitious thief can make quite a bundle selling the valuable wood. The chef took giant bites of my peach cake while telling me, quite frankly and with a full mouth, that the search for a pastry chef for Quince had been reduced to two candidates. One was me, and the other was a young woman I would surely know, who had the only other résumé that could even begin to compete with mine. Bernadette Chapman.

Bernie.

I felt the blood drain from my face as I heard the unmistakable buzz of an outlaw chain saw in my ears. I started to say that Bernie was now the pastry chef at Acroama, but the chef of Quince waved for me to pause. He swallowed another huge bite of my cake, wiped his thin lips, and explained. "Bernie is unhappy at Acroama, as I believe you know. She's looking for another job. By the way, this cake is delicious, though I would reduce the sugar slightly and serve it with a coffee sauce, not the crème anglaise you have here. Is changing the recipe a problem for you?"

I was stunned and must have looked it, for I suddenly realized that he was staring at me, waiting for me to answer him, and mistaking my shock about Bernie for shock about his comments concerning my cake. With effort I relaxed my face and answered him. "I, um, I, uh, about the cake, yeah." The chef frowned at me, and I quickly pulled myself together. "I have no problem reducing the sugar or changing the sauce for you," I managed to say. Play the game, Nancy, I reminded myself.

The chef seemed satisfied with my answer. Then he asked me what happened at Acroama. He wanted my side of the story before he passed judgment. I explained briefly and cautiously, not sure where this chef's allegiances lay. He gave me a chance to give my opinion of Bernie. I was honest, but not scathingly. I told the chef that Bernie and I didn't work well together and that I found her "disruptive," but didn't go into detail. At the end of the interview I left with the impression that the chef was genuinely confused. He said he would call me with an answer shortly.

I walked away from Quince feeling that I shouldn't have been so nice. How dare he put me on the spot! Why should I have to explain or defend myself? Bernie already had a job, *my* job. Eric and I were both out of work. Why did Bernie have to compete with me for the few decent pastry positions available? Okay, so it's a free country and she could apply for any job she wanted, when she wanted. But why *this* job, *now*? All the way home on the subway I composed different angry speeches in my head directed at the Big Unscrupulous Chef in the Sky, an imaginary villain who represented everything that was unjust in the restaurant world—speeches I didn't have the nerve to deliver to Bernie or to the chef at Quince.

A few days later I received a phone call that made me regret even more not speaking my mind. It was the chef at Quince calling as a courtesy, to tell me that he had hired Bernie for the pastry chef position, but not because he didn't think I could do the job as well. What had settled it for him was when he spoke to the chef at Acroama, who had given me a bad reference. Ironically, the chef at Acroama had no idea that he was handing the job at Quince to his own pastry chef, Bernie, by default, and I felt some small satisfaction knowing that he had bitten off his nose to spite his face. Still, I felt the steam of bottled anger rise behind my eyes and press against the top of my head.

I challenged the chef at Quince, however meekly. "How can you take a reference from a chef who employed me for a handful of months, and not take a reference from the other chefs on my résumé who have known me for years? I did a great job at Acroama and the chef and I had a falling-out only when he laid me off, did he tell you that? Did you call Seth Rubinowitz?" I asked him, barely controlling the urge to slam the phone down.

The chef at Quince dismissed my questions. He had already made up his mind and I knew by then all too well that when chefs make up their minds, nothing anyone else can say will change them. I hung up the phone—too gently—and put my face in my hands. The cat jumped up and sat in my lap, purring, lowering my blood pressure as I imagined racing out into the wood toward the sound of the whining, murderous saw. Too late. My walnut tree was gone.

Seth called me a few days later when he heard what had happened and tried to comfort me. "I gave you a four-star recommendation," he told me, "I just want you to know that. But this guy believes the chef at Acroama. What can I say? It stinks, but it happens."

Ironically, Eric and I enjoyed the rest of the peach and honey upside-down cake, which I would never have bought the ingredients for on our tight, unemployed budget if I hadn't had to bake it for Quince. We portioned it out in thick, luxurious slices for breakfast, relieved to break the monotony of oatmeal. Between interviews, Eric played his guitar and I started the sketches for a large painting I was going to title *Biological Clock,* a subject that had been preoccupying me lately.

After a month, as the humid weather gave way to dry autumn days and cool nights, Eric told me he couldn't see holding back his chef's career for his music, or vice versa. The next door that opened for him, whether it was musical or culinary, he would enter. He would leave it up to fate. He pushed hard in both directions, waiting to see which one would yield fruit. And so, a few short weeks later, he accepted a position as executive chef of a café and bakery downtown, left his band, and put all his energy into his cooking career.

Even though Eric seemed satisfied with his new position, it didn't inspire me to do the same and risk having to choose between art and baking once and for all. I kept looking for a job that would let me have a life as an artist as well as a chef. And I comforted myself that maybe the real measure of my worth wasn't a reference or a résumé, but a tree, the one whose knotty branches included the hardheaded-thick-skinned-as-an-Austrian-billy-goat blood of generations of women who survived against the odds, like Bella.

Peach and Honey Upside-Down Cake

For the peaches:
5 or 6 ripe peaches
1 cup sugar
Water
¼ pound (1 stick) unsalted butter, softened

For the cake:
½ pound honey
½ cup black coffee
1 egg
½ cup sugar
¼ cup canola oil
Grated rind and juice of ½ orange
2 cups flour, sifted
1 teaspoon baking powder
½ teaspoon baking soda
¼ teaspoon each ground cloves, cinnamon, and allspice
¼ cup chopped walnuts (optional)

Preheat oven to 325 degrees. Grease a ten-inch cake pan, not a springform. Line the bottom of the pan with parchment paper and grease the paper.

Prepare the peaches: *Peel, pit, and slice the peaches in half. Place peaches, cut side down, into bottom of pan until the entire pan is filled. Do not overlap. Cut fruit to fit pan if necessary. Place sugar in heavy sauté pan and add enough water just to cover. Place pan over high heat. Cook sugar until it bubbles and turns amber colored, about five minutes. Add softened butter all at once and swirl pan to combine; do not whisk. Pour caramel over peaches and bake until peaches are tender, about 20 minutes. Allow time for peaches to cool before preparing cake batter, about 1 1/2 to 2 hours.*

Prepare the cake: *Place the honey and coffee in a saucepan and heat to combine. Set aside to cool. Mix egg, sugar, oil, grated orange rind, and orange juice in a large mixing bowl. Sift flour with baking powder, baking soda, and spices. Add flour to egg mixture in three parts, alternating with honey/coffee mixture and beginning and ending with flour. Stir only to incorporate each addition. Do not overbeat. Add walnuts, if using them, and mix gently. Pour batter into cake pan over peaches and bake about 1 hour, until a knife inserted in the center of cake comes out clean. Cool cake in pan 10 minutes, run a knife around the edge of the pan to loosen the cake, then turn out onto a serving platter.*

Swing Cook

Ten

"In the Crimea, near Balaclava, there is a Walnut Tree
which is said to be a thousand years old, and which
annually furnishes no less than eighty thousand, and
sometimes as many as a hundred thousand nuts.
The produce is shared amongst five Tartar families."

TREE GOSSIP,

FRANCIS GEORGE HEATH,

1885

 f you had asked me to choose between waiting tables
and working as a pastry cook ten years before I lost
my chance to be the pastry chef of Quince, I would
have chosen to be a waitress, no contest. It was very
romantic to be a young artist waiting tables, very New York City,
very counterculture. Now that I was thirty-five years old, though, it
was still very New York City, but a different view of the city. Very
bags-under-the-eyes-middle-aged-waitress-in-sleazy-neighborhood-

greasy-spoon-wearing-orthopedic-shoes New York City. More bitter and bored than bohemian.

Interviews, interviews. I could give up my life for pastry or I could demote myself to Starving Artist. I interviewed for pastry positions that would overshadow my life like a ninety-foot tree heavy with nuts, shriveling every other plant in its shadow, and I applied for waitressing jobs that would leave me as empty as a squirrel-ravaged grove. I was unsure which way to go, uncertain which would be better, which was the right choice, until one day, when I received a small envelope in the mail, postmarked Florida.

My mother and father were by then all settled into their new home in Pompano Beach—and the envelope was from my mother. It contained the usual things: a short letter, an article from a magazine about an artist she thought I would be interested in, a small sheaf of recipes she had cut out from various newspapers with my tastes in mind, and tucked inside a folded recipe, one of her poems, handwritten on a sheet of cream-colored notepaper. I separated the poem from the rest of the papers, and first began reading a pie recipe.

As I scanned the new pie recipe my mother had sent, I remembered baking pie with my mother, and I could still see my mother's hands looking through her recipe file for her pie recipe.

Apple pie. This one is Grandma Rae's.

And so like my mother's. By the time my mother was my age, she had four children and had been with my father for seventeen years. By the time my grandmother was my age, she had two daughters and was married for eleven years. I remembered how the spoons and bowls and packages of baking ingredients would take my mother back like a hypnotist waving a watch on a chain in front of her face. The stories, the stories.

Grandma Rae had two sisters. Dotty and Rae were prim and proper, but Aunt Goldie was full of the devil!

As my mother told the stories, we baked, and as we baked, the stories were told.

Oh, Aunt Goldie was a character! She was always laughing. She loved to dance! She did the shimmy in dance contests, and won a bottle of champagne!

The stories were the precious gems of our inheritance that we took out of the box together and held to the light, watching the colors dance against the walls.

When Goldie did the Charleston, she would stand still with her legs slightly apart, raise her skirt, and make her thighs jiggle to the music! We kids loved it, but it horrified Rae and Dotty, who didn't think that was very ladylike at all!

I laughed, hearing all of them giggling like children in my memory, imagining Grandma Rae and Aunt Dotty buttoned up tight in their girdles and slips, their dresses pulled demurely over their knees, outraged at Goldie's glorious shaking thighs.

If I close my eyes and concentrate, I can still hear Goldie laugh.

Goldie's pie, if we had a recipe for it, would be as full of mischief as the one full of blackbirds, set before the king.

Nathan forbade Goldie from going out to dance. Oh, he was terrible. She used to sneak out anyway, to spite him.

But when the pie was cut open, Goldie didn't fly free.

She married a button sewer who worked in a men's suit factory, and had a little boy.

Goldie's pie was still pie.

I was so proud to be part of this baking club, this sweet heredity. In some ways, I wanted to be just like my mother, my greataunts, and grandmas, to follow in their illustrious baking footsteps, to inherit the apple pie recipes, the time-honored toque, the apron as soft as sifted cake flour after hundreds of years of washings; to smooth the underside of my fingers with a rolling pin until they curled around it instinctively, even in sleep, to know the feel of dough so well that a mere touch revealed the dough's exact defi-ciencies or excesses. Didn't this make my choice of what to do next obvious? In other ways, though, those old recipes would never work for me. I put down the pie recipe my mother had sent me, wondering if I would ever be able to use it, and picked up her poem.

When we kids were growing up, my mother wrote her poems in her spare time—in between washings and ironings and shopping trips and errands. Hidden inside the drawer of her bedside table was the small notebook where she wrote—stealing a few moments from her life to write about her life. This is what artists do. But be-fore my mother wrote in her notebook, first the beds were made, the dishes were dried and put away, the food for that night's dinner was chosen and brought home. The time she had for poetry was at the bottom of a pile of dirty clothes. When I moved to New York City to live alone and wait tables to support my art career, I had done more than just let the laundry pile up. I had taken that pile of laundry and turned it upside down—poems on top.

Many nights after work I would find myself sitting in the mid-dle of a floor that desperately needed a mop, in a pair of jeans that was long overdue for a scrub, adjusting the dusty lamp to throw more light over a drawing or painting. This wasn't just bad house-keeping on my part, it was an act of subversion, a political state-ment, a giant leap away from my mother's clean, organized house that I admired and missed so much but would never give up my art to have. It was *my* recipe for apple pie, and it barely resembled my mother's or grandmother's recipes anymore. Her poem, though, was another matter.

My mother's original poems are sweet and spare. I love to read them. "Poem for you!" she had written on the page above it cheer-ily. It was entitled simply, *"Nancy—1992."*

> Two hats she wears
> Beret and Toque
> Pursuing careers
> In Arts Baroque.

> Two hats she wears
> As she creates
> Artistic fares
> On "afters" plates!

Two hats, I read again, feeling the poem touch me as if my mother's arms were gently wrapped around me. Suddenly the answer to my dilemma was very clear. Two hats, yes, and both of them fit me to a T. So why was I trying to take one of them off?

I tried to peer into the plaster-smeared window of a new restaurant on one of the tiny side streets in the East Village. I had been walking around for hours, handing out résumés. This was Eric's idea—that my best shot would be approaching the new restaurants before they advertised jobs. I didn't want to get dressed, I didn't want to go out, I didn't think anything would help my predicament. But I did go, reluctantly, through SoHo, the West Village, and East Village, and up into Chelsea, following the trail of a list of new restaurants compiled by top critic Bette Brown in the slick pages of *City Magazine*. By the time I got to the Fig Tree, I had rattled off my spiel so many times that I could think about something else while I spoke.

"My name is Nancy Ring. (Shake hands, smile, say hello.) I'm looking for work and—" Meanwhile I was thinking about whether Eric and I had enough oatmeal to last a few more meals, and that it was fortunate I hadn't known I was going to get laid off from

Acroama when I bought my extravagantly expensive new shoes, which turned out, ironically, to be great for interviews. At the Fig Tree I had to climb over piles of construction debris and paint cans to get to the sooty little kitchen in the back of the restaurant. I gingerly tiptoed through the dining room, trying to avoid smearing my leopard print and brown leather shoes with fresh plaster or wet paint. When I got to the kitchen, Violet was the only one around—a tall, slender, exquisitely pretty woman. She had extraordinary eyes, at least one size larger than the average person's, and the color of a pale blue summer sky, with fine blond hair that framed an unlined oval face. She looked like the lovely, unassuming barmaid in Manet's painting, *A Bar at the Folies-Bergère*. But Violet was no barmaid. She was the chef.

I tried to explain diplomatically why things hadn't worked out at Acroama. "I know the chef of Acroama," Violet said.

I felt my shoulders tense, rising half an inch, until she added flatly, "And he screwed me too."

My shoulders went back down. Shocked, I opened my mouth to say something, but she stopped me by raising her hand, the palm facing me. "Don't get me started about him," she said, "I don't like to bad-mouth people. Let's just put it this way. You don't have anything to explain."

Not all walnut trees crossed the borders of countries and continents solely because their seeds were flooded there or carried by rodents. Some of them had human help. Violet was just as surprised that I couldn't find work as the Polish Reverend Paul C. Crath was when he emigrated to Canada in 1917 and found no walnut trees growing there. Since the weather in North America was perfect for walnuts, he purchased several tons and had them imported. Violet was convinced that the climate at the Fig Tree would be very beneficial to me. She hired me on the spot.

The food at the Fig Tree would be updated Mediterranean, like

Dover sole wrapped in grape leaves with pickled lemon followed by
pumpkin flan. Spanish figs would be highlighted—Violet wanted a
signature fig entrée and dessert. The situation was perfect—the
restaurant's pastry requirements were small enough so that Violet
didn't need a full-time baker. I could work for Violet and wear both
of my hats. Two days each week I would be Violet's pastry chef. I
would start in one week at the beginning of October, testing recipes
for the restaurant's opening mid-month. And three nights each
week, after the restaurant opened, I would do something I swore I
would never do again.

"The apple pie is made with tart, Granny Smith apples that are
sautéed in butter, lemon zest, and cinnamon and then baked in a
crust with caramelized figs."

I adjusted my tie. The nicest thing about the uniforms at the Fig
Tree was that they were unisex. I had the same elegant long tie and
black pants as the men. When I told the other waiters about the
confining dress I had to wear at Bistro Redux, one of the gay waiters, Charles, said, "Well, I have to agree with you. If the girls are
wearing dresses, then I want to wear one too." It was then I knew I
was among friends. Still, I was nervous. I had been waiting tables
only for a few weeks by then after a three-year absence, and I didn't
have my old nonchalance in action yet.

Earlier in the evening, the curly-headed, sweetly ineffectual
manager had taken me aside and asked me if I liked the candles she
had put on all the tables. I said yes and that I thought that candle-
light was romantic.

"I don't know," the manager fretted, "I can't decide if candles
are the way to go."

Don't worry about the candles, I thought, worry about the service and the kitchen. Worry about the waiters: nervous Charles and

overbearing Joey and temperamental Liz. Worry about Sandy, the busboy, who could barely speak English or the high-strung cook, Cal, who would sooner throw a plate at your head than serve it when the restaurant got busy. Worry about the pizza oven that sometimes fluctuated a hundred degrees in temperature while food was baking. Worry about me. Me who hadn't even carried a tray in three years until a few weeks ago.

"The pie is great and has no calories," I kidded the ladies at my table, trying to make the dessert sale and raise my check average.

I knew the minute I saw this table of six fashionably skinny, stylish women that they weren't going to eat and enjoy Violet's incredible cuisine. I predicted they were going to pick and share and order things dry with sauce on the side. And that's exactly what they had done. A true test of my selling abilities would be to interest them in something delicious and decadent.

"Have you tasted the pie?" a woman in a mink headband asked me suspiciously. This was a mink *head*band, not *hair*band, mind you, wrapped around her forehead like she was Jimi Hendrix come back to life as Greta Garbo.

"Actually, I made it," I confessed to their incredulous stares. "I'm the pastry chef."

This same scenario occurred over and over at the Fig Tree, and much to my surprise, I enjoyed it. I loved telling the customers that I baked as well as waited tables while pursuing my art career. I loved being this amazing balancing act, this person who drew outside the grid and who made up life to suit her as she went along. In the mornings of those days when I didn't have to be in a chef's coat baking salty buckwheat breadsticks at six-thirty in the morning, I was in my studio, painting.

"One apple pie, six forks."

The lady in the mink headband ordered dessert for the table. I hid my smile by pretending to rub my nose. Then they ordered an assortment of coffees and teas that sent me running in several directions at once: one mint tea, one regular, one half decaf coffee and half regular coffee in the same cup, one cappuccino no cinnamon, and two espressos, one in a large cup with steamed milk on the side, the other without lemon peel. My pen ran out of ink in the middle of the order and I tried to memorize the last three. Then I raced off, muttering the order to myself, and retrieved my extra pens which Joey and the bartender had borrowed. In the waiters' station I tried to organize the order.

There were no forks in the silverware bin, so I yelled to the dishwasher to sort and rinse the clean silverware, which lay next to him untouched while he arranged and rearranged the pot shelf to his liking. Then I grabbed the boxes of teabags. The mint teabag ripped when I tried to shake loose the string attached to it, and the tea spilled all over the station and into the cups. After I cleaned that up, I realized that we were now completely out of mint tea and had to run down to the basement storeroom to get another box. Meanwhile, one of the other waiters emptied the decaf coffeepot and left it sitting on the burner with about a quarter inch of coffee in it. While I was making a new pot of decaf, Charles told me that the bartender was getting annoyed because my espressos were ready and getting cold at the bar. Cursing, I ran to the bar, where the bartender picked one of my pens from my pocket while my hands were filled with the espresso cups.

When I delivered the espressos, the ladies told me with some annoyance that their pie had arrived but not their forks. They had ordered the busboy to get them forks, but he had brought napkins instead. I apologized and ran back into the kitchen to get the forks, where I found Joey, with his thick Italian accent, a fork in one hand and a napkin in the other hand, lecturing Sandy, the Ecuadorian busboy, who spoke only broken English. "Fork" (with emphasis on the *f* and *k*), "nap-keen, fork, nap-keen." Why neither of them had brought the forks to the table I will never know. Then I ran back to the bar to pick up the steamed milk, but by the time I arrived, it had found its way to somebody else's table. For a second, while the bartender steamed another pot of milk for me, I leaned on the bar and took a deep breath, trying to calm down. I should have known this wouldn't be a good night. It had started off all wrong when something Violet said—or, rather, the way she had said it—had made me apprehensive. She had announced gravely at the beginning of the shift that there would be an important, mandatory kitchen meeting three days later on Tuesday evening.

Kitchen meetings were usually nothing to worry about—just a mild scolding about cleaning up after ourselves and a reminder to sign in and out if we wanted to be paid properly—but the edge in Violet's voice made it obvious that this was no ordinary meeting. Working in the dining room and in the kitchen might have had its advantages, but it also had its shortcomings. For one thing, my chances of running into trouble were doubled.

The Northern Nut Growers Association, the Wisconsin Horticultural Society, and individuals like George Carson of Toronto helped the Reverend Crath distribute his walnut trees so successfully that farmers' interest in the trees reached an all-time high. Contests during the 1950s produced some named varieties. Ashworth, Broadview, Burtner, Colby, Fickes. I felt as proud of my new position as a grove owner handing out cigars over the birth of an exceptional Carpathian walnut bearing his name. Unfortunately, though, Violet didn't have any societies or associations to help her get what we needed at the Fig Tree.

It wasn't Violet's fault that things became difficult just a few short weeks after the restaurant had opened in mid-October. Violet did the best she could, peeking in the old ovens to make sure the breads didn't burn on one side, or that the cheesecakes weren't lopsided on the crooked shelves. She worked hard to keep the kitchen clean, despite the fact that it was hopelessly infested with mice and cockroaches and coated with a stubborn film of soot from years of neglect. The owner, Carl, had spent what little money he had renovating the dining room of the restaurant, but spent nothing on the old, dilapidated kitchen. Not surprisingly, we still hadn't received the benefits we were promised, and Carl and his friends drank up a lot of the profits. Fat, balding, gregarious Carl Sparks was like a wind-up toy that had been wound too far. Though I had never had a wind-up toy that drank. It wasn't long before his relationship with refined, quiet Violet was as chilly as the autumn winds outside.

I could hear Violet and Carl arguing during their meetings, but I couldn't hear exactly what they were saying, just the sound of their voices—Carl's usually slurred from his lunchtime nip of Spanish cabernet—interrupting each other. Sometimes Violet would work silently in the kitchen after one of these arguments, angrily tearing the outer leaves off hundreds of baby artichokes.

"What's wrong?" I asked her Monday morning when I was working in the kitchen.

"Oh, it's just Carl, he—" she started to say, and then stopped, looking at me as if she weren't sure whether she should be confiding in me. Reserved and quiet, Violet was always the professional. I was standing close enough to her to see the fine, perfectly painted stripe of her black eyeliner following the curve of her lower lids. Her skin was like porcelain, smooth, unlined. If I were so inclined, I thought, I'd fall in love with her. Everything about her seemed so controlled, nearly flawless. "Forget it," she said abruptly, going back to her artichokes. "It's nothing. I'll work it out."

I really liked Violet and wanted to help her succeed. I kept thinking how much her success would mean to us as women. Although there were a lot of women in the kitchen by then, there still weren't enough at the top. Violet looked up again from her artichokes, and suddenly continued the conversation she had just ended. "It's just that I'm not sure what I should do about the Fig Tree—what any of us should do." I waited for her to explain, but she didn't say anything else.

The daytime sous-chef, Marlena, and I were working on the apple pie filling while Violet prepped her artichokes. Marlena was juicing oranges for cooking the figs, and I was sautéing the sliced apples in batches, draining off the juice that sweated from them as they cooked. Later, I would reduce the juice into a sweet, thick syrup that would be added back into the filling along with the figs. I caught Marlena's eye. She shrugged at me silently in response to Violet's cryptic remarks.

Another giant case of apples was delivered while we worked, and Marlena and I both groaned in anticipation of the heavy work of peeling and slicing all forty pounds of the bright green apples inside it. Ordinarily, the prep kitchen would take this work, but we needed the apples right away for another batch of pie filling and the prep cooks were already up to their ears in sacks of carrots and potatoes to peel for Violet.

"We'll flip a coin for it later," Marlena said.

This was one thing I appreciated about Marlena and Violet— they wouldn't just give me the extra prep work to do simply because they were above me in rank. In Violet's kitchen, everyone was equal. Marlena and Violet were old friends and I loved cooking with them; the storytelling and camaraderie of women reminded me of the kitchens of my childhood.

I'm the kind of person who doesn't make mistakes for a long, long time and then suddenly I'll have a full day of blunders. My first day in the kitchen at the Fig Tree with Marlena was one of those days. My chocolate seized, my egg whites fell, my batter broke. Mortified, I waited all day for Marlena to tell Violet to fire me. I didn't know what was wrong with me that day—maybe it was just being in a new kitchen again, or maybe I was still preoccupied about Acroama. I apologized again and again for my sudden ineptitude. Marlena was completely unruffled. "This kitchen is really too small," she said. "You'll be fine once you get used to it." Marlena must have had a feeling I was a better chef than my first day exhibited, and fortunately for me, she followed that feeling. I kept my job and her respect.

I owed Marlena more than simple gratitude for believing I could bake. She generously taught me the pastry recipes that Violet wanted to get me started and organized the whole baking department before I came since I worked in the kitchen only two days each week. She was in charge of the pastries, breads, homemade pastas, and the complicated appetizers, in addition to being Violet's right-hand woman. I liked Marlena's quiet, calming presence, her large hazel eyes crinkled in conspiratorial laughter. Marlena had also had it up to her toque with the inequities of most New York City kitchens.

"Heads or tails?" Marlena asked, dragging the case of apples closer to the prep table. I chose and she flipped the coin into the air. Then she grinned. "You lose," she said.

A case of apples weighs forty pounds. If you have something on your mind that's unresolved, you really must peel a case of apples. Peeling apples gives you time to think, to work things out. The fastest way to peel apples (undoubtedly you won't have much time, because if you are peeling a whole case of apples, you are probably a pastry chef, and if you are a pastry chef, you will never have enough time), as I was explaining, the fastest way is to peel the tops and bottoms off all the apples first, then peel down the sides. Then you slice them all in half with your biggest, sharpest chef's knife and use a melon baller to scoop out the cores. Don't borrow the cook's apple corer because it leaves behind the seeds and you will have to go back and do the work twice.

Be careful not to leave any seeds for the executive chef to pick out of the filling and scold you about—you are busy enough without having to stop and make excuses. Turn the apples on their flat sides and line them up all in a row and expertly rock your chef's knife, guiding it with the knuckles of your other hand (fingers curled in!) slicing, slicing, slicing, thin, thin, thin. You will fill at least one bucket almost as high as your hip. When you are very good at it, the whole job should take you about an hour and a half, and still the chef will shout at you that it takes too long. Tell him or her to hire another prep person to do it for half the money that you are being paid and watch the chef walk away without listening to you. Unless it's Violet. Violet never shouts at you and you love her for it. If it's not Violet, and you're being yelled at and walked away from, sigh loudly. Begin again, each morning. Shhh, shhh, the peeler will tell you as you swivel the blade down the apple skin. Shhh, shhh, it's not so bad, shhh, shhh, no need to cry.

One thing I learned as a pastry chef is that if you don't cover the dough on a pie as it bakes, the edges may burn. And if you don't put enough flour in the filling, when you cut into the pie, it will run.

I should have made a ceramic mold of Winnie's thumb back at Prairie. She had the perfect thumb for crimping pies, long and shaped like a teardrop. It made beautiful crimps, elegant and tapered like rose petals. My thumb makes a round crimp, like the petals of a daisy. With a sharp, pointed knife, I cut steam holes in the top of my pie in a symmetrical pattern of slits, and then placed it in the walk-in to chill the dough before it was baked. Then followed a light brush of shiny egg white and a heavy sprinkle of sugar. A pie is like a portrait of a baker: the imprint of her thumb, the heaviness or lightness of her handful of sugar. Whenever I bake pie, my mother's voice comes back to me again.

Grandma Rae and her sisters all graduated high school, which was a big deal in those days. They all worked, too, but after they had children, they became housewives.

The thumbprints on these pies were so like the prints of generations of women before me. They may have held jobs, but with rare exception they never had careers or lived alone, without children, as I did. I couldn't help wondering whether any of them had regretted it, especially my college-educated mother, who peppered her conversation with the Latin she had learned while pursuing her pharmacist's degree. But she insisted her life was spicy enough.

Between you kids, my vegetable garden, my bird feeder, and the collection of puppies and kittens all of you children were always dragging home, I had enough to do, believe me.

I was the one who wanted to change the recipe. I was the one who was most relieved that she kept her pharmacist's license current "just in case." I was the one who wanted to hear, over and over, about the day my mother rebelled.

Enough was enough. I just left everything undone—my baking, my chores, and ran away one day, on my bicycle.

Like Goldie sneaking out to dance.

I was mad at your father.

And she wanted to run free, do the shimmy, shake her thighs. For all the injustices piled up like dirty dishes in the sink, for all the opportunities missed like socks lost in the laundry.

No, I was angry because we were invited to a family wedding, and your father refused to go with me. Because it was a wedding on my family's side, and he wasn't interested. He didn't care.

So she rode off on her bicycle, and my little brother ran down the street after her, yelling.

Runaway Mama! Runaway Mama!

She rode, her dark curls flying behind her, her eyes as shiny as apple slices in syrup, hissing clouds of steam escaping from the slits in the top crust of her pie. Then she snuck back to get her car.

I went to the drive-in movies. And to dinner, with your little brother. You and the others were having takeout because we should have been at the wedding. I didn't care what your father ate.

But she came back later that night, to continue making the beds and sorting the socks and baking her pie. It was me who left the dishes in the sink and the socks unsorted so that I could paint. It was me who kept going, driving north on Highway 35, toward the city, driving to let the steam fly off. And I was determined to never circle back.

Runaway Mama! Runaway Mama!

That's me.

When I came home at midnight, your father was asleep. But I didn't let him forget that night for a long time.

Sometime after, she wrote in her notebook:

INDEPENDENCE DAY

I am Yours

Yours am I

In Your mind's eye

We are We

For all to see

In Their mind's eye

But I am Me

Me is I

In My mind's eye.

Seven A.M., Tuesday, a cold November morning. The kitchen, how-ever, was hot, as usual. I had my hands deep in a mountain of pale, thick pie dough, scraping it violently from the sides of an uncoop-erative, unbalanced, heavy metal bowl much too big for me. Mean-while, I was trying to wipe my damp forehead on the sleeve of my chef's coat. Apple pie wasn't very Spanish, but Violet loved the rus-tic look of my deep-dish pie, brimming with fruit. After the addi-tion of caramelized figs to the filling, I liked the pie even better. It was improved, just as my life had been since I had divided the pie of my time into nice neat slices: one for art, one for baking, one for waiting tables. Despite the tension in the restaurant, I was feel-ing better these days, but Cal, one of the line cooks, wasn't. Sweat was dripping in his blue eyes; sweat was sticking his starched white chef's coat to his skin. He had enough work for three cooks that morning and the owner of the cramped, dilapidated, bug-eaten ex-cuse for a kitchen in the Fig Tree had dared to call him to make his breakfast.

Carl's sunny-side sizzled in a black cast-iron pan while Cal mut-tered, "Goddamned froggy-lookin', hunched-over, underpayin', no-good, cheatin', greasy-egg-eatin', drunk slave driver." He flipped the eggs with the motion of one muscular arm. Gritting his teeth, he stuck the yellow pupils with a long-pronged fork, scrambling them, rebelling against Carl's demands.

A plume of smoke rose black and choking from my caramel pot that I would have sworn I was watching with as much interest as I was watching Cal. I grabbed the scorching handle with my batter-covered hand, then flung it to the side. "Shit!" I hissed, wringing my seared hand while the pot careened into the side of a plastic drum of olives, spilling them in an oily wave over the side of the table. Just then the rising temperature sent my proofing yeast dough overflowing in a fury over the top of its squeeze bottle in an eruption of custardy lava.

"Let's go outside," I pleaded to Cal as I mopped the oil and olives and dough. Cal smacked the old floor fan, swaying over him, skeletal and useless. It started and stopped, then started again before hopelessly sputtering out. Over the roar of the clogged vent fan in the oven hood, its motor gagging on the thick heat and years of grease, I yelled, "Please?" Cal was in charge of the kitchen during the day, and it was up to him to decide if it was okay to take a break. The apple pies were in a slow oven, and the fish, with their throats cut, were dreaming on ice.

Cal put the plate of glistening mangled eyes on the shelf above the stove, and grabbing the soiled sleeve of my jacket without hesitation, pulled me with him out the heavy back door into the sweet cold slap of November air. Fava, the mouse, who hid under the stove, must have watched with tiny whisker-shivering anticipation as the shadows of our heavy soles disappeared from the crusted rubber floor mats. Out of the corner of my eye I saw his small, dark shape dart across the floor just as the door closed behind us.

Outside, Cal lit a cigarette and sighed, leaning against the frozen door, cooling his back, talking out of the side of his mouth with a mist of frosted breath and smoke.

"Ah, that's better," he exhaled. We both laughed bitterly, standing on the three-foot-by-four-foot patch of stained cement surrounded by iron bars in a rotting alley that constituted our porch and our sorry garden. It faced the back side of a brick apartment building revealing voyeuristic views of torn shower curtains, neglected knickknacks, and a cat's furry back flattened against a greasy pane. But the air was cool and the demands few in our backyard, and if we craned our necks, we could see above our rotting alley, above the pails of yesterday's carcasses and peels and skins, and the excrement of pigeons and rats. We could see the flap of one pure white wing throwing a floating shadow down into the courtyard as it passed overhead for an instant in a square of sky no bigger than a pound of butter, but blue.

"I'm gonna quit," Cal confided in me for the fortieth time, to which I responded, "You won't have to," to which he replied, "What, you mean they're gonna fire me?" to which I said with an enigmatic smile, "No, I mean I think everyone is getting fired together."

Without waiting for me to finish the "ther" at the end of "together," Cal cried, "You mean including Violet?" He paused to sneer, unbelieving.

"I don't know," I said. "Nothing's definite, but I'll bet you Violet will tell us what's going on at the kitchen meeting," to which Cal exhaled without inhaling his last cigarette puff, and tried to say "Tonight?" in a cloud of smoke. "Yes," I coughed, waving away the cloud, and Cal said, "Sorry," and I said, "That's okay."

Then we didn't say anything else. Cal bent down to drop his cigarette carefully so it wouldn't roll away on the slanted cement, stamped it out with the blackened left heel of his sneaker, and straightened up enough to look me directly in the face, sarcastically raising one soot-smeared blond eyebrow.

Violet and Terry, her night sous-chef, who had just arrived in the late afternoon to take Cal's place for the evening, were tossing the raw carcass of a butchered duck back and forth between them across the metal table in the kitchen. Charles, crisp and neat in a newly pressed tuxedo shirt and long tie, followed the duck carcass as intently as a referee at a Ping-Pong championship, back and forth.

"This is its butt, and this is its neck," said Terry emphatically, pointing to the ends of the bird with a soup ladle full of tomato sauce that sloshed over the side a little. He reached up easily and absently hung the full ladle on the pot rack above his head.

"No way!" Violet stuck a fork prong into the opening at one end of the bird. "*This* is its butt and *that* is its neck!"

I knew Violet was right from all the years I had studied anatomy in art school, before I became a pastry cook, but I didn't say anything. I crossed my arms over the front of my chocolate-encrusted chef's coat and watched the argument from a distance with Cal, who whispered close to my ear, "Terry's so full of shit." Terry was what you might call a know-it-all. Pigheaded. Arrogant. Combined with good-looking and a dash of farmboy charm, that made him a damned good recipe for what they also call in the food world "up and coming." Cal, fresh out of Detroit and with a propensity for a bad attitude, was clearly jealous. But Cal had his good points too—his brutal honesty and bizarre sense of humor, which could be cultivated only while growing up tough in city streets. Cal had a bad boy's charm.

Terry stuck his head closer to the bird and looked intently inside. Then he straightened up too quickly, banging his head on the ladle. Oily, thick red sauce dripped down his face.

"Fuck!" he yelled.

Violet burst out laughing, loud and giddy, and that's when we all stared at her, including Terry, with the sauce in both eyes, blinking furiously. Violet never laughed out loud. She was always poised and calm. If everyone was laughing, she would smile shyly and turn away, always focused, always reserved. But that was hardly my first indication that something besides sauce was boiling in the kitchen. Violet checked her watch, cleared her throat, and regained her composure quickly. Her voice became suddenly serious.

"Kitchen meeting, now," she announced. "Get everyone together immediately."

When she had us all assembled, Violet told us that Carl had instructed her to reduce all of our salaries by 30 percent. "Oh, my God," Cal moaned, putting his face in his hands. Everyone started protesting at once, and Violet raised her hand, asking them to hear her out.

"In Carl's *opinion*," she said, "my payroll is too high and my menu is too expensive and complicated."

"But isn't that what they told you they wanted?" interrupted one of the cooks. The other cooks began to talk over each other again; Violet waved them to be quiet once more.

"My only other alternative is to simplify my menu so that I need fewer people and can fire nearly half of you."

I glanced at Cal and his jaw dropped. Over shouted protests, Violet started to explain. The cooks quieted. Carl had promised her carte blanche when he hired her and Violet had taken the job under what she now believed were false pretenses. She had been told that the restaurant would be a showcase for her ideas. Carl had lured Violet in with the promise of exposure and a lie about rich backers as bait, and now he wanted to throw her back in the water or make her perform like a trained seal. He told her that he wanted to put chicken-fried steak on the menu, and plain spaghetti and meatballs. This last remark was greeted with gasps and moans from the cooks. Carl also told Violet that he couldn't afford to give the staff their benefits (louder moans), which didn't surprise Violet, since he had already bounced two of her paychecks (more gasps).

"After a lot of thought," Violet said very slowly, "I have decided that perhaps I should resign."

There was silence. Terry spoke first, measuring his words out as carefully as cayenne pepper. As her night sous-chef, he was second in command, and the job of chef would naturally fall to him if Violet should leave. "If you leave, Violet, I'm leaving too."

"Me too," said Cal quickly, on the tail of Terry's words. It was the first time I had seen the two of them agree. One by one, all the cooks, including Marlena and me, voiced their solidarity for Violet's position.

"What are we talking about here?" Violet looked as pale and exposed as my peeled apples. I had never seen her look unsure of herself, and it scared me. She had become a role model for me—I needed her to be unshakable, resolute, in control. "Are we talking about what I think we're talking about?"

"We're talking about a walkout," Terry said, his face serious. Violet was sitting right next to me, bolt upright in her seat. Her blue eyes darted around the room, back and forth over the faces before her, never resting anywhere. Finally she said that she didn't want to walk out without first warning Carl. The cooks howled, but she raised her voice over theirs. She didn't think walking out without warning was fair, and she was afraid it would blacklist her with other restaurants. Cal argued that a walkout had to be a surprise or the effect would be lost. Violet wouldn't budge.

Violet told us not to compromise the quality of our work while waiting for her decision. "*If* we go out," she urged us, "we go out having done a great job."

Violet turned to me. "I have to talk to you after the meeting. Stay here when the others leave."

I felt like a child who has been told to stay behind after the rest of the class is excused. I glanced at Marlena, who only shrugged. Everyone stood to leave, too quietly.

Then Terry said in a loud voice what I was already thinking, "Well, I for one think it's about time somebody stood up for what's right in the kitchen."

What Violet told me in private was that Carl had decided to buy cheap desserts from a bakery and get rid of the pastry department. This meant firing me. Violet raised her arched eyebrows at me, and I looked back at her, dismayed. "I'm sorry," she said to me, "you're not being fired from your waitressing job, just the kitchen. If I had my way, I would keep you. I hate buying desserts. They're never as good as having my own baker to make pastry fresh just the way I want it." I'd known this was coming, but it still took me by surprise when it was suddenly a reality. "I think I'm having déjà vu," I said, thinking of Acroama. I was suddenly a full-time waitress again by default. Violet apologized to me again and told me how glad she was that I would still be working there, as she considered me to be one of her best waitresses. I was happy to get this compliment, but even so it was like cold cream on a sunburn—underneath, it still hurts.

"Don't worry," Violet said. "I might be able to do something about this, but I don't want to say anything yet. It depends on—well, it depends on something kind of awkward." I waited to hear more, but she said only, "I can't talk about it right now." Then she changed the subject.

"How's Eric?" she asked.

"Oh, he works days now," I told her. "We see each other only when I'm not waiting tables at night." This was my chance to talk to Violet outside the kitchen, where we didn't have to be self-conscious about our professional demeanor. This was especially true for Violet, who needed the mostly male crew to respect her not just as a co-worker, but as their boss. What mixed feelings the men who are sexist in the kitchen must have for the women! Obviously they have no problem with a woman wearing an apron, cooking, but the very words "professional kitchen" must fill them with a profound confusion. Professional *anything* is surely the domain of men according to them, but professional kitchen?

"Do you have a boyfriend?" I asked Violet, suddenly realizing that because of her struggle to maintain her leadership, she rarely spoke about anything personal at work. Maybe Violet had some insights about relationships that would help me.

"No," she said, looking unhappy for a moment.

"That's weird," I said. "I thought someone like you would have a string of admirers." By anyone's standards, Violet is attractive. Especially in the kitchen, with an armful of carrots or beets, the fresh green tops waving in her face like a lush bouquet. Combined with her success, her attractiveness made me think she must be extremely popular with men.

"Why?" she asked, looking perturbed. "Why does everyone think I would have no trouble getting boyfriends?" She sounded angry. "It's not true," she said with an edge to her voice I had never heard before. She sounded defensive. Her porcelain brow wrinkled in a frown.

I had never seen this insecure side of Violet, and it surprised me. It's easy to idealize someone you don't know well because they're successful. Love is a universal problem for women, I thought, whether we're dropouts or executive chefs. Maybe men felt threatened by Violet. Curious, but sensing her distaste with the topic, I dropped it.

My mother had no stories to tell me about how Great-Aunt Goldie had found her bedroom window locked when she came home from her night out dancing, so she moved to a big city alone, worked as a waitress to support her dream to be a dancer, didn't marry until she was forty, and had her first child at forty-five. My friends and I were living that story ourselves. Hopefully we would be able to hand down our own pie recipes someday, with accurate measurements and foolproof results, like Grandma Rae's. Until then, we were improvising at best.

Remember, there are as many different recipes for apple pie in the world as there are bakers.

Somehow I would learn to substitute, that's all. Make do.

Maybe my mother couldn't tell me any stories that fit my life exactly, but hadn't she told me the stories about Great-Grandmas Esther, Bella, and Reba? Wasn't the blood of these strong women my blood—and hadn't all of them made it clear to me that a woman is in no way handicapped if she has to go it alone? Too clear. My mother had shared a bedroom with her sister until she went to college, where she had a roommate. Then she married my father, and shared a bedroom, of course, with him. She complained to me once.

I never had my own room.

And that was all I had.

Somewhere between what I perceived as my mother's martyrdom and what she perceived as my selfishness, I knew there must be a middle ground. I watched Violet work, her time eaten up by the restaurant, leaving her barely enough for sleep, let alone a life. Meanwhile, I ran through the tunnel of my two jobs and my art studio, never looking left or right, hardly noticing the time passing. Days and days slipped by where Eric and I barely saw each other.

The change in me was a gradual thing. It's not as if I woke up one day after all those years of ambivalence and thought, now I'm ready to get married. It was more like making caramel for figs. It cooks down and down, seeming to take a long time. You get tired of watching it; it seems to take so long, you might even stop paying attention. And then very suddenly, it's turning color, darker and darker, fast, until it's just the right shade of brown, and if you don't pull it off the flame immediately it's going to burn. That's how it felt to me when my heart caramelized. I wanted a commitment from Eric or the caramel would burn and the black smoke would fill my kitchen and choke me.

When I mentioned marriage to Eric, though, he bristled. The next few times I mentioned it, he got so panicked, his hair nearly stood up on end, like a porcupine with its needles sticking out, ready to defend itself. And the next time he let those needles fly.

"Don't pressure me!" he raged. He picked up the nearest object, a vase that sat on our coffee table, and smashed it, startling me. "When I'm ready, you'll know!" I accepted a sweet apology later for the broken vase and frightening behavior, and reassurance that he loved me enough to marry me—someday—but no immediate change of heart.

Okay, I decided, that's it. I would tolerate my status as a significant other silently only until the next October—the third year anniversary of our first date.

Of course, by the time I was making my fig apple pie for Violet, that meant there was less than a year left before I presented Eric with the same ultimatum my grandmothers gave me. *I just want to dance at the wedding before I'm too old to dance anymore.*

The next morning I made a few phone calls looking for work to make up for losing my baking shifts. My chipper, generous accountant, John, who loves artists and always helped me when things got difficult, threw me a life saver. Once an aspiring actor, John empathized with those still in the trenches. He offered me a couple of days—temp work playing receptionist—filing, making copies, and reciting, "Tax Doctor, may I help you?" until I decided what to do. Hesitantly, I questioned him about the pay. Artists don't end up with demeaning jobs like waiting tables because they love the abuse, they do it because the money is good. The more enjoyable jobs, without overtime or undue pressure that would leave one with the energy to make art, in clean, well-lit offices with respectful bosses like John usually don't pay enough to buy necessities as well as expensive art supplies.

"How much do you make when you wait tables each day?" John asked me.

I told him. "Well, that's what I'm paying too," he said. John is what my grandparents would call a *mensch*. Gratefully, I accepted.

To be honest, working for John two days in his office at Broadway and Fifty-fifth Street, closer to home, was much less pressure than baking had been. Invigorated, I cleaned up my studio and started the tentative initial underpainting for *Biological Clock,* and sorted through my flat files, digging out and perusing my sketchbooks.

In the meantime, I kept my three shifts waiting tables. On one of those nights near the end of November, Violet suddenly burst into the dining room, having run upstairs from her basement office. She was out of breath and paused a moment to compose herself before telling us her news. There were a few customers seated at the bar, but the busy part of the night was still ahead of us. Violet called the cooks to come out of the kitchen and hear what she had to say as well. Marlena was among them.

"I just received a phone call from our publicist," she said. "He tipped me off that we are in the process of being reviewed by Bette Brown. We're not supposed to know, but now that we do, I think it's important for us to really be on our toes. He said that she has already been here twice for lunch, and is due back again for dinner the night before Thanksgiving."

"That's tomorrow night," Marlena pointed out. I shivered.

Critics never make reservations in their own names—you're not supposed to know who they are, which is ridiculous, because many people know basically what they look like. However, even if someone at a restaurant is familiar with the critic, if that person is not present when the critic comes in, then he or she won't be recognized. I could see some of the waiters who worked lunch looking at each other nervously—who had waited on her? Violet didn't work in the daytime—Cal did and he obviously hadn't seen the critic before. The lunch manager must not have known either. Then I felt my own blood pressure begin to rise. I was scheduled to work the night before Thanksgiving. I tried to calm myself down. I'd never met Bette Brown in person, but I figured somebody who worked at night must have.

Violet told us that for the time being, at least until the review came out, we would put off deciding whether or not we would walk out on our jobs at the Fig Tree. We would all concentrate instead on gearing up for Ms. Brown's imperial visit.

My mother began planning her Thanksgiving dinners a month or more ahead of time. Except for the turkey, she would try to serve an entirely different meal each year. We used to call it her "one-woman show." She would work up recipes and cook them beforehand, then pick the ones she thought were best and write out her shopping lists. Several days before the holiday, she would polish the silver and make sure she had the right serving dishes and utensils for each dish. The day before Thanksgiving, she would bake the breads, biscuits, and desserts. That night, the eve of Thanksgiving, she would iron her massive embroidered linen tablecloth and matching napkins, have my father help her put the extra leaves in the dining room table to make room for all the guests, and set the tables. There was the long, formal dining room table set with my mother's bone china, crystal glasses, and sterling silver flatware, and a children's table, in the next room, set for ten. Flower centerpieces, candles, and favors for the children.

At last the holiday would come, and the critics would all arrive. My mother need not have worried. My grandparents, aunts, uncles, and cousins were thoroughly appreciative, and the reviews were always excellent. Not that they lied to make my mother feel good. The food was wonderful. My mother can cook like nobody's business. And if plates were ever pushed away before stomachs were completely full, it was only because they were saving room for dessert.

My mother never made up her own baking recipes. Her talent is mostly for savories—her turkey giblet gravy is second to none—but she also has a talent for collecting. She tirelessly collected as many of the family's baking recipes as she could, learned them, and funneled them down to me, along with the stories.

If only we could use those recipes now, at the Fig Tree. The review that Violet had coming was doubly scary because Violet wasn't just trying to re-create the recipes of the past, but to invent her own individual style of cooking, against which there was no precedent to measure her. Dried cherries in the mousse, white chocolate in the cheesecake, caramelized figs in the apple pie. Rebellion in the kitchen. Now, there's a recipe that my mother couldn't hand down to me.

"Are you worried about Bette Brown coming in?" I asked Marlena when she passed through the dining room again carrying one of the apple pies from the downstairs walk-in to the kitchen. It was about seven-thirty P.M. by then, and Marlena, who started at six-thirty in the morning, was working late. Violet and she had a lot to go over in preparation for Ms. Brown's dinner the following night. Marlena had seen Bette Brown in person once, but wouldn't be working when the critic came in. She paused to speak to me, the pie cradled in her apron.

"Well, I think we're doing a good job," Marlena said without answering the question.

Marlena assured me that my presence in the dining room instead of the kitchen on that night would be just as important to the review. I couldn't help feeling left out, though, having been demoted to the sidelines. I was also worried because the restaurant had been open only about a month, and many of the waiters and kitchen staff were novices. The more experienced ones, like Charles and me, would be expected to pick up the slack. This was something I still wasn't confident I could do. I started to voice my concerns about the subject, but was interrupted when Marlena heard Violet calling her again from inside the kitchen.

"Gotta go," she apologized.

I hurried back to my station, where I was just starting to get busy, and glanced at the kitchen, where Marlena was headed. Violet appeared in the doorway, accepted the pie Marlena handed her which she must have been waiting for, then stood there gazing at the dining room for a moment as she often did about this time of the night. She would be counting heads, assessing how long it would be before the kitchen got hit with a rush. I tried to imagine what she was feeling. There she was, a pretty woman with love troubles wearing an apron and holding an apple pie, like any of the women in my mother's stories. The very next night, though, she would be a powerful executive chef in charge of an entire restaurant about to be reviewed by a famous critic. And none of us knew then that the venerable critic's visit would be as wild as one of Goldie's thigh-shivering shimmies.

Fig Apple Pie

For the crust:

2 yolks

½ teaspoon vanilla extract

2⅔ cups unbleached flour

½ cup sugar

½ teaspoon salt

1¾ sticks unsalted butter, cut in small pats

2 to 4 tablespoons ice water, as needed

1 egg white for brushing crust before baking

Sugar for sprinkling crust before baking

For the figs:

12 ounces dried figs

1½ cups orange juice

½ cup honey

For the apples:

7 pounds Gala or Granny Smith apples, about 17 apples weighed whole

½ cup sugar

1 tablespoon Calvados or other apple liqueur (optional)

Zest and juice of 1 lemon

1 tablespoon plus 1 teaspoon cinnamon

½ teaspoon powdered cloves

Butter for sautéing, about 12 ounces

2 tablespoons all-purpose flour

2 tablespoons whole milk

The night before: *Lay out butter pats on parchment-paper-covered sheet pan and freeze. Measure dry ingredients for crust and refrigerate or freeze as well.*

Prepare the crust: *Beat yolks and vanilla extract together. Place dry ingredients in bowl of electric mixer fitted with a paddle and combine on speed 1. Add frozen butter and combine until butter is the size of large walnuts. Add yolk mixture. Strain water from ice and drizzle slowly into dough until a fistful of dough feels moist and clings together. Bits of butter should still be visible. Divide dough in half and wrap in plastic wrap. Refrigerate several hours or overnight.*

Prepare the figs: *Place figs, orange juice, and honey in a saucepan and bring to boil over medium-high heat. Stir constantly until figs are caramelized and the liquid reduces to a thick syrup, 30 minutes or more. Cool.*

Prepare the apples: *Peel, core, and slice apples thinly. Combine with sugar, liqueur, lemon zest, lemon juice, and spices. Sauté in batches with butter over medium heat, covered, stirring occasionally, until apples are tender but still firm. Drain well and cool, reserving liquid. Return liquid to pan and reduce to a thick syrup. Fold syrup and figs into apples. Add flour and milk and mix well.*

Assemble the pie: *Oil a 10-inch glass pie pan. Flour a board and roll dough out into a circle that hangs over the edge of the pan*

by two inches. Line the pan with the dough. Fill lined pan with cooled fig/apple mixture. Roll out second ball of dough larger than pan and cover apples. Crimp the edge of pie as desired. Cut slits in top crust for steam to escape. Refrigerate pie until dough is firm again. Preheat oven to 400 degrees. Brush top of pie with egg white and sprinkle with sugar. Bake pie 30 minutes. Reduce oven heat to 350 degrees. Bake pie 1 hour more, turning once to ensure even color. To prevent burning, cover edges of pie with foil if necessary. Pie is done when top and bottom crusts are medium golden brown. Cool pie on a rack.

Eleven

*". . . in several places 'twixt Hanw and Francfort in Germany, no
young farmer watsoever is permitted to marry a wife til he brings
proof that he hath planted, and is a father of such a stated
number of Wall-nut-trees, as the law is inviolably
observed to this day for the extraordinary
benefit which the tree affords
the inhabitants."*

THE NORTH AMERICAN SYLVA,

EVELYN,

1663

Busy nights in restaurants leave the realm of the ordered, the reasonable. When they are extremely overwhelming, they take on a life of their own, directing the actions of everyone involved like a child playing with dolls—on a chaotic whim, a caprice. It was just such chaos that took over on the night that Bette Brown came to review the Fig Tree. The night was so hectic, so frantic and strange, I sometimes wonder now if it happened or if I dreamed it.

I skidded into work ten minutes late and snuck into the back of the restaurant, successfully avoiding Carl. We set up the dining room early and endured one of Carl's embarrassing pep talks.

"We're a mean, lean restaurant machine!" he bellowed. "Each and every one of you is a gear in that machine, and you must be well oiled and running like clockwork. If one gear slows down or gets rusty, the whole machine will break down. Now, tell me: What are we ?"

A few of the waiters answered wearily, hardly in unison, "A lean, mean restaurant machine."

"Egad," Charles whispered to me.

"Charles!" Carl cried out, startling us. "Perhaps you would like to be the one to wait on Bette Brown this evening." Charles turned ashen.

Charles Pearl's height and booming, eloquent speaking voice belied his baby face and soft, swaying gait. He was an actor, but his dream was to do voice-overs for commercials on television or radio. This way he could act without being seen. Charles was shy. If Charles was on the menu, he would have been bouillabaisse, elegantly seasoned and full of flavor, but with the absurd heads of the crayfish staring out from the edge of the bowl, feelers quivering.

"I couldn't, Carl," Charles protested. "If I have to wait on her eminence, I'll hyperventilate and pass out in her lap. I always faint when I'm under stress. I can't help myself. It's a problem I've had my whole—"

"Oh, all right, Charles, don't get your boxers in a bunch over it," Carl scoffed.

Carl shifted his gaze to me, and I could feel my breathing quicken. Luckily, Liz saved me.

"Give me the old bat," Liz cackled, reapplying her black-red lipstick in the bar mirror, "I'll make sure she gets her money's worth."

Liz had a lot of finesse—she was a concert cellist working her way through graduate school at Juilliard, and she was also an excellent waitress with ten years of experience. Though as petite as the tiny, twirling ballet dancer in a music box, she was tough and unforgiving.

Slowly, the room filled, then began to swell with people. By the time Carl spied a woman who resembled Bette Brown's description stepping out of a cab on the street in front of the Fig Tree, the restaurant was packed. Violet, the only one of us who had ever actually seen the critic in person, was too busy to come out of the kitchen, so Carl ran back to the stove where she was working and described her to Violet—large, middle-aged, short red hair with bangs, Cleopatra-style. Violet said, "Yes, that's her. Give her to Liz."

"Thank God it isn't me," Charles whispered to me, and pranced happily back into the dining room, where he was busy entertaining the customers at his tables with his refined elocution.

Carl ran back through the dining room and barely made it to the hostess stand just as Bette Brown and her retinue came through the door. I made a point of walking close to the door on my way to the bar area to pick up drinks and listened in. "Good evening, ladies and gentlemen," Carl puffed, and gestured grandly behind him to the checkroom. "Our delightful coat-check girl will take your coats for you and your table will be ready in a moment." But the dingy, long-legged coat-check girl, Maryanne, missed her cue. Maryanne wanted to be a model and was known to disappear into the bathroom several times each night to redo her makeup in case a famous photographer or agent should arrive at the restaurant and discover her. Carl called her again over his shoulder, never taking the smile off his face or the beam of his eyes off Ms. Brown, but beginning to grit his teeth.

"Maryanne, darling?"

As Ms. Brown and her guests stood awkwardly in the doorway,

Carl suddenly lost his strained smile and his patience and swung around. "Maryanne!" he yelled into the coatroom. Suddenly Maryanne came running up the stairs leading to the rest rooms, apologized to Carl, and began taking coats from the smugly amused party.

Ms. Brown's entourage was then led by a fawning Carl to one of Liz's tables. When Ms. Brown complained of a draft, Carl moved her to another table in Liz's station. When she complained that the new table was now too near the waiters' station, Carl moved her again. Finally, an inelegantly perspiring Carl returned in a huff to the front of the restaurant.

"Where were you?" Carl rebuked Maryanne in a hoarse whisper. Carl had sworn not to drink that night so that he would be on his toes for Ms. Brown. His temper was shorter than usual. Carl wasn't a mean drunk. He was mean *until* he got drunk. Maryanne flinched and began to slink back into the coat room behind her.

"No, you don't!" Carl grabbed her by the arm and pushed her in front of the hostess's stand again. "Just for that, you are taking over the door as well as the coats so that I can work the room." He shoved a huge pile of menus into her skinny arms. "Here. Make yourself useful." He thrust his face into hers and exaggerated each word for emphasis. "Seat people."

As he strutted away from her, I heard Maryanne mutter under her breath, "So you can work the barstool is what you really mean."

The bartender and I exchanged amused glances, and I hurried back to my assigned station. I was working next to Liz's station, so I could see and hear everything at Ms. Brown's table, and I admit I frequently craned my neck that way to see how things were going with the critic. My curiosity was all too soon rewarded.

While Ms. Brown was reading her menu, Sandy ostentatiously placed an overflowing bread basket on her table, then backed away, bowing. I cringed in embarrassment and turned away—it was too painful to watch. A moment later, as I was taking an order from a table nearby, I smelled something burning and sniffed the air around me. My customers also became concerned, and began sniffing loudly. I tried to calm them by saying it was probably just a small mistake in the kitchen. That's when Ms. Brown began to yelp, and I turned around to look. Sandy had placed the basket too close to the candle and the edge of the napkin holding all the breads had caught fire. While Ms. Brown and her guests were engrossed in their oversized menus, they didn't see the fire getting higher and higher. Sandy ran to the rescue and poured ice water from his pitcher all over the flames, drenching the table and flooding the place settings. Aghast, I looked back toward the bar, where I saw Carl chugging a double brandy. Uh-oh, here we go, I thought. Carl, appropriately contrite after his alcoholic infusion, moved the appalled Ms. Brown once more.

Carl stalked over and reprimanded Liz, who immediately turned on Sandy, who then complained in speed Spanish to an uncomprehending Joey. Carl went back to the bar and ordered another drink. My customers laughed nervously, then everyone seemed to calm down. But then, it's always calm just before a storm.

On my way to the kitchen I passed Charles, enunciating each Spanish word in the specials with a perfect, flowing accent to a large table of new customers. He winked at me over the heads seated at his table. Just as I was placing the finishing touches on the plates I was picking up—a lemon wedge on the sole, a soup spoon beside the mussels—Charles came in humming with pride.

"Oh, I have the most wonderful duchess and her court on one of my tables this evening!" Charles effused, assuming the comic, pompous voice he used to amuse me. "She's a pip! Ordering everything in sight. What a check it promises to be. And you, my dear, shall share the bounty!" All of us waitpeople at the Fig Tree pooled our tips and then split the money at the end of the night.

"Good thing," I laughed, "because judging from what's going on at Bette Brown's table, we're not going to see much from there!"

"Oh, dear," Charles said, then added, "Well, I shouldn't worry. That Liz could charm the pits out of peaches. She'll smooth things over." Then he turned his attention to Violet. "Ms. Chef, could you possibly send out a little something special to my table number seven?"

"Who is it?" Violet asked.

"Well, I'm afraid it's nobody," Charles apologized, "but they are so wonderfully enthusiastic and I just thought—"

"Oh, all right," Violet mumbled. "Come back in ten minutes and I'll have something ready." Charles helped me pick up the rest of the dinners for my table and we were in the process of delivering them in the dining room, when we overheard Ms. Brown telling Liz that she was outraged about how long she had been waiting for her dinner. It turned out that since Ms. Brown's table had been moved so many times, Joey had become confused about her table number and brought her dinners to the wrong table—one of mine—where my customers had started to eat some of them.

"We ordered this chicken and this steak," a woman at the table told me after flagging me down, "but these other dishes are wrong."

I accepted the offending plates and then ran into the kitchen, only to discover Liz, Violet, and Carl in a heated debate about table numbers. Helplessly, I stood by with a poached filet of sole in each hand.

"Where did you get those soles?" Violet asked me in exasperation.

"Joey brought them to my table!"

"Oh, Jeezuz." Liz covered her mouth with her hand, pulling her lower lids down with the tips of her long fingers and rolling her exaggerated eyes to the ceiling.

"Liz, run out and apologize to Bette Brown immediately, and tell her I'm sending her . . ." Violet looked around desperately, then grabbed a bowl of mussels that was about to be sent to another table out of Joey's hands. "Tell her I'm sending her these mussels on the house while her meal is recooked." Even thick-skinned Liz was starting to feel the heat. Shaking, she took the mussels and clattered out of the kitchen with Carl on her heels, berating her.

"Cal!" Violet yelled. "Take over expediting for me so that I can help the cooks redo Bette Brown's dinner!" Violet had asked Cal to work that night as swing cook. That's the cook who's not assigned to any one station, but instead does whatever needs to be done. Violet squeezed into a spot at the crowded stove and rolled up her sleeves.

Meanwhile, all Liz's attempts to smooth things over with Bette Brown by making little jokes and apologizing were greeted with hostility and disdain. While serving the complimentary mussels, she nervously dropped a mussel next to Ms. Brown's plate. In an effort to retrieve it, she knocked Ms. Brown's drink into her lap. I winced and once more looked away.

"Do you have any idea who I am?" I heard Ms. Brown snap at Liz.

"Yes, ma'am," Liz answered with a tone of regret, and ran to get Ms. Brown some extra napkins.

Charles, whose section was separated from Liz's by a fortuitous brick divider atop which sat a huge arrangement of fresh flowers, was blissfully unaware of the hysteria surrounding the critic's table. He breezed by me and, before I could say a word, he winked at me and proudly boasted, "My royal party on Table 7 is at this very moment savoring the flavor of our fabulous chef's sublime salt cod croutons and wiping their plates with a piece of Marlena's crusty, warm homemade semolina bread in shivering anticipation of an array of piping hot, artistically prepared entrées. Even now our Joey is describing each plate to them with the charming gusto of an Italian opera singer. And I'm on my way to the bar at the lady's request to retrieve another bottle of this delicious Spanish white wine." He held up an empty bottle of a very expensive vintage for me to admire. "Oh, I just love it when they coo!" he exulted before he hurried off. I didn't have the heart to tell him what was going on.

Meanwhile, Violet told the cooks to put a rush on Ms. Brown's order. All would have been well, but the addled cooks mixed up the tickets and fired someone else's order ahead of Ms. Brown's, and all these dishes were delivered to Ms. Brown's table. Not only were there not enough dishes, but none of them was what she and her guests had ordered. Violet, too mortified to show her face, hid in the kitchen, furiously prepping artichokes. When Ms. Brown finally had her dinner served to her, Carl was slumped over his bourbon, whimpering incoherently to the bartender. As I picked up drinks for one of my tables, I heard him slobbering, "We're history. We're out of business. She's going to destroy us."

By the time Liz and Joey cleared Ms. Brown's unfinished cold entrées, most of the other customers in the restaurant were gone. I was about to place coffee and tea on a table nearby, when Charles breezed by on his way to the tip jar. He waved a fifty-dollar bill in my face.

"Lucky seven!" he beamed. "And they complimented me on my voice!"

But it wasn't over by a long shot for Liz and her unhappy customer, who sarcastically asked Liz if she had graduated from high school. I paused in my coffee service for a moment, biting my lip, and wondered when Liz's feisty temper would flare. Liz pushed her jaw out ever so slightly, and I braced myself. But she was still trying to be diplomatic. Through her clenched teeth, she politely answered that she was a musician, studying at Juilliard. What I overheard next made me stop in my tracks, despite the tray of undelivered coffees I held in my hand.

"Well, I hope your violin lessons are going well, because this certainly isn't your calling," Ms. Brown taunted.

At last, Liz went for the bait, raising her voice slightly. "Lady, I'd be happy to trade places with you and you can show me how it's done."

Charles passed behind me with a full bus tray of dishes and whispered near my ear, "Catfight! Sic her, Lizzie!"

"Do they train you for this job, or do you make it up as you go along?" Ms. Brown clearly wanted to start something.

"Here, I'd like to see you do it better."

Liz took off her apron and shoved it at Ms. Brown. Then the dam broke, the waters exploding through the weakened walls of Liz's tolerance in a torrent of pent-up emotion. Once Liz started, I knew she couldn't stop. There was too much injustice to be avenged, too much insult to be vindicated, not just for her, but for all of us.

"You know, I don't give a shit who you are. I just want to say that I have never in all my years as a waitress waited on such an ungracious, ignorant cow. Accidents happen, you know, and it's the civilized person who can accept an apology without looking for someone to crucify. I'm not here to take your abuse, and I'm not here because I'm too lazy or too stupid to do anything else. I'm here because I believe in myself. And just for the record, I am not taking violin lessons. I am a concert cellist with a summa cum laude degree and more ability in the little finger of my left hand than you probably have in your entire body. And you know what? You can take your pretentious old fat ass and just walk yourself right out of here."

Ms. Brown's face turned an exquisite shade of red, like blood-red filet mignon. But Liz wasn't quite finished. As Ms. Brown waddled and stomped over to Carl, Liz shouted at her back, "You're just jealous because I'm young and talented! *And I have sex!*"

Ms. Brown confronted Carl at the bar, where he was busy crying into his fourth double bourbon. Not wanting to miss one word I followed with the forgotten coffees—forgotten by me as well as by my enrapt customers—still on the tray in my hand. And it's a good thing I didn't deliver those coffees, because I would have missed the biggest shock of all.

Ms. Brown stood before Carl, puffed up and shaking in a self-righteous rage, and declared, "My name is Louise Knollman Edermeyer, and I want you to know that I have seen some bad service in restaurants before, but I have never been set on fire, drenched with ice water and liquor, waited on by buffoons, and treated with such outrageous rudeness and—" It was here that Carl's face changed, maybe even brightened, and he interrupted Mrs. Edermeyer.

"Did you say Edermeyer? You're Louise Edermeyer? Theo Edermeyer's wife? Of Edermeyer Fish Company?" Carl started to hiccup and laugh simultaneously. "And you're not Bette Brown?"

"Betsy who?" Mrs. Edermeyer shouted at Carl, her jowls quivering. "No, I am certainly not! And I suppose you think this is funny! Well, you listen to me—Theo will hear about this, and you can be sure he'll tell every single supplier in the restaurant business!"

Carl grabbed Mrs. Edermeyer's hand and shook it vigorously, sputtering, "Mrs. Edermeyer, it's a pleasure to meet you. A real pleasure. I'm so sorry about your experience this evening, and I would like to extend my heartfelt apology. This is wonderful, I mean, terrible," Carl flubbed. A high-pitched, giddy laugh escaped him. "Please, accept your meal on the house. Please come in for another meal on the house, for you and the whole Edermeyer family. Come in whenever you like. For free." He kept shaking her hand, while Mrs. Edermeyer composed herself with effort and accepted Carl's offer. "For your friends too." Carl laughed.

Then Carl turned to Liz, his face closed down and the sound of his voice, suddenly double bass, made me jump. "Liz! You're fired!" Liz didn't even flinch. She flipped her dupe pad on the bar with a bored expression, pulled her hair out of its bun, and tossed it over her shoulder as she walked slowly toward the stairs leading to the waiters' locker room. "No sense of humor," she said to no one in her best Bette Davis-imitation voice.

Just then, an odd look crossed Carl's face. He must have realized, as I was suddenly realizing, that if the publicist had been correct, then Bette Brown had surely been in the restaurant that evening. By then everyone had gathered around the bar.

"If Bette Brown came in, where was she?" Carl asked in a panic, jerking his head left and right like a bird. None of the waiters replied. I tried to go through the customers I had waited on that evening one by one in my head, wondering if any of them could have been the critic. But all I could summon to mind was Edward Hopper's bewildering painting, *New York Restaurant,* in which a diner's face is blocked partially from view by the back of his companion's head in a crowded dining room. This scene included even me, the anonymous waitress, identifiable only by the back of her starched white apron and enormous bow. In the ensuing silence, Carl turned to Maryanne and took her firmly by the shoulders.

"Maryanne!" He held his face an inch from hers to make sure he had her complete, if fuzzy attention. "Do you remember seating anyone who looked like the description of Bette Brown?" It was then that Charles started to speak very slowly.

"A lady with short red hair," he said, looking at Mrs. Edermeyer.

"Yes!" Carl cried out impatiently.

"Perhaps a little younger and more sophisticated than Mrs. Edermeyer," he continued. Mrs. Edermeyer bristled, but it was clear that Charles wasn't trying to insult her. He began to turn white.

"Perhaps the hair a little more auburn and thinner"—he paused to swallow hard before he managed to say in a weak voice—"and the bangs not so even in length?" to which Maryanne cried out, "Yes! I sat a lady like that on Charles's Table 7!" And Charles fainted.

By the time Charles came to, we realized what an extraordinary time Bette Brown had had at the Fig Tree. I ran into the kitchen to tell Violet and the cooks, glad to be the bearer of good news. Everyone had walked past Charles's table dozens of times, but we were all so convinced that Liz was waiting on the critic that not one of us had even so much as remarked on the similarities between the two women. The cooks, hilarious, made me repeat three times what Liz had said to Mrs. Edermeyer, but Violet, though smiling in her controlled way, didn't really laugh. When the kitchen settled down, she took me aside.

"I had to fire Marlena this afternoon," she told me. "I wasn't given a choice. Carl just didn't like her or her salary. But when I told Marlena that she had two weeks to look for another job, she quit."

My ebullient mood collapsed. This must have been what Violet was hinting about the other night. I knew exactly how Marlena must have felt, and momentarily I lost an iota of faith in Violet. I had idealized her as a Joan of Arc in the kitchen. I wanted her to fight, to stand up for us. Instead, she had crumpled under pressure, sacrificed Marlena in our war against the unjust practices of the restaurant world. Then again, Violet had worked her whole life to become an executive chef. The Fig Tree was her baby, her masterpiece, the culmination of years of hard work and perseverance. I couldn't expect her to jeopardize all that without some hesitation.

Torn between my empathy for Marlena and my support of Violet as a woman chef, I couldn't pretend to know who was wrong and who was right. Violet told me that since Marlena was gone, I could have my old schedule back, baking two days in the kitchen in addition to my three waitressing shifts. A flood of mixed emotions overwhelmed me. Then I saw Liz heading out the front door and ran after her, relieved to have an excuse not to make my decision right at that moment.

"Liz, wait," I called. Liz stopped and turned her head to look at me impatiently, her back still facing me, as if she were sure I wanted only to add to her misery by criticizing her behavior further. Liz and I didn't always get along.

"I just wanted you to know I'm sorry," I said.

It was Thanksgiving eve—cold, and just beginning to snow. Big, soft flakes fell around us. Tired and strung out from the crazy night we had just experienced, I imagined we were two figurines in one of those glass domes full of fake snow. Somebody had just shaken us up but good, and put us back down to be blinded in a dizzy flurry.

Liz leaned back against the brick wall of the restaurant and laughed. For a second, I thought she was laughing at me, but then she said, "Don't be sorry. I've wanted to do that for a long time."

"Me too," I confessed. Liz grinned. "It felt great!" Then we both laughed. Liz raised her hand and we slapped our palms together, hard.

On the way home in a taxi, I decided I would talk to Marlena and make sure there were no hard feelings before I took back my baking shifts. Knowing Marlena, I was certain she would be supportive of any decision I made. Besides, at that point, there wasn't any right or wrong anymore. Just battles and casualties. And the fight wasn't over yet by a long shot.

Yankee Stadium. The hiss of the grandstand microphone, then a few short, blaring, distorted shouts and the loud roar of the crowd. Must have been a home run. Six blocks away, Great-Aunt Dotty couldn't close the window in her small, cluttered kitchen to block out the noise—too hot today. So she pointed the creaky, noisy fan in the direction of her stove where she was making blintzes, and flipped the radio dial, hoping to hear something besides the morning serials and soaps.

Crackle, *Our Gal Sunday,* crackle, shhhhh, crackle, then the sweet voice of Pat Boone, shhhh, crackle, then the melting tones of Eddie Fisher, singing the praises of his sweet Papa. If only velvet croons could smooth over real life, Dotty thought, unhappily reminded of her own papa, Nathan. She patted her short curls gently, feeling her fifty-two years in her aching hands this morning and regretting how hard she and her husband, Willie, worked to pay the rent on their small apartment. The girls would do better than this someday, she reassured herself. The youngest, Constance, was already a teenager, though, and the oldest, Joan, married and gone. Someday was nearly here.

Dotty sighed. The butter in her fry pan was nearly the right temperature for blintz crepes, hot but not browned. She stirred the crepe batter. Perfect. No lumps. She picked up the bowl of blintz filling she had made and smashed it a few more times with her potato masher. On special occasions, she sprinkled walnuts into the bowl of cheeses and sour cream. Guests were coming today. Dotty pulled the bag of Diamond walnuts from her pantry and scooped up a generous handful. A tablespoon of sugar, a little vanilla. Everything was ready. Just then, Constance came into the kitchen and watched her mother reach for the icebox door, which opened backward toward her, like a prayer book. Great-Great-Grandma Gootah's brass candlesticks, the ones Dotty used for Shabbos, graced its top like the ornate wooden dowels sticking out of the top of a Torah scroll. As Dotty placed the cheese filling for the blintzes on a shelf, Connie had a momentary view of the icebox door shelves loaded with the Milky Way bars, chocolate chips, and chocolate candy that her mother loved so much. As slim as long-handled wooden spoons, Dotty and her three daughters were the envy of other women who hated to watch the Bogen women eat as much as they liked and never get fat.

Connie reached for the yellow plastic pitcher of orange juice as her mother held the icebox door open, and before she could avert her eyes, caught a glimpse of the plate that stood on the second shelf.

"Ugh, brains." Connie winced.

Connie knew the plate of brains in aspic was for her father's dinner, but she still hated to see it there whenever she was thirsty or hungry. She pictured her father, eating the brains, sliced and cooked in congealed schmaltz and onion, and ending his meal, as he always did, with a shot of schnapps. Suddenly, Connie was six years old again, a little girl whose large brown eyes were exactly the height of the second shelf of the icebox, where the brains sat, daring her to look, a little girl with a key around her neck coming home after school to an empty house. Dotty worked as a secretary for a man who imported spices.

She felt guilty about working so much, neglecting the children.

No, she didn't, she enjoyed it.

I'm telling you her husband forced her to work!

Are you kidding? He was ashamed! Why should she have to work unless he didn't make enough money himself?

She was ahead of her time, that's all.

Everyone had an opinion. But nobody complained when Dotty came home with free bags of spices. Connie watched her mother for a moment as she checked the clean cotton towels she had ironed and laid out along the kitchen counter for the finished crepes, a thin

red stripe along the edge of each one. How did she do such complicated work in this kitchen, Connie wondered—the clothes drying
rack hanging from the ceiling, that ancient stove, the pitted aluminum sink, the stained, beat-up breadboard under the counter—
everything cramped, too close, and too old. Connie held the glass of
cool juice to her warm face for a moment, lifting her long, straight
brown hair off her neck with her free hand. But then, she hadn't
come in the kitchen just for juice.

"Ma," Connie said, "I got into Music and Art." Music and Art was
the high school in the city devoted to teaching art to gifted students.

Dotty sidestepped Connie's statement as expertly as she ladled
crepe batter into the hot pan and swirled it around, pouring off the
excess with one precise motion.

"Check the pilot light under the icebox for me, Connie, I think
I smell gas."

Connie bent down and stole a cursory glance at the little dancing blue flame under the icebox, then sat down at the kitchen table.
At thirteen years old, Connie had already reached her full, extraordinary height of five foot ten inches, but she knew it was useless to
try to intimidate her much shorter mother. Dotty had earned the
respect of her daughters, and with that respect, she towered over all
of them.

"Ma, I have a form from Music and Art that you have to sign before I can go there."

"Don't park yourself," Dotty scolded gently as she turned the
pan over and flipped a perfect crepe onto one of the cotton towels.
"You could help me with these dishes." Dotty wiped her face with
the edge of her apron. It was hot enough to melt butter without a
stove. Too hot for a spring day. Another cheer arose from Yankee
Stadium. Perry Como delivered a static-filled croon. The fan
creaked.

"I want to be an artist, Ma," Connie persisted over the ruckus.

This shouldn't have surprised Dotty. Connie had been recognized over and over for her talent at school, where she painted scenery for the school plays, and excelled in drawing and painting.

Dotty poured more batter into the hot pan. "I will not sign that form, so you can just forget about it. You will go to the local high school and college and become a teacher," she said.

"I don't want to be a teacher," Connie replied. "That's what *you* want." She twirled the radio dial until she found the rock 'n' roll station. Bill Haley and the Comets were belting out "Shake, Rattle, and Roll."

"The local high school was good enough for your sisters, and it's good enough for you," Dotty stated, and flipped another perfect crepe out onto a towel. She reached over and turned down the Comets' volume.

"It's *not* good enough for me," Connie defied her mother.

Dotty turned her head to look at her daughter's beautiful face, her full lips, her eyes the color of dark, bittersweet chocolate frosting. No, Connie didn't understand. The girls must not defy their mother, they must defy the yentas who yelled in the stifling courtyard, they must defy all the kitchens cracked and corroded with age. Dotty's family never belonged in this neighborhood; that's why she bleached and pressed her housedresses until they crinkled with stiff creases, that's why she scrimped and saved, that's why she bought yards of felt from a relative's hat factory to sew circle skirts for the girls instead of buying them. Skirts without the fashionable appliqués, which were too dear to buy. The girls must rise above the squalor of a tenement courtyard like the clean cotton dresses strung all in a row high on Dotty's clothesline. Artists were crazy people, like that strange child, Miriam Rosenthal, who lived on the first floor with her meshuga mother—crazy and shiftless.

Dotty used Constance's Hebrew name only when she was especially angry. "Sarah, I won't let you go to school with a bunch of hopheads."

Connie glared at the funnel-topped grinder that she used to help her mother grind calves' liver. Resentment stewed inside her as she thought of all the afternoons she had spent working in her father's luncheonette. Connie would stand in front of the penny candy counter, making sure that no one stole. And this was how they thanked her.

"Artists are not hopheads," Connie steamed, "I should know. I'm one of them. And I want to go to art school more than anything."

The crowd beyond the window roared. Dotty flipped another crepe onto a cotton towel. The radio blared. Dotty turned around completely for the first time to face her youngest daughter. Connie saw her mother lock her jaw, deepening the fine wrinkles around her mouth that betrayed her youthful hazel eyes and long, elegant nose, a face as pretty as an ivory cameo. A cameo worn around the neck of a strong-willed matriarch.

"Do something useful," Dotty said quietly, handing Connie a broom from the tiny closet next to the sink. "Go sweep the floors before Aunt Rae and Aunt Goldie get here." Then she turned back to her stove and poured the last of the blintz batter into her pan.

Connie took the broom from her mother and left the kitchen, her knuckles white where she gripped the broom handle.

Dotty flipped the last blintz crepe onto its waiting towel and wiped her tired fingers painfully on her apron. She put her pan in the sink and ran water in it, then turned around to study her daughter's back as she swept the hallway. Where did Connie get such crazy ideas? she thought angrily, placing her hands on her hips. Behind her, a row of carefully made, delicately beautiful, pale round crepes laid out on clean, starched towels elegantly graced the sagging counters of her aging tenement kitchen.

About two weeks after Bette Brown had dinner at the Fig Tree, a full-page rave review appeared in *City Magazine,* complete with a glossy color photograph of a proud Violet surrounded by her stunning dishes. Needless to say, the restaurant was packed every night of the week after the review, and the furor among the cooks about walking out died down. For a while we all believed Carl when he said that soon all the wrongs would be righted, and keeping up with the hectic routine of a busy restaurant during the crowded Christmas season became everyone's priority.

One night when I came dragging home from waiting tables at the Fig Tree, I was surprised to find Eric soaking in the bathtub. It was unusual for him to be awake so late. He said he couldn't sleep. It was also hard for me to wind down enough to sleep right after work, so I decided to join him in the bathroom—not to take a bath with him, but to sketch him. I grabbed my drawing pad and charcoal from my studio, and went to sit on the edge of the tub. The lines of Eric's stomach and legs were clear under the water, seeming to disconnect from his chest by a quarter inch or so at the point where the water cut across his body. His skin blushed in the heat, giving it a damp sheen like a runner's glow. I followed the angle of his smooth hip down to his thigh, the edge of my charcoal whispering along the paper. Eric lay back quietly, letting me study him.

I guided the charcoal around the contours of Eric's body on my pad, smoothed the lines with my finger to soften them, then began working from the edge of one thigh upward with more pressure on the charcoal. While there are innumerable paintings of nude women painted by men, there aren't too many of nude men painted by women. Gazing at Eric with my charcoal in my hand, I thought of Hopper's *Moonlight Interior,* a soft, sensual painting of a nude woman near an open window. Then I thought of Alice Neel's revealing, stripped-down portrait of John Perreault. How did I want to portray Eric? Nude like the Hopper, or naked like the Neel?

"So, what do you want to do for the holidays?" I asked Eric as I worked. Ever since two of my siblings moved to the West Coast and the heads of the family went south, I'd been joking that I spent every holiday in the post office. Mailing their presents was the closest I would get to celebrating with my family. Eric's immediate family lived far away as well, except for his sister, who spent holidays with her in-laws. My Aunt Norma still lived in New Jersey and invited us year after year, but the three-hour round trip was too daunting to us in our exhausted condition. Then again, most of my friends complained that the members of their families couldn't be in the same room together for more than ten minutes without someone having an argument or insulting someone else. Maybe we were better off this way. Still, it was lonely sometimes. Eric and I had learned to keep our spirits up by planning something special just for the two of us.

"I'm tired, Nan," he said, leaning his head back gently on the edge of the tub. "I don't know. I haven't really thought about it." The way he spread his muscled arms on either side of the tub, opening his chest, made me want to climb in and lie against him, feel the contour of his body against mine. Definitely Hopper.

"Seems like you're not interested in the holidays at all this year," I said.

"Well, maybe I'm not." No, Neel was the way to go. I mercilessly sketched in the nervous, pulsing vein at Eric's temple.

"Not even Christmas Eve, the birthday of the woman who may someday be your wife?" Despite the fact that I had sworn to suffer in silence, I had begun dropping hints again, not day in and day out, mind you (I was too proud for that), but now and then, when I thought he might be receptive. I reached over and playfully drew a charcoal line on the ring finger of Eric's left hand, then softened his temple in my drawing. Hopper.

"I'm too young to die—I mean, get married," Eric said impatiently, with eyes the color of rising lake water in a storm.

Neel.

He rose from the tub abruptly, splashing the drawing. Eric was nobody's muse. He grabbed a towel, and as it left the bathroom, Eric's dripping back said to me, "This conversation is getting stale."

I dropped my face into my hands. When had I turned into this person who pressures her boyfriend about getting married? Eric was good to me, he didn't deserve it. There had been a few more fights over it. Heated, door-slamming fights.

I walked into the living room and sat on the windowsill, my heart feeling as overworked as a painting that's been scratched out and started over so many times that it may no longer be salvageable. Through the glass I watched the smoke drift thinly out of the chimneys of the buildings across the courtyard. This time of year I was usually as cheerful as a construction-paper snowflake fluttering in the wind on a string behind a child. But now the sights outside my window that usually brought me so much pleasure in winter— snow-draped rooftops right out of one of Hopper's landscapes, water towers silhouetted against a midnight-blue sky—tore my fragile construction-paper limbs.

Edward Hopper, I reminded myself as I sat brooding, wasn't known just for *Moonlight Interior,* but also for his disturbing paintings of couples that portrayed more loneliness than love. I put down my charcoal. Not everything could be reduced to black and white. The nicest thing about Eric, I realized, was that he was there. He was always there, and even when he left, he came back. So many of my friends, even my married friends, complained that they felt alone in their relationships, that their mates never seemed to be present emotionally or available physically. Eric was all of that, and more. Besides, he had told me a dozen times since our very first fights that as soon as he was ready to be married, I would be the first to know. There was no sense trying to bake blintzes with an undermixed batter full of lumps.

Never rush a recipe.

An ascetic, well known during medieval times, once atoned for his sins by drinking nothing for days on end but the warm water in which he had boiled a walnut. That was one way to make it up to Eric. The other way, and the way I was sure Eric would have chosen had he been consulted, was to never pressure him again.

Stop that crying.

Connie had become so accustomed to hearing those words from her mother that she barely ever cried anymore. Tears had no effect on Great-Aunt Dotty. Connie knew there was only one way to get what she wanted from her mother. If Dotty insisted on standing in Connie's path, then Connie would simply find a way around her. Connie quietly returned the broom to the kitchen, where Dotty was busy frying her blintzes, grabbed her house keys, and headed for the door. She would go visit Harriet. Connie had been spending a lot of time at Harriet's lately. As she marched purposefully there, she remembered a conversation she had had with Harriet several months before. It was the previous fall, a cool October day when the leaves on the trees were just starting to glow with brush strokes of vermilion and cadmium yellow against a Prussian-blue sky.

"What's the matter with your mother?" Harriet had asked. "My mother thinks artists are degenerates," Connie despaired, picking absently at the somber dark yellow bedspread. "Besides, Miriam Rosenthal is an artist and her mother is a little wacky, so that means artists' mothers are out of their minds. What would people think of her if she let me be an artist?"

Harriet shook her head sympathetically, even though she didn't have the same problems. Her family held the arts up as high as a mezuzah hung on the door frame to bless the house, and Harriet was about to apply to Music and Art herself—with her parents' enthusiastic approval. Her polished wood baby grand piano had as honored a place in the Rifken living room as a famous painting had in the Metropolitan Museum of Art.

"Oh, cheer up, Connie," Harriet said. "Let's go get Teddy—he'll know what to do."

Harriet's older brother, Teddy, was already a senior at Music and Art. Handsome and refined with wavy, dark hair, he would have made as good a model as an artist. Teddy told Connie that if she wanted to be an artist, that was, of course, what she had to do. When Connie protested that she couldn't possibly work on her portfolio, which was required for admission to the art school, in her home under Dotty's disapproving eye, Teddy suggested the only alternative.

"Do it here!" he said with the indignance of someone pointing out the obvious.

Harriet and Teddy's parents agreed, and for the two months, Connie spent her meager allowance and what she could borrow from her friends on art supplies. She couldn't afford costly oil paints or canvas, but she did manage to buy enough to make the ten pieces of art required for her portfolio. After school and on the weekends, she sat in Harriet's room, carefully inking in the intricate letters on a sheet of calligraphy spelling out her name, drawing Harriet's striking portrait, penciling the fine lines and foreshortened forms of her hand, and sketching the ruffle of trees around a wooded section of the park near her house in poster paints. In the meantime, she signed up to take Music and Art's admittance test. No matter how badly Connie wanted to be an artist, and no matter whether or not her mother approved, she wouldn't be attending Music and Art if she couldn't impress the school with her portfolio and pass that test. There was another obstacle to pass before the exam, however. Music and Art required two forms: one granting Connie permission to take the test, and one—if Connie passed the test—to attend. Both had to be signed by her mother.

Blintzes are easy to make once you get the hang of it, the sense of just how much batter to pour in order to make each crepe the same thickness, none too thick and none too thin. Once a skilled baker gets the feel of it, she can make blintz after blintz, each one an exact duplicate of the one before. Connie went into her mother's kitchen when her mother wasn't there and pulled a pen from her mother's cup—her mother's pen, the leaky blue ballpoint that her mother's own hand held daily. And with that pen in her hand so close to her mother's hand, Connie signed the form herself that would allow her to take her entrance exam—with the ease of an experienced blintz baker.

At last Connie's portfolio was finished and the day of the test neared. To transport her artwork to the school, she would need a case of some kind. Connie counted what little remained of her money and resigned herself to buying one of the inexpensive large red cardboard envelopes that the art supply store sold. It wasn't the most professional-looking solution, but it would have to do because it was all she could afford. Teddy and Harriet had assured her that it would be fine. A few days later, as she was measuring her work to make sure it would fit in the envelope, Teddy came in the room with a large brown package behind him.

"Connie, this is for you from me. Good luck."

Inside the package was a brand-new, large, professional black portfolio, the kind that tied with smart black ribbons on three sides, the kind Connie had yearned for in the art supply store, the kind that she had only dreamed of one day being able to afford. Teddy beamed as Connie joyfully placed her heart's labors into the portfolio.

Music and Art was housed in an old Gothic building that if served on a silver platter, would be an ornate and imposing cake fit for the coronation of a queen. Teddy advised Harriet and Connie not to take the subway on the bitter cold January day of their exam. This was a day too important to waste energy. Instead, he pulled around the front of the apartment building in his shiny black '47 DeSoto, opened the doors for them as grandly as the most dedicated chauffeur, and drove them right up to the school. Then he waited outside under the tangled shadows of the bare tree branches swaying in the wind on St. Nicholas Terrace until the tests were over.

I dug the point of my carving tool into the edge of the soft linoleum block and pushed gently, following the black lines of the drawing I had transferred onto the block. The point of my smallest silver carving blade, making a groove no bigger than the width of fine spaghetti, dug out the inside lines of a drawing of a pinecone. I was making cards to mail out as holiday presents. A slender ribbon of the brown linoleum lifted from the block and began to curl backward over my tool. I brushed it away and kept digging. The linoleum was as soft as fresh clay—it made no sound as I carved it, gliding my tool easily around the details of my drawing.

I was on the phone with my friend Carole as I worked. I held my breath and guided my carving tool around a tight circle in the drawing on the block.

"How's every little thing?" Carole asked.

"I have good news and bad news," I said, exhaling. "Which do you want first?"

"Well, let's have the good news first," replied Carole. "That way I'll be in a better mood when I get the bad news."

I laughed, picturing Carole's usual deadpan delivery, as poised as a shiny brown cat. "Remember that group show at a renovated school building downtown that I applied for?" I held my linoleum block up to the light. At a certain angle I could begin to see the way the block would print—black where the linoleum was raised, white in the negative spaces where I had carved. The top half of a pinecone winked back at me for a moment, filling me with a pleasant anticipation bordering on impatience. I could hardly wait to see the rows of identical prints coming off the finished block like Great-Aunt Dotty's blintzes flipped one by one from her pan.

"Yup, the three-person show," Carole said. Since I didn't have much new work to show yet, sharing the gallery space with two other artists would make it possible for me to exhibit sooner.

"Well, I got it," I bragged, brushing the linoleum ribbons off the surface of the block. "Three of us sent slides of our work to an address we got off a telephone answering machine, cold. It's just short of a miracle. I got the acceptance letter a few days ago."

"Great news!" Carole effused. "I feel wonderful. Now hit me with the bad news."

"Eric and I had another fight about getting married," I confided.

She scoffed. "Oh, don't even worry about it. He's probably just setting you up. I'll bet he's going to propose soon."

I let out a derisive sound, like the crackle of calves' liver popping in a hot oiled pan. "Fat chance. Especially since he's hardly ever around here anymore. All he does is work. In fact, he has to work on my birthday—on Christmas Eve. And he's not even trying to get out of it. I'm telling you, Carole, this year he's just not into it. I can't figure it out, but somehow he's different. He's not teasing me about it or hinting around about surprises or anything like he usually does. And besides, he's started referring to marriage as the M word. Most of the time he won't even say that, as if it were a curse that would cause him to expire instantly simply by passing his lips."

Sure, why should he buy the cow when he can get the milk for free?

"What?" Carole said.

"Oh, nothing," I answered, "I was just remembering something my grandmothers used to say. Anyway," I continued, "I decided not to bother him about it anymore. I haven't said anything since, not a word. And he hasn't either."

"He's just a very good actor," Carole suggested optimistically.

"Well, I hope you're right," I said, "but if he's acting, then boy, did he miss his calling. His performance is flawless."

Carole was silent a moment. "Well, I'll expect an invitation to your show" was all she said.

Edward Hopper's wife, Jo, confirmed that a painting entitled *Two Comedians* was actually a portrait of Edward and herself. In it, two pantomime actors stand, taking their bows, on a dark stage. I couldn't help wondering, as I carved my block, if Eric was about to bow out of his pantomime too.

L'chaim.

Clink. Great-Uncle Willie, Great-Aunt Dotty, and her two sisters, Great-Aunt Goldie and Grandma Rae, lifted their glasses for a toast before dinner. The girls lifted their milk in the jelly jars their mother had cleaned and saved. Blintzes, crisply fried, shining with butter. Dotty passed a platter loaded with sliced cucumber, quartered tomatoes, and iceberg lettuce.

Pass the sour cream.

Take! Eat!

Next time, my house. I'll make roast chicken.

Connie and her older sister, Ellen, exchanged glances, both suppressing giggles over Aunt Goldie's roast, so smothered in Dotty's free paprika that once baked, it looked more like dark-stained mahogany than chicken.

Get the roaster from Rifken, he's got the best.

I wanted to make you pot roast, potato pancakes, and noodle kugel, like I usually do for my guests, but it's too hot to run the oven.

Stop! Your blintzes are to die for.

Besides, it's nearly Shavuot and blintzes are traditional.

Connie heard every word as if for the first time. Despite the argument she had had with her mother in the kitchen that morning, knowing that she was accepted to Music and Art had left her feeling lifted and exhilarated ever since. She felt full before she was even halfway through her dinner, holding her excitement in her belly like a blintz wrapped around a warm dollop of fresh cheese. When she had finished what was on her own plate, Aunt Goldie reached her fork across to take a little bite of Rae's blintz.

Thou shalt not steal.

Thou shalt not bear false witness against thy neighbor.

Thou shalt not covet thy neighbor's blintz!

Connie was confident that the argument with her mother that morning was only a minor setback. Persistence had always paid off in the past. She silently beamed across the dinner table at Ellen, who was happily enrolled in City College with a minor in education. Ellen, who loved children and classrooms perfumed with the smell of chalk. And their older sister, Joanie, had moved away to live a life not very different from her mother's—married early, a young mother working as a secretary for a stocking manu- facturer. Ellen knew now what Connie had been doing all these weeks, why Connie went to Harriet's house so often. In private, she had backed Connie up in her initial decision to go to art school, though she hadn't an inkling of what Connie was up to in the meantime.

After dinner was over, and the aunts and her sister had moved into the living room to watch the postcard-size screen of the table- top television, Connie approached her mother and father in the kitchen. Willie always did the dishes after dinner and the girls dried. Connie watched her father's strong forearms dip the pink-and-gray- speckled pottery into the soapy water in the sink, a dish towel tucked into his waistband to keep his trousers dry. Sounds from the television drifted in from the other room.

Tonight we have a really big show.

Connie leaned against the washtub where her mother's laun- dress, Bertha, scrubbed her family's laundry on a washboard once a week. The blintz towels were wrung out to hang on the clothesline, where they dried into twisted, wrinkled clumps. Dotty pressed them afterward, into smooth blank canvases ready to be painted with more blintzes. After the argument that morning, Connie was loath to bring up the form to be signed again, but in her heart she had no choice. This time she was direct.

"Ma, please sign this form," Connie said, placing the permission form from Music and Art on the kitchen counter. She began to dry her mother's fry pan.

"I saw Mrs. Green today," Dotty answered. She bunched up the used paper napkins and threw them away, then pulled the embroi- dered tablecloth, just for company, off the wooden kitchen table and replaced it with her checkered oilcloth.

"You have to sign this form for me." Connie had no intention of letting her mother change the subject this time.

"Mrs. Green told me to tell you that a girl with lips as full as yours shouldn't wear such bright orange lipstick."

Connie instinctively touched her lips, painted with Tangee Orange, her favorite lipstick color, as bright as cadmium orange oil paint straight from the tube. Funny, wasn't it, Connie thought bitterly to herself, that the bright red shade of lipstick that Dotty preferred had a name much more provocative than Connie's full orange lips—Revlon's Cherries in the Snow. Connie knew her mother would not appreciate the irony. She straightened her back and asked her mother the only other question she could think of now.

"Just whose side are you on?"

Connie's father remained silent throughout the conversation, something he did when he had nothing to say that was any different from what Dotty had already said. Connie knew when to quit. Without waiting for a reply, she left the kitchen.

It is suggested that another reason the Jews ate blintzes on Shavuot is because they didn't have time to slaughter animals and kosher the meat after they left the Sinai. Connie didn't have any time left either. When the guests were gone, the television screen was dark, and the kitchen was empty, she went to the table, took her mother's leaky blue ballpoint pen in her hand once more, and flipped out another perfect blintz.

The summer waned. Connie's secret swelled inside her, filling her up so completely that she feared the others would smell it on her, like a strong perfume. Still, the subject never came up. Finally, near the end of August, Dotty asked Connie when she started classes at the local high school.

"I don't start at the local school. I start at Music and Art."

"No, you don't."

Connie had prepared for this moment and she pulled a piece of paper from her mother's kitchen notepad.

"Then here is the name of the principal of Music and Art," Connie said, writing the phone number down with her mother's blue pen. "You can call him yourself and explain why I'm not coming."

It was a bluff, and like any bluff, it could backfire. Connie waited nervously while Great-Aunt Dotty stared at the paper that Connie had placed in her palm. Then Dotty dropped her arms to her sides and looked hard at her daughter. It's true, blintzes can be turned out of the pan in perfectly identical rows. But not daughters. Dotty knew her recipe would fail in the principal's office. She didn't say another word.

"September fifth!" Connie cried out triumphantly as she raced from the kitchen, a freshly washed dress blown from the clothesline to fly high above the tenement courtyards in the dancing wind.

I returned home from the Fig Tree late the night before my birthday and crawled into bed, aching and exhausted. Eric was unconscious, snoring lightly, and I fell asleep almost immediately. In the morning, I woke up first, and leaned over Eric to peer at the clock. It was late.

"Eric"—I shook him—"I thought you had to go to work."

"Happy birthday," he mumbled, "I don't have to go after all."

My paper snowflake lifted a little, but then fell with his next remark.

"Nan, get up and make breakfast. I'm starving."

"What d'ya mean, get up and make breakfast? This is *my* birthday, *you* make breakfast."

"No way, you're the baker. Let's have blintzes."

I stared at the back of his curly head, his neck still smooth as a child's, deceptively innocent. This was the last straw: He's here but he's not going to be *present*. So much for the Eric-is-always-available theory.

Eric turned over and pulled me close to him, pressing his lips to my ear. I thought he had decided to reconsider his behavior, until he whispered, "Please make blintzes."

"I can't believe you!" I protested, pulling myself away from him.

"Please. Please. Please," Eric repeated. His arched eyebrows lifted their wings, entreating. For a moment, I hesitated. What difference did it make now if I did or didn't? If I were alone today, I would have to cook for myself anyway. Fine, I thought angrily, I would start out my thirty-sixth year cooking and waiting on someone. Why should my birthday be any different from the rest of my year?

"All right," I said, turning my back to him, and marched into the bathroom to retrieve my robe from the hook on the back of the door. I didn't even stop to brush my teeth or wash my face, or bother to comb my hair. Who cared? In the kitchen, I pulled out Great-Aunt Dotty's blintz recipe, then reached for the bag of flour on the kitchen shelf above me. I paused and looked toward the window for a moment. Our kitchen window faces an air shaft, like so many kitchen windows in the city. We've covered it with a self-sticking opaque paper that lets in a diffused light, while protecting us from the prying eyes of our too-close neighbors. I felt even more trapped at the sight of that milky window without a view.

Eric had pulled on a T-shirt and sweat pants and followed me into the kitchen by then. As I started to open the flour bag, he said, "Wait."

"Wait what?" I asked him, standing with the bag of flour in my hands. Eric looked like he was trying to figure something out, something really difficult.

"Maybe we should have some coffee first," he finally said.

"Coffee?" I stared at him, my hands poised on the edge of the flour bag. "Eric, c'mon," I said, trying for some semblance of capitulation, "you got me out of bed saying you want me to make blintzes and that's what I'm gonna do. It takes a few minutes to mix the batter, so go ahead and make coffee while I do it, if you want."

I unfolded the top of the bag of flour and dug around in one of the kitchen drawers for my measuring cups. Eric sighed deeply and loudly. He cleared his throat. When I looked at him, he said, "What?" as if I had gotten his attention, and not the other way around.

"What is up with you?" I asked in exasperation. Then I dug one of the cups into the flour. It stuck. I looked in the bag. A dark shape was buried in the flour.

"Eric, there's something in the flour," I said, still believing I was telling him news he didn't know.

Eric took a few steps back from me and covered his mouth with his hands. His eyes were smiling.

"What's so funny?" I said, starting to get suspicious. I pulled the object from the flour and it turned out to be a small package wrapped in paper and tied with ribbon. I smiled. "Eric, what is this?"

Eric had given me birthday presents in the kitchen before—chocolates, kitchen gadgets. Maybe it was some special ingredient for the blintzes. He was absolutely silent while I tore off the paper. Suddenly I was holding a small, soft, very serious-looking black velvet box in my hands. It was unmistakable. My whole body felt like a blintz frying in hot butter.

I said, "Is this what I think it is?"

Later, when we told the story again and again to each other, Eric would say that I turned every shade of red it was possible to mix with my palette knife.

I opened the box, revealing an intensely glittering diamond ring, and fanned myself with a kitchen towel.

Eric's proposal came out, "Will you m-m-m-marry me," but I didn't mind. I was so proud of him. He said the M word. And he didn't die.

I did finish making the blintzes, and just as I was about to roll the crepes and fry them, I threw a handful of walnuts into the filling.

One of the greatest pleasures of my life turned out to be wearing my engagement ring while I waited tables. My female customers never failed to comment on it, sometimes to the chagrin of their male companions.

"Nice ring, doncha think, honey?" one woman chided her date openly.

The other waitresses and I had a good laugh over it. What was curious to me was that at one time in my life I would have said that I had no desire to have a diamond ring. Sometimes I even made excuses for the rock I wore on my finger, defensively telling others that I never really put much significance on a diamond ring. In some ways, that was true, though I believe now that it depends, in more ways than one, on where you find it.

In the months after I got engaged, waiting tables remained little more than waiting tables, even with the ice on my finger as well as in the glasses, and things at the Fig Tree deteriorated daily. More than once Carl's drunk friends had to be thrown out of the restaurant by the police for disturbing the other customers. Carl became increasingly critical of Violet and Violet began to simmer with resentment. Despite the glowing review, we never received the benefits or fair salaries we had been promised. Slowly, the talk about a walkout resurfaced and began to bubble at the edges of the Fig Tree's kitchen. All it would take was just a little more heat to make it boil over.

Great-Aunt Dotty's Blintzes

For the crepes:
2 eggs at room temperature
2 tablespoons melted unsalted butter
½ cup milk, and more if needed
½ cup water
1 cup flour
1 tablespoon sugar
Pinch salt

For the filling:
¾ to 1 pound farmer cheese
¼ pound cream cheese, softened
1 egg
1 tablespoon sour cream
1 tablespoon sugar
1 teaspoon vanilla extract
¼ cup chopped walnuts (optional)
Butter for frying

Prepare the crepes: Beat eggs and butter together. Mix together milk and water and add to egg mixture. Add flour, sugar, and salt through a sifter, gently whisking until batter is the consistency of whole milk. Add more milk to reach desired consistency if necessary. Do not overbeat. Rest batter at least 30 minutes or overnight in the refrigerator. Strain. Heat a slope-sided crepe or sauté pan, preferably nonstick, 7 or 8 inches in diameter, over medium to medium low heat until very hot. Ideally, the pan shouldn't be so hot that it sets the batter immediately upon contact and makes the crepes too thick, nor so cool that the batter won't set at all. Lightly brush skillet with butter or canola oil—no more than $1/4$ teaspoon of fat should be used for each crepe in a nonstick pan. Quickly pour 3 tablespoons crepe batter into the pan, then tilt and swirl the pan around to spread it thinly. Pour off excess if necessary. Cook until set. Flip out onto a clean towel to cool.

Prepare the filling: Combine filling ingredients with a potato masher or fork until well mixed. Mixture will not be completely smooth. Put a heaping tablespoon of filling in each blintz and fold each one top down, sides in, and bottom up, to form a package.

Fry the blintzes: Fry each blintz in small amount of butter in a hot pan until lightly browned and crisp. Be careful not to burn the butter. Serve hot with sour cream and apple sauce if desired, or with berries and powdered sugar. Yields one dozen blintzes.

Twelve

"My maiden aunt . . . carried a three-shelled walnut with her
in her handbag all through the Second World War,
and was convinced that it protected her."
CORRESPONDENCE FROM P. H. WALDEN, NORTHAMPTONSHIRE,
<u>COUNTRY LIFE</u>,
MARCH 8, 1990

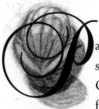

apa Max always knew that there was one more family story yet to be told. When he left Slonim with Great-Grandma Esther and Great-Grandpa Jacob and his family, he left behind a half brother, Berel, who was a son of Great-Grandpa Jacob's from his previous marriage. Berel's mother had passed away years before Jacob married Esther Hanna, and Esther embraced Berel as one of her own sons. But Berel did not want to move away from Slonim when the rest of the family fled for Argentina. He had a wife who was already pregnant with his child. So Berel remained in Slonim.

The families stayed in touch. Until the Second World War began, Grandma Rae and Papa Max received letters regularly from Berel. Abruptly after the start of the war, though, the letters stopped.

So much of almost every Jewish family's history was lost in World War II—records destroyed, homes confiscated or burned, photographs lost, tombstones savagely broken and used for cobblestones. Our true past, even our real names before they were changed on Ellis Island, became a mystery, like a drawing that has been erased, leaving behind only a ghostly, unreadable image. But Papa took a chance that not all of our history had been lost. After the war was over, he went to the displaced persons bureau and inquired after Berel.

No one can say for sure where the history of the walnut begins. There are paths to follow, overgrown and blocked from sunlight, that lead back to long-deserted clearings where walnuts once lay: the cool stone priests' table in the Temple of Isis in Pompeii, where the eruption of Mt. Vesuvius in A.D. 79 left the temple in ruins and the walnuts uneaten; the dark, ancient caves of Shanidar in Northern Iraq, where pollen analysis and actual finds revealed walnuts along with eggs, fish, and cereal to have been sustenance for the Middle Paleolithic cave dwellers; the green shores of the upper Great Lakes, where walnuts, their cousin hickories, and acorns were left behind as early as 2000 B.C. Digging into the past of a Jewish family, a past as disrupted by the Second World War as the Temple of Pompeii by the eruption of Vesuvius, can unearth similar kinds of isolated fragments, leading everywhere and nowhere. Papa was told that Slonim had been utterly ransacked and plundered during the war and that its records were scattered like so many burning ashes in the wind. The bureau was unable to find anything.

While Charles and I were waiting at the bar one night for our drink orders at the Fig Tree, we overheard Carl conversing with a couple of women seated near the bar. They were sisters, regular customers, and favorites of Carl's. Eccentric ladies, basically harmless, who came dressed in matching outfits, and who liked to drink and smoke. They were also investors in the restaurant, which made them V.I.P.'s. On slow nights, which were unfortunately more and more frequent, Carl loved to schmooze with them, buying them (and himself) round after round of dry Rob Roys, two lemon peels apiece.

"We'll have the crab cakes," one of the sisters told Carl, pulling at the collar of her red turtleneck. "They sound really interesting." Carl often took the orders from his friends, then handed them to the waiter for that station.

"Well," Carl said with his haughtiest snort, "if you really like crab cakes, you won't like the ones my chef makes here."

Charles and I looked at each other uncertainly, then back at Carl. What could he be up to?

"I love the ones you get in Maine in the summer," the other sister said, pushing up the sleeves of *her* red turtleneck.

"That's just what I mean!" Carl cried in drunken bravado. "The crab cakes here are all gussied up with nouvelle inventions, sun-dried this and that and essence of so-and-so. Not the traditional thing at all. And no tartar sauce, just some kind of puree or coulis or other such nonsense."

Charles's jaw dropped open and we stared at each other in disbelief. How did Carl expect to fill the restaurant when he was knocking his own chef to the customers? Especially these customers, whose money and interest meant a lot to Violet's future.

"I'll tell you what," Carl volunteered without being asked, "I'll go into the kitchen myself and make them for you, and I'll kill two birds with one stone because I can teach the chef how to make them at the same time."

"More like three birds," Charles whispered to me, nodding in the direction of the two red-breasted sisters and the preening Carl. "And Violet will be throwing the stone, not Carl." We both snickered quietly.

Carl excused himself to go to the little grocery next door and buy ingredients. The bartender loaded our trays with our drink orders. Suddenly Charles looked at me, panic-stricken. "We've got to warn Violet!" We picked up our trays, delivered their contents as quickly as possible, then hurried into the kitchen. Too late. Carl was already behind the stove, unpacking a brown paper bag that held an assortment of mundane ingredients from the bodega next door—a box of cornflakes, a can of condensed cream of mushroom soup, a jar of mayonnaise, and a jar of commercial pickle relish. Violet stood with her arms crossed over her chest, a belligerent look on her face, just as we had expected. When we burst into the kitchen, she looked over in our direction and her eyes met first mine and then Charles's, understanding at once that we knew something she didn't.

The other cooks stood around looking uncomfortable while Carl pretentiously lied to Violet that he was forced to come into the kitchen because he had been receiving numerous complaints about her crab cakes, and now he would just have to show her how to make the "real" thing. Violet's embarrassment was as obvious as a naked green salad while her meticulously trained staff stood around witnessing her humiliation. When the whole mortifying display was over, Violet cornered Charles and me in the waiters' station.

"Tell me everything that happened," she demanded. We related our story. Typical of Violet's composure, she didn't respond, only listened to what we had to say and returned to her kitchen. Soon we knew, though, that Violet wasn't being passive. She was just waiting for the pan to get hot before she really started cooking.

Violet called each of us aside about a week later and spoke to us privately. When it was my turn, she sat me down with her in the dining room at one of the unset tables before the restaurant opened. We both wore our chef's whites. Violet was blunt.

"Nothing has changed and things are only getting worse for us here. This is the end. I'm going to walk out. What are you going to do?" she asked me.

"I'm going with you," I said without hesitation.

"You don't have to do that."

"I know."

Solidarity has its own language. A handshake, almost a smile, but not quite. Even though we were happy to fight for what we believed was right, our elation was tempered by the obvious consequences. I had promised myself ever since I was fired from Acroama that I would never again keep a job that I didn't want simply because I was afraid to be unemployed. There was nothing else to say. Within a week Violet and her entire kitchen staff, including me, walked out of the kitchen at the Fig Tree for the last time.

Being jobless by choice had a different feel to it than being laid off or fired, especially since we were all unemployed in protest of unfair treatment. Our unemployment had a larger purpose as well—to get for chefs, especially women chefs, the same humane schedules, fair pay, and benefits of other professions. We weren't the only ones. We heard through the industry grapevine about other incidents from time to time. A pastry chef and her assistant walked out of a busy restaurant in SoHo; another pastry chef walked out of a café in Murray Hill. A prominent chef and his entire staff walked out of an Upper East Side hotel over conflicts with the management, and three chefs, one after the other, walked out of a new restaurant in my neighborhood. A leading industry magazine ran an editorial page admonishing the restaurant business to take stock of the abuse it doled out to its workers. Unfortunately, though, it would take a lot more to shake up the restaurant world than a few brave cooks and a little outspoken journalism.

Violet found a backer and began plans to open her own restaurant, where she could operate fairly even if the majority in the restaurant world didn't. The rest of us scattered, looking for jobs separately. We vowed that when Violet was ready, or sometime in the future, we'd all work together once more. In the meantime, I kept painting, living for and dreaming of the day when I could support myself with my art. Until then, I found another survival job at a melting-pot-style American restaurant near where I lived called Cook & CakeWalk. Two days baking mousse cakes and blueberry tarts, three nights waiting paper-covered tables laid with steak knives and extra napkins for the baby-back barbecued ribs. No candles—just glasses of crayons for the kids.

From the minute I took the job, the chef at Cook & CakeWalk was constantly fussing with my dessert menu. Every time I presented him with a menu, he would shake his head and look uncertain. The chef was tall with a long, delicate, thin face like a sage leaf drooping on its leggy, overgrown stem. One afternoon, I presented him with a dish of cookies to sample that we were considering. He munched thoughtfully while he read over my ideas for the new spring menu.

"I don't know," he said, biting into one of the walnut tuiles I had shaped, still warm, into an elegant curled coronet. "There's something missing here, I just don't know what it is."

I didn't either, but I found a clue in an unlikely place.

On one of our days off work, Eric and I made a trip to the tenement museum on the Lower East Side. It was a hot day, so we were happy to duck into the shady basement of the slim building on Orchard Street and sit on the cool metal folding chairs to watch a slide show about the history of the tenements. Across the street was a gift shop and a display of things that had been found in the tenement buildings while they were being renovated. There were seltzer bottles and thimbles, shoes and sewing needles and bits of clothing. But the object that held my gaze the longest was a tapered wooden rolling pin. How many hands had held that pin and baked handed-down family recipes that were now scattered or gone, perhaps forgotten?

As soon as I returned home, I dug out my own rolling pin and the notebook where I keep all Grandma Rae's recipes. Since the New Year, Grandma's health had been deteriorating rapidly. There was talk that she might not make it to the wedding. I stared at the book of family recipes, thinking, how can these help me now? The chef had approved my sophisticated walnut tuiles for a plate where they would be served artfully shaped and filled with out-of-season berries flown in from Chile, along with scoops of three exotically flavored sorbets, and accented by a stylish spiral of raspberry coulis squirted from the fine tip of a squeeze bottle. I had watched the chef tuck a dainty sprig of fresh mint into the cookie for a garnish. He was especially pleased, he said, because the tuile recipe had no added fat in it, and because the fat in walnuts had recently been reported to be 70 percent polyunsaturated, unlike other nuts. That made the tuiles and sorbet the perfect answer to his customers' unending requests for a dessert that was lighter and more suited to their new, "nineties" lifestyle. No, my grandmothers' recipes were far too rustic, old-fashioned, and plain for the modern urban fare at Cook & CakeWalk.

Then again, artists agree that the best subjects are the ones you are most familiar with. I tore the rugelach recipe out of my notebook and put it in the pile I was collecting to develop my menu for work. Maybe I could use it somehow.

Berel Yakimovsky, his wife, Risha, and three of their five children sat huddled together inside the cellar of their house within the walls of the Jewish ghetto in Slonim. Outside, a November fog filled the ghetto like the steam from a hot pan thrown under cold water. The flame had been turned too high under Slonim, Berel thought, since June, when the city fell to the Germans, when Abraham, one half of Berel's twins, had suddenly disappeared. Berel had been hiding, just like this, in July also, during the Germans' first *Aktion*. All Jewish men older than fifteen were ordered into the street carrying everything they owned, only to have their clothes and belongings loaded onto trucks and their naked bodies beaten with sticks and taken away. When that woman, the shoemaker's daughter, came running back, hysterical and screaming, with her story of a mass grave and twelve hundred murdered, Berel, like the others, didn't believe her. How could it be so, in this civilized world, in 1941? God wouldn't keep poison like this on the shelves of His kitchen.

How Berel longed for the way Slonim used to be, with its sleepy tree-lined cobblestoned streets crowded with horse-drawn wagons stopping at the bakery or outdoor market for a little rugelach or a thick stalk of horseradish, or tethered at the magnificent seventeenth-century stone synagogue for Saturday-morning prayers. Not that it was always peaceful—too much salt had been thrown into Slonim's sweet recipe more than once already. The Jews were persecuted in Slonim as early as 1660, and some of the pogroms since then had been extremely violent. That's why the community had obediently paid the two-million-ruble fine the Germans imposed in the middle of the summer. But that was before the ghetto had been established in August, before all the leaders of the *Judenrat* went missing and were reported murdered after refusing to cooperate with the Germans. Now there was less and less reason to obey quietly. Sixty people had been taken from the ghetto to work for the Germans a few months ago and had never returned. Rumors spread that the workers had dug three big holes on the outskirts of the city intended for more graves, and then were shot and thrown in. The only difference between this rumor and the others was that Berel was starting to believe them.

Yellow tickets had been handed out in the ghetto as part of the second *Aktion*. The ones who had received the tickets would be allowed to stay in the ghetto, and the ones without would be taken away. Only Berel's daughter, Golda, the other half of the twenty-one-year-old twins, had received a yellow ticket. The suspicion in the ghetto had gotten so strong, though, that even some of the ticket holders had decided to hide. After agonizing over the decision for hours, Berel had finally taken Golda's round face in his hands, so like his own with her large, dark eyes, but with her mother's curving, full mouth, and told her that it was safer for her to stay upstairs. Then he had answered her protests with a kiss on her smooth forehead, gathered up the little ones, taken Risha's hand, and walked with them down into the basement.

In expectation of a raid on the ghetto, the Jews had built bunkers in the ground and connecting tunnels through the basements of the ghetto buildings. Before the German soldiers had passed through the front gates of the ghetto, followed by a mob of Lithuanians and Ukrainians carrying axes and sticks, the ghetto streets and houses emptied into the secret bunkers, basements, attics, and barns. Berel tried to stretch his long arms around his family as they hid in the cellar.

And I am praying, God.

They couldn't possibly hurt her, because she is a woman like a pale half moon, thin and stooped but luminous. My wife. They couldn't possibly hurt the children either. Five children, five little teacups, two of them twins, exactly alike, one already gone. The other three smaller and mismatched but still able to catch the moonlight in their milky bowls.

They couldn't. How could they? Little cups full of light.

Berel heard the shouting—loud, squawking words like the cries of the huge birds that swept through his garden and yard, looking for prey. The German soldiers had been searching the ghetto for hours.

"Jews! Come out of hiding! Come out!"

The voices neared, faded, neared again. Berel watched the frightened eyes of the little ones, shining with choked-back tears. Above them, suddenly, the wooden floorboards shook with the footsteps of heavy boots. Furniture turned over, a crash so loud it vibrated the walls of the cellar. Berel felt himself gasp—the effort to hold back his breath was too much. He tried to quiet the children, but they were afraid, so afraid. They heard Golda's high voice pleading between the dissonant caws of the soldiers' words, then the door of the cellar being yanked, the weak hinges ripping away. Risha gripped Berel's hand like a vise as the family was dragged from the cellar and out onto the street.

Golda, Golda, you are slipping from my arms, I am supposed to hold you here, I am supposed to keep all my children in the circle of my strong arm, in the circle of the pale light of my wife. When did my arms get as short as broken pot handles, when did the shelves splinter, when did the guns like glinting metal spoons start crossing in the air, pointing at us?

Berel defied the German soldiers and refused to let his family board the trucks that were waiting to take them away. When the soldiers tried to take them forcibly, the family resisted. In the struggle, Berel and Risha and the three little children were pushed to the ground. The soldiers formed an impenetrable line between Golda and the rest of her family. Golda felt the day turn dark, as if hundreds of crows had filled the sky and blocked all the light, as if thick curtains had been hung in front of her eyes that beat with the pulse of a pounding heart. A heart beating with the speed of machine-gun fire.

Don't look, my heart. We are smashed on the floor of the house that they dragged us from. Don't watch! They have us in their beaks, they're going to drop us, they're going to break the teapot, they're going to spill the boiling water, the red, red boiling water.

Now.

Golda watched, not wanting to watch but unable to look away as her family was murdered in front of her eyes.

Golda was roughly dragged back into the house, thrown to the floor, and ordered not to leave until the *Aktion* was over. She pressed her face to the window and watched in agony as the bodies of her family were thrown into a truck and driven away.

With difficulty, Golda slowly raised her heavy head. How long had she wept? It must have been days, weeks possibly. But when she stumbled out of the house into the startling glare of daylight, she learned that it was only late in the afternoon of the same day. The German soldiers had ended their search. The rumor had spread that the ghetto would be completely sealed off sometime very soon. No one would be permitted to enter or leave, not for any reason, not even the men, who were usually permitted to work for the Germans each day in the city.

Polish sympathizers from the town came to the ghetto to tell the Jews that they had seen the people the Germans had taken away in the *Aktion* being murdered in the Chiplova fields and thrown into the three big holes dug by their fellow Jews three months before. The soldiers had played music to drown out the screams, and ate, drank, and played cards between shootings. Even after hearing this, some of the Jews insisted that only the ones who had resisted could have been shot. How could anyone believe that nine thousand people could be so heartlessly executed?

Golda believed. She had witnessed the inhuman coldness of these murderers with her own eyes. And she believed that if the ghetto were sealed off, it would mean only that the biggest slaughter of all was yet to come. She remembered her twin brother, Abraham, telling her before he disappeared that he was planning to run away and join the partisans in the Slonim forest to work for the underground against the Germans. The reports from the forest were hardly better than the situation in the ghetto. There was anti-Semitism even among the partisans themselves—some of them had been in labor or P.O.W. camps, where they were saturated with anti-Semitic propaganda. Rumors spread that the Jews who fled to the forest were cowards, hiding. But it was also rumored that Jewish partisans had raided the famous Romm printing plant in Vilna and melted down the old Hebrew type into bullets. Surely cowards had no use for bullets. According to the stories, the rebel fighters had plenty of guns to fill with those bullets. When the Red Army retreated, they purposely left behind soldiers to organize the partisans. These soldiers were reported to have close ties with Moscow and received regularly parachuted supplies of automatic weapons, explosives, and mines, as well as radio receivers and food. It was said that the Germans didn't have enough forces to keep control everywhere and still maintain a strong effort on the raging eastern front. The partisans had a chance.

Golda had heard that young people had flocked to the forest from all around, especially those from the ghetto who had lost their families. There was no time for mourning now. With Abraham's words echoing in her memory, Golda made up her mind to try to find him. Somehow, she had to get past the German soldiers at the gates and leave the ghetto before it was sealed off. As hard as she tried, however, she couldn't push her mind past the horrifying picture of her family's last moments. In despair, she lay down on the floor of the house and began to weep once more.

In the early morning she awoke from a restless sleep when she heard the door to the house open behind her. Terrified, she crept behind a large bureau and peered into the semidarkness. Then she heard a familiar voice calling her quietly.

"Abraham?" Golda whispered in disbelief. "I am dreaming. It can't be you." Golda touched her twin brother's face, longer and thinner than her own but with the same full mouth and knowing dark eyes. She smoothed her hand over the waves of his thick dark hair in awe, sure that she must be touching a vision in her state of shock.

"You're not dreaming, Golda," Abraham whispered. When Golda tried to tell him what had happened to their family, Abraham shook his head and made her stop.

"I know everything," he said. "There's no time to talk. If I'm caught, we could both be killed. Listen carefully, because I have to go before it gets too light. In a few hours the men will be allowed to leave the ghetto once more to work at the carpenter's shop. Below the carpenter's workroom is a whole basement filled with weapons they have been collecting and stashing there. When the men get to the carpenter's today, they're not going to work. They're going to take the weapons and escape to the forest to join the underground. Golda, you must wear Papa's clothes and disguise yourself as a man. Then you must go out to work in the morning with the carpenter's men. You'll blend in with the crowd and—"

Golda started to protest, but Abraham gripped her wide shoulders and made her listen to him.

"You're a big girl, and strong, Golda. No one will notice you in Papa's baggy overcoat. When you get to the carpenter's, don't take a weapon. You don't know how to use it and it will only make you vulnerable to thieves. Enter the forest at night. Never stop moving;

keep going all the time and try to travel in the dark. You will have good clothes, so don't sleep, because the forest is dangerous. They'll kill you for your boots. Come to Volcha Nora, about thirty kilometers outside Slonim. My partisan group is Sechors 51. My partisan name is Anton. I'll be waiting for you."

"Why can't I go with you now?"

"It's too dangerous for two. Alone, we have a better chance."

Then Abraham embraced Golda, left the house, and disappeared into the slate-colored dawn.

Shortly afterward, the German soldiers sealed off the ghetto for the last time, and the following June, 1942, the ghetto Jews hid in their cellars and bunkers during yet another *Aktion*. The Germans, determined to rout out the Jews once and for all, set the ghetto on fire. Thousands died in the flames and smoke. The ones that escaped were shot down in the surrounding fields. Out of fifteen thousand Jews that had once lived in the Slonim ghetto, only eight hundred survived.

One of those survivors was a woman, who, with her thick dark waves stuffed inside her father's felt cap and her heart hammering as loudly as a carpenter's workshop, had walked unrecognized through the heavily guarded front gates of the ghetto before it was sealed.

Zenya hoisted her short-barreled rifle, her *Karavyanka,* onto her shoulder and walked quietly through the dense bushes just beyond the tracks of the Slonim-Volkalvisk railroad. Just the night before, she had knelt in these bushes for hours, waiting for the German patrol to pass by, signaling the arrival of the enemy train. Zenya's raid unit had five Soviet partisans, a Belorussian scout, and herself. Zenya chuckled to herself quietly, remembering how all of them had fallen asleep from exhaustion in the bushes in the predawn hours. All except Zenya. She alone had stayed alert, seen the patrol, and awakened the others in time to assemble the bomb. But that's why Zenya was the lookout. She was good.

They had successfully blown up the tracks the previous night and derailed seven cars loaded with German artillery, including three cars of soldiers. That night's train was just as important—all soldiers.

Zenya hiked up the loose men's pants she wore over her thick boots and kneeled down to peer through the dark bushes to where the charred, wrecked cars from the bombed train still lay next to the tracks. She had changed so much since she joined her twin in the partisan camp that it almost seemed as if Golda were another person from another life. When the train was derailed the night before, most of the men aboard had been killed. Tonight they hoped to be as successful. "What would you think of that, Golda?" Zenya asked herself ruefully.

At a flicker of light in the darkness ahead, she abruptly stopped her conversation with herself and hid more completely behind the bushes heavy with new leaves. It was spring and the night was mild, but Zenya shivered anyway. More flickers, tiny orange lights that shone brightly for a moment, then receded. Cigarettes. There were people out there. German people. Zenya quickly ran back to the place where the others were waiting, and whispered that they would have to move the site of the raid farther down the tracks. They couldn't risk being seen there. The scout told Zenya that about fifteen kilometers away there should be a more deserted spot near the tracks to assemble the bomb.

As Zenya and the other partisans walked carefully through the dark bushes down the tracks, she couldn't help thinking that every day she was still alive was a gift. There were moments when she hadn't been as confident as she was that night, like the first time Anton had put a rifle in her hands over a year ago when she joined him in the forest. She had been the only woman in a group of shoemakers, teachers, doctors, and scholars who had traded in their books

and tools to be rebel fighters. Sechors 51 was one of the most famous partisan groups—famous for their ideals and high morals, for
their bravery and determination, for their loyalty to one another.
Members of the group were known to have traveled hundreds of
miles to help their comrades escape the labor camps or ghettos. It
made sense for Anton to be part of that group.

Among the partisans, Zenya was still considered a "gun car-
rier" and not a real gunner, like Anton. Many groups would not accept a woman at all, least of all one who had so recently learned
how to hold a gun. Partisans were expected to be capable of constant physical exertion, often having to march long distances with
little food and live out in the open in all kinds of weather. Needed
artisans were accepted without guns or age limits: tailors or type-
setters or locksmiths. Otherwise, only the strong and healthy were
preferred, or those who could read maps, handle explosives, or ad-
minister first aid. Or cook. Zenya joined the Chipayav group,
which already included four women, who worked in their outdoor
kitchen as cooks. But partisans were also valued for their sincerity
and honesty, for their loyalty and ruthless determination. Zenya
stirred all of that, and more, into her soups for the camp. Soon she
was as valuable for her help with their raids as she was with their
recipes.

In the months since then, Zenya had seen many a train derailed.
By the time she walked with her unit along the railroad tracks
where they hoped to ambush another train, she had hardened into a
courageous, smart saboteur. Zenya checked the area around the
railroad tracks where the scout had led them, carefully searching for
signs of anything that could prevent them from carrying out their
plans to bomb the train. When she was satisfied that everything was
safe, the partisans hunkered down in the bushes once more to wait.
An unbidden memory of a time when she had worked with a doctor
in a partisan medical unit blinded her eyes.

One day the doctor had to amputate the hand of a partisan named Patia with a saw, without anesthesia. In the same struggle in which he was injured, his wife had been killed, and he kept screaming her name. Zenya winced, seeing again in her memory the blood from the amputation spraying the doctor's face. But the doctor never lost his nerve, and he saved Patia.

Of the other horrors, far worse than that suffered by Patia, Zenya and her partisan brothers and sisters were completely unaware: They didn't know about the concentration camps. Knowing wouldn't have made it any easier, though, to live in the forest in fear, under constant danger. At least Zenya had the company of the other women when they cooked together on the camp cook stove, stoking the campfire and one another with stories. It comforted Zenya to think of the camaraderie of those women as she squatted uncomfortably in the dark bushes near the railroad tracks, waiting for the ill-fated train.

"We raided a rich ballroom and stole all the food and wine set up there for a big wedding," laughed Rashka one night as she stirred the soup for supper.

"Such bragging!" Zenya teased her, gently letting the peeled potatoes from a bowl plunk into the broth. "I'll tell you a story to brag about. I heard the Ukrainian police were poisoned by their cook, Nadia, when some partisans got to her and convinced her to help."

"Nadia is also a partisan?" Dvora asked. She tightened the tablecloth, stolen from the ballroom, that she now used as an apron.

"No, just a peasant," Zenya answered.

Rashka spat into the fire angrily. "Those bastard peasants," she hissed, "who traded Jews for salt!"

"The partisans killed those peasants, I know for a fact." Zenya nodded with a small, satisfied smile. "And their cows—God forbid the Germans should eat them." The women smiled together. Then their eyes became serious, reflecting the orange campfire as it crackled and smoked in the darkness. Not all the stories were about successes.

Dvora said quietly, "The partisans in the Carpathian Mountains suffered heavy losses."

Losses under the black walnut trees, whose roots were drunk with spilled blood. Losses that made Zenya want to fight even more. Zenya's group routinely damaged trains and train tracks, and ambushed the roads to steal cars. They stole food and other goods from storehouses on Polish estates where the Nazis had hidden them. The pilots who dropped supplies to Zenya's unit had complimented them on how well-stocked their kitchen was. This was a point of bittersweet pride for the partisans, especially the Jewish partisans in the Russian units, who were known to volunteer for the most dangerous operations such as stealing food from right under the Nazis' noses. In this way they deliberately built reputations as frightening rebels, not cowards, and avenged the slaughter of their people.

Zenya was no exception. Her name had been posted for bravery in that day's camp newspaper after the previous night's bombing. The other women were so jealous, they arranged to take turns between cooking and going out on raids. Tonight, though, the commander had ordered that it was still Zenya's turn. Zenya felt her chest relax when she thought of the good position she had secured with her new commander, Vlasov, because of her loyalty to his unit and her record of participating in so many successful combat and ambush raids. But there were still more trials to bear. Zenya winced at the sudden memory of a girl's face with a defiant chin—young— too young to be a spy under interrogation by commander Vlasov. There had been two girls—both had admitted finally that they were from a spy school in Baranovitch. Zenya wasn't surprised—the way the oddly dressed girls behaved had made the whole camp suspicious. One was burned alive.

What had surprised her more were Vlasov's words as he held the other terrified spy in front of her, words that still rang in Zenya's ears along with the sight of the menacing long-handled knife that he thrust into her hand.

"Take it, Zenya! Kill her!" he had cried. "People like that spilled the blood of your parents."

"But you didn't kill her, did you, Golda?" Zenya asked herself, a sad, ironic smile on her lips. "It seems you haven't left me for good." The girl was killed by others.

A small light, like a star falling toward her, caught Zenya's eye as she watched the railroad tracks. Zenya was the first to spot the train. Half a world away at the same time, Frida Kahlo painted her self-portrait *Thinking About Death,* in which her dark, serious eyes gaze out of a forestlike background. In the middle of her forehead is a circle enclosing a skeleton. How far away the two women were from each other at that moment, yet how close in fighting spirit. A few minutes later, the train cars were thrown from the track, burning in a searing flash of flames and smoke blacker than the night sky, and the explosion, for just one moment, drowned out the screams in Zenya's heart. If she and her brother lived to see the end of the war, Zenya vowed, they would leave this blood-soaked country behind and never return.

One spring evening, Papa Max's brother, Meyer, breathless from running six blocks from the bus stop, repeatedly rang the doorbell of Max's home in Hillside, New Jersey. Grandma Rae and Papa Max were in the kitchen finishing up dinner with their younger daughter, Norma. They were startled when they answered the door and Meyer burst into the living room, flushed and gasping. He excitedly waved the tissue-paper-thin envelope of an airmail letter in his hand.

"Come into the living room. Sit. Relax," Grandma Rae ordered Meyer. Max and Rae each took one of the high-back, upholstered chairs near the couch, where Norma sat down. Norma's pretty face was uncannily echoed by the painting above her, one of two photographically realistic oil portraits of her and her sister, Dottie, that hovered over the couch like protective angels in gilt frames. Meyer stopped to wipe his fogged wire-rim glasses with a handkerchief from his back pocket, then patted his balding head before he wearily lowered his short, stocky limbs into the welcoming couch cushions. He placed the letter he carried on the marble coffee table next to Rae's rococo pink-flowered ceramic candy dish filled with hard candy twisted in colorful cellophane wrappers and chocolates in gold foil.

"Have some candy or chocolate," Rae insisted. When everyone refused, she shrugged and took a piece herself, unwrapped it, and chewed regally while Meyer spoke.

"Fanny's cousin was visiting the Slonimer shul in the city," Meyer began, still struggling to catch his breath. Ever since the family moved out of the city, they no longer regularly attended the synagogue established by immigrants from Slonim, the synagogue where Esther Hanna had been so honored and loved. Once in a while, though, somebody from the family, like Meyer's wife, would visit their old friend, the rabbi.

"And Fanny's cousin gave this to us." Meyer paused to slip his reading glasses back on his long, sloping nose before he handed the letter to Max so that he could read it himself. Max opened the thin envelope and noticed the postmark from Israel: April 1954. Then he carefully unfolded the thin pages, scanned the letter quickly, and translated from the Hebrew for Norma and Rae: "I am looking for my family . . . can you help me, blah, blah, left Slonim before the war." A list of names followed: "Esther Hanna, Jacob, Max." He broke off and caught Meyer's eye for a moment, then continued to read the rest of the names. "Meyer, Isadore, Lillian, Lazur, Louis, and Elya Yaki—" He stopped again, but Meyer completed the reading for him, smiling and looking directly into Max's startled hazel eyes.

"Yakimovsky."

"Who's Yakimovsky?" Norma asked. Although a full-grown married woman with an infant son, at twenty-one, she was much younger than her hard-lived immigrant ancestors had been at the same age.

"Who's Yakimovsky?" Papa mimicked Norma, laughing with Meyer. Of course, the person who wrote the letter had no way of knowing that the family's name had been changed when they arrived at Ellis Island on the S.S. *Tintoretto*. The trail of the family was as hard to follow as a walnut's. Whether walnuts originated in Stone Age Switzerland or Neolithic Iraq, or whether they spread from Persia to Italy, or from India to China, changing their name along the way from *bannut* to *karuon basilikon* to *Juglans regia* to *walh-hnuta*, one thing is clear. Yakimovsky came to New York City from Argentina as Kasofsky and ended up in New Jersey as Kasoff.

Rae stood and took Norma's heart-shaped face into her hands, smoothing back her long, auburn hair.

"Who's Yakimovsky?" Rae repeated in a playful, high voice, laughing and placing her hands on her daughter's thin shoulders. "You're Yakimovsky, that's who!" Then Max ran to the closet to get a piece of stationery and an envelope to write a letter in reply to the person who inquired after the Slonim Yakimovskys. His hand shook as he carefully addressed the envelope.

"To: Zahava Ravitz."

Like Max, Zenya had also changed her name once more. A new name to suit a new life.

Near the end of May, as the nights grew warmer and longer, and the deep royal-blue sky of winter dusk softened to a hazy cerulean, my art exhibit went up at the renovated school downtown. One or two artworks from each show were chosen by the gallery director to be displayed in the gallery window overlooking the street in hopes of luring passersby. I was happy to learn as I approached the gallery the night before the opening of my show that my intensely colored drawing of Papa Max had been chosen for the window. Papa smiled at me as I pulled the heavy front doors of the gallery open.

I had stopped by the gallery to drop off an updated résumé and artist's statement to be included with the others at the receptionist's desk during the opening. But I was glad to have an excuse—I also came to have some time to myself in the gallery before the opening crowd filled the space with noisy conversation and jostling bodies. Just me alone in the quiet gallery with my work.

Even though I always labor long and hard on my artwork and am very familiar with each piece, nothing compares to the feeling of seeing it for the first time on bare white walls in a clean, spare gallery space. It's as if I had never seen it before. Even though its beauty and successes as well as its weaknesses are accented, the overall effect is one of extreme pleasure. I strolled through the show, enjoying the solitary sound of my footsteps on the newly waxed floor, admired my fellow artists' works, and inhaled deeply the heady ambiance of our accomplishment.

Next to the drawings and paintings, each artist's name was printed on the wall in big block letters. I walked directly in front of my name and regarded it proudly, remembering again why I go to all the trouble I do in order to make art. As I stood there, though, I suddenly felt a doubt.

The rebel Zenya had no choice but to leave behind gentle Golda, so steeped in the values of the past, in order to survive. Without Golda, though, Zenya would have become as cold and heartless a murderer as the enemy she fought. Golda and Zenya haunted me, but I couldn't put my finger on Zahava, even though without Zahava there would have been no future at all. All my life I felt as though I were just like Zenya, a rebel hell-bent on survival, dismissing my past as easily as I dismissed my traditional great-grandmothers' long skirts. I wanted to follow Zahava's lead, but I knew I had yet to find my true name.

Our opening the next night was successful insofar as we had a good turnout, though nothing sold. A small review appeared in a local paper written by a high school student, grammar forgiven. This was par for the course at an alternative gallery on the fringes of the art world as well as the city. Even though I was satisfied to get the exposure for my work, I still felt like Cinderella at the ball as I watched my carriage change back into a pumpkin and ended up at my survival job the next morning. The other two artists in the show also worked at restaurants in the city: one, a bartender, the other, a waitress.

In the gallery, the three of us held our glasses of cheap Chablis high and began a series of high-spirited toasts. "To us! To art! To the gallery!" We drank and celebrated and laughed. "To the restaurant world," I said finally, with a bittersweet smile, "for supporting so many artists."

The glasses soberly clinked.

As the Red Army closed in on the Germans near Zenya's camp, the partisans feared that the Nazis would try to kill everyone in their path as they retreated. One day when Zenya was on patrol, she and her comrades spotted soldiers coming toward them at a distance in the forest. The partisans hurried to take cover. Zenya steadied her rifle against her body to free her hands, and slowly focused her binoculars. Through the lenses she saw the welcome red stars of the Russian Army on the approaching soldiers' caps. Overcome with joy, she yelled to the others in celebration. Over the next few weeks she and her group watched in relief as the German soldiers fled, starving and barefoot.

Anton left the partisans to join the Red Army and continue the fight, even after the war was officially over. The Germans may have already started retreating, but the rampant anti-Semitism encouraged during the war continued. The Jews were still in danger in certain places and needed help. A few weeks later he wrote to Zenya at her partisan camp, where she stayed with the others until they decided what to do next. He began his letter "For me, the war hasn't ended yet."

And would never end. Soon after Anton's letter arrived, Zenya received the unbearable news that he was killed in the struggle. Her grief might have been eased when more news came confirming that Slonim had been liberated by the Red Army, but it wasn't. Zenya began to cry and couldn't stop crying. Commander Vlasov asked her why she was so upset.

"Did someone insult you, Zenya?"

When Zenya was unable to answer through her tears, one of the other women told the commander that Zenya cried because she didn't have a home in Slonim anymore, because her family was lost to her forever. She cried because now that the war was over, she realized that she was completely alone, and she had nowhere to go.

Zenya kept her promise to herself to leave Poland. She moved to a survivors' station, where so many of the homeless and bereft congregated after the Holocaust, to look for a connection, for warmth, for any shred of a way of life that had been discarded like so much scorched stew scraped from the bottom of a pot. At the survivors' station she worked in the children's home. There she fell in love with Peritz Ravitz, who had also lost his entire family in the war. Together they made their way, illegally, to Israel. That's where Papa's letter found her, living on a kibbutz with her new name, her husband, and three children.

The tears ran down Zahava's face as she read Max's reply to her letter. For the first time since Anton died in the forest, she had blood relatives, family, from Slonim, from her home.

After I returned home from my opening, I set my alarm clock to wake me so I would be a little ahead of time to work at Cook & CakeWalk the next morning. My menu problems were still unresolved, and I would need an early start. Then I fell asleep and began to dream.

Artists often dream about their own work, any artist will tell you that. It's our subconscious—we're always fishing around in there and sometimes we catch something too big for us to handle, so it pulls us back in, the other way. But this dream was a little different. In the dream I painted a picture of my forthcoming wedding. The painting depicted Eric and me in our wedding clothes, and my grandparents and great-grandparents in their antique wedding clothes, holding our hands. Only two things were unusual. One, the deceased ancestors were upside down, and two, when I painted their feet at the top of the painting, I painted inky-black stockings and black shoes sprouting from their wedding whites, like dark, muddy, uprooted stems branching out from beautiful white flowers. Then I woke up.

Unlike other confusing dreams, I didn't have to wonder too long about it in the morning—those muddy, nourishing roots, those lives sometimes so like mine, sometimes so unlike mine, but still connected. As much as I had tried to ignore those roots, baking fancy French tuiles in a modern restaurant kitchen, I couldn't forget them. Were all the ovens in my future filled only with trays of pretentious tuiles? Tuiles had a rich past, yes, but it wasn't mine.

Back at work, I looked at my hands as they baked, always held in the old, creased hands, the way new dough is cradled in a baker's canvas-lined bread basket, then marked with the basket's weave as it rises. So what if I were an artist without children, who hardly ever—okay, never—went to temple and hung linoleum block prints out on her clothesline instead of laundry. That wasn't going to stop me from figuring out that maybe the trick to rising without losing my basket's identifying weave was to first fall back in. I dug out my menu for Cook & CakeWalk and tentatively began one more revision.

At Cook & CakeWalk, I had an assistant, Dee, an eighteen-year-old woman from the Philippines. At first I didn't want to hire her, mostly because she had never worked in a restaurant kitchen before. She also looked physically weak to me and wore a lot of makeup to her interview. Looking at the heavy black eyeliner she painted, cat-style, well past the outer edge of each eye, I couldn't help thinking that a restaurant kitchen, with its sweat and tears, is no place for the fragile and vain.

The chef and I interviewed her together. We kept questioning her about her motives. Did she have any idea what she was getting into? She insisted that she was used to working hard in her high school's vocational baking program and she wanted to bake more than anything. There was something about her I liked. She was about the age a child of mine would have been had I given birth to one when I was as young as my mother was when she first started having children. And now, here I was, with a career, and the children I might have had when I was younger were my assistants. Dee confided in me, when I asked how her family felt about her choice of career, that she had recently lost her young mother to ovarian cancer. Now she felt a fire blazing in her telling her to live life fast before it was burned up. She needed a wing to be taken under. I reminded myself that I, too, had had no experience when I got my first job baking at LaCoupe, and I gave her a chance. As she left, the chef forbade her to wear her makeup in the kitchen.

"Why?" I asked him after she was out of earshot, curious if we were thinking the same thing, that a kitchen is not a nightclub.

"Because me and the guys won't be able to concentrate on our work with a gorgeous woman like that all made up and distracting us." I had to laugh. "Sexist pig," I kidded him. "That's me," he admitted freely, enjoying my indignant reaction. The lines were drawn, and not just on Dee's eyes. I spent many an afternoon after she was hired chasing hopeful bees away from the honey so that we could finish our work. Not that she needed my help.

It turned out that wrapped around the fine bones of this young woman's body was a lot of wiry, strong muscle and a tough skin. She was smart and plucky and wanted to know the reasons for everything we did. When I told her to cream the butter before adding the sugar, she asked why, when I told her always to add eggs slowly to butter, she asked why. I gave her the textbook answers, most of them having to do with physics and chemistry. Many times I warned her to slow the big mixer down before she added flour to a batter. One day she poured a bucket of fresh flour into a mixer slapping eggs and butter on high speed. The flour puffed back out at her, covering her face and uniform in a billowing white cloud.

"That's why," I laughed, stopping the mixer for her, then I added, "Actually, you want the mixer on low so that the dough isn't overworked once the flour is added. If you overwork it, gluten can form, and that makes the cookies tough."

She went back to scraping the dough down the sides of the heavy mixing bowl. The things she asked me! Why were croissants crescent-shaped? Why were linzer tarts filled with jam? It was a tradition, a history, I told her, as old and venerable as any art, that was passed on just like any heritage. You learn the old ways, keep what you need, and discard the rest in order to become yourself. This I said in an offhand way, as if I had always known it. Really, though, it had come to me just the moment I said it, in the same way that a drip of paint, purely accidental, can suddenly resolve a difficult painting.

You should never forget where you come from, never forget the struggle, never forget the lives that were lost.

No, Zahava, I vowed to her in my mind, I will never forget. And for the first time, I realized what I had to do to keep that promise.

Walnut Tuiles

½ cup sugar
¾ cup chopped walnuts
½ cup flour
¼ cup plus 2 tablespoons water

Prepare the tuile batter: *Grind sugar and nuts in the bowl of a food processor until very fine. Transfer mixture to a mixing bowl. Add flour and mix well. Add water, and stir in gently by hand until incorporated. Allow batter to sit at least fifteen minutes.*

Bake the tuiles: *Preheat oven to 325 degrees. Use a parchment-paper-lined or nonstick sheet pan, or a tuile mat purchased from a specialty baking shop. Spread batter thinly onto pan in desired shape with the back of a spoon or with your fingers. Experiment with the thickness of the batter; tuiles should be light and thin, but not so thin that they have holes or break, and they should not be so thick that they lose their delicate quality. Experiment with different shapes as well—the shapes for tuiles are limited only by the imagination of the baker. Circles are a shape recommended for first-time tuile bakers. Bake tuiles until they are set and light golden, about 8 minutes, then remove them from oven and immediately fold into desired shape while still hot. This may burn fingers a little and takes some practice. One technique that works well is to bake circles, then lift them with a spatula and fold them quickly over the curve of a rolling pin, forming tacolike shapes, or fold them into the curve of a small bowl, forming cups that can be filled with berries or ice cream. If tuiles become too cool to shape without breaking once they are finished baking, then return them to the oven for a few moments to warm them before trying to shape them again. Cool and store in an airtight container away from moisture and humidity. Yields approximately one dozen round tuiles, four inches in diameter.*

Thirteen

"Karuon *meant a nut in general; the walnut, strictly speaking,*
was karuon basilikon, *'kingly nut.'"*

FOOD,

WAVERLY ROOT,

1980

hen I presented my revised menu to the chef at
Cook & CakeWalk, he read it over quietly, vaguely
wagging his head neither yes nor no as his eyes pe-
rused one item and then the next. Suddenly he
stopped and pointed to the fig and sun-dried cranberry rugelach
with lemon ice cream.

"This is it!" he cried out in triumph. "This is what I've been trying to get out of you, what I've been looking for all along. Something that tells me about *you,* who you are, where you come from."
The chef was Jewish too. He looked at me wide-eyed, the leggy sage
leaf leaning toward the sun, and took hold of my shoulders. "This is
great!" he cried. "You'll make rugelach, and I'll make latkes, but

we'll change them a little to update them, use different, more American ingredients, and serve them along with your tuiles and my foie gras. These are our roots. It makes so much sense." He started to spin me around and dance with me, laughing.

I couldn't help laughing too. It was true. This was it, what we had been looking for all along. With a circle of fresh dough on my pastry board, I prepared to roll rugelach—a little bit differently—from my grandmother's recipe. I smoothed some flour down the length of my wooden rolling pin, sprinkled a little on the board, and rubbed some into my hands. My hands, and all the hands that bake with mine.

Three smacks to the top of the cold dough with my pin to soften it, and suddenly they appeared, as if summoned magically from the past. There they were, seated around my mother's big dining room table set for a holiday and impossibly extending from my pastry table, filling the small pastry kitchen from end to end. It was all so familiar—Grandma Selma's glittering diamond bracelet and red fingernails waving, and Papa Eddy with a fat cigar and a handful of aces. Papa Max telling stories and Grandma Rae sitting up tall in her corset, great-grandfathers pulling up chairs to talk shop or take another piece of rugelach, Great-Grandmas Esther Hanna and Reba and Bella trading recipes and tenement gossip with Zenya, the guest of honor. And Great-Aunt Dotty blushing as Goldie stands up to raise her skirt and dance—

And all the voices repeated the words that Grandma Rae used to say:

If we live long enough, we always come full circle.

As the wedding approached, Grandma Rae became even more ill. Gone was her high, teased black beehive and her bright red painted-on mouth. Now her lips were pale, her hair was white, lying limp against her gaunt cheeks, her skin as pale as unbaked dough. She sat, more and more, with her eyes closed, shutting me out. I began rolling my dough out into a perfect round—three short rolls out from the center, then a quarter turn, three short rolls, another quarter turn. With every roll of my pin, it seemed, Grandma grew thinner and thinner.

In my memory, Grandma's hands and my hands stirred the rugelach filling in a pot and added a handful of walnuts. We call the English walnut English because it's imported to us from England. It's not native to England, though, any more than Papa Max is native to Argentina. In more ways than one, we're all just passing through. There's no sugar in Grandma Rae's rugelach dough.

It doesn't matter, because the filling is so sweet.

That's just what Grandma would have said about life too. With the pot of filling on the stove, I returned to my rolling. I lifted the edge of the rugelach dough and dusted the pastry board beneath it with more flour and sugar. How could I move beyond my mother's and grandmothers' lives without being held back by the past like dough sticking to a pastry board, flattened down by the heavy pin of history? And if I loosened myself from that past, would I leave behind the things I needed most, would I be rolled out so thin that I would tear under the slightest weight? Each time I returned to the holiday table in my mind, I had to stretch my memory farther to fill the empty chairs. And if my memory could no longer fill those chairs, I would lose much more than my recipe for rugelach. I listened expectantly for my ancestors' voices to continue guiding me. There was no reply. Unnerved, I scraped the warm filling from the pot with a wooden spoon into a bowl.

Dried cranberries and figs made fine stand-ins for the raisins Grandma Rae specified for her rugelach. As I finished scraping the filling from the pot, though, the differences between our recipes were suddenly unimportant. I could change Grandma's recipe anytime I wanted without abandoning it completely. What fixed my attention instead, just then, was the one ingredient that I hadn't changed.

Papa Max could crack open walnut shells in his bare palms, and would challenge his six brothers to walnut-cracking contests which he always won. He once taught my father the trick—if you've got a large, strong hand, just line up the nut-shell seams of two nuts before you press them together, hard. I have a nut-cracking tool, fashioned with ornate designs and made of a solid, fine silver that I use to crack open the walnuts that I draw and bake. Because my hand is small. But not too small. Papa's strong, large hand is always open around mine, and Grandma Esther's around his, and so on, from me all the way back, as far as we can remember, and from me all the way forward, as many times as we can tell the stories, into as many hands as we can place the recipes. And the walnut shells are already cracked, the sweet meat ready to be eaten, lying in the open shells, nestled in all of our palms.

When I had rolled out a circle of dough of just the right thickness, I sprinkled the cooled, sweet filling onto it, and cut it into sections. Then my hands and their hands rolled each one up, around and around.

Soon there will be a great-grandchild baking rugelach!

Oy, gavolt, leave Nancy alone. She just got engaged!

All right, so it couldn't hurt, to give a little push in the right direction.

And that's how I know I can always return to that noisy, crowded holiday table.

If we live long enough, we always come full circle.

Because I can still hear them.

Fig and Sun-Dried Cranberry Rugelach

For the pastry:

½ pound unsalted butter, softened
½ pound cream cheese, softened
2 cups flour
Pinch salt
1 egg white, beaten, for brushing dough
before baking

For the filling:

¾ cup brown sugar, packed
½ tablespoon cinnamon
2 cups chopped dried figs
½ cup sun-dried cranberries (available at specialty shops)
Grated zest of 1 lemon
2 ½ tablespoons lemon juice
Pinch salt
1 ½ cups walnuts, toasted and chopped

Prepare the pastry: *Beat butter and cream cheese until smooth. Add flour and salt, mix gently. Do not overwork the dough. Divide dough into five pieces and refrigerate until firm.*

Prepare the filling: *Cook all filling ingredients, except walnuts, until the sugar has dissolved. Cool.*

Assemble the rugelach: *Line a cookie sheet with parchment paper or grease it and set aside. Working with one piece of dough at a time, roll dough in equal parts of flour and sugar. Roll dough out to a circle 8 inches in diameter. Sprinkle dough evenly with some filling and walnuts. Cut the circle into quarters, then cut the quarters into three triangles. Roll each rugelach up from the large end of each triangle to the small pointed end. Place rugelach with the points tucked under on the prepared cookie sheet. Continue rolling all the cookies and placing them on the sheet pan. Rest the cookies in the refrigerator until firm. Preheat oven to 350 degrees.*

Bake the rugelach: *Brush each cookie with egg white and sprinkle with sugar. Bake until the cookies are golden, 10 to 20 minutes. Yields 60 cookies.*

A B O U T   T H E   A U T H O R

Painter, poet, and pastry chef
NANCY RING lives in New York City
with her husband.